Democracy in the Making

The Open Forum
Lecture Movement

Arthur S. Meyers

UNIVERSITY PRESS OF AMERICA, ® INC.
Lanham • Boulder • New York • Toronto • Plymouth, UK

Copyright © 2012 by
University Press of America,® Inc.
4501 Forbes Boulevard
Suite 200
Lanham, Maryland 20706
UPA Acquisitions Department (301) 459-3366

10 Thornbury Road
Plymouth PL6 7PP
United Kingdom

Library of Congress Control Number: 2012938397
ISBN: 978-0-7618-5926-0 (clothbound : alk. paper)
eISBN: 978-0-7618-5928-4

For Marcia—
who knows the reasons why

Contents

Preface

My quest for the Open Forum began in 1991, when I was researching Hammond, Indiana, of the 1920s and 1930s. I came across articles in the local newspaper on a series of public lectures in the city. As the programs were held at Temple Beth-El, I asked congregants if anybody remembered them. A former member learned about my request and brought me all of the program brochures for the nineteen years of the lectures. They listed dates, speakers and topics, from the beginning in 1924 through the end in 1943. The series had to stop during World War II, probably because gasoline rationing made it difficult for people to attend.

With the brochures in hand, I was able to follow the lectures through the newspaper. As I continued my research, I learned the programs were part of a national public lecture movement, begun at Ford Hall in Boston in 1908 under Baptist auspices. I then discovered that nine scrapbooks of newspaper and magazine articles on the Ford Hall Forum and the national movement were in the American Baptist Historical Society in the American Baptist-Samuel Colgate Historical Library in Rochester, New York. Through the bulging scrapbooks, I was able to follow the movement in Boston and as it spread through New England and across the nation.

In my research, I found that there is little or no discussion in modern studies of the Social Gospel, the progressive era, and adult education about the Open Forum, the founder George W. Coleman, Ford Hall where it began, or local Forums that developed around the nation.

Kevin Mattson, in *Creating a Democratic Public; The Struggle for Urban Participatory Democracy During the Progressive Era* (State College: Pennsylvania State University, 1998), sets the early Ford Hall series within the broader context of public lectures of the period, noting particularly the impact of World War I. He provides significant insights into the role of participatory deliberations in later twentieth century America. However, his focus is on the "democratic public" deliberating civic issues. As a result, he does not examine the wide array of other lectures that were presented, such as on religion, the arts, sciences and humanities. He also does not explore the Social Gospel underpinnings of the Open Forum or the spread of the movement to several hundred small and medium-sized communities beyond Boston.

Maureen A. Flanagan, in *America Reformed; Progressives and Progressivisms, 1890s–1920s* (New York: Oxford University Press, 2007), draws from Mattson in briefly examining "The Public Forums Movement." Her emphasis is also on civic issues rather than the broader adult education goal of Ford Hall and the Open Forum. The uniqueness of the locally-planned Ford Hall series, with the completely open question period after the lecture, as well as in the national movement that evolved from it, is not shown clearly when it is placed in this context. Flanagan also writes that "the public did not direct or decide upon these forums; they were mainly to listen and learn." This was not true at Ford Hall in Boston, or in Terre Haute and Hammond, Indiana, where broad-based planning committees developed programs based on local interests.

The Ford Hall Scrapbooks at the American Baptist Historical Society revealed that the lectures began in many communities around the country. However, letters to public libraries and historical societies could not often confirm whether the lectures took root deeper than an opening address by Coleman. A few local records were retrieved, such as in Haverhill, Massachusetts.

An overview of the movement is in Arthur S. Meyers, "A Bridge To the Future: From the Boston Baptist Social Union To the Beth El Open Forum," *American Baptist Quarterly*, XIV (September 1995), 225–40. Local series are examined in Trudie Casper, "San Diego's Open Forum—Birth and Death," *Journal of San Diego History* 26 (1980) 126–32; Meyers, "'A Cross Blazed In Every Park Of Hammond': The Vision and Courage of the Beth-El Open Forum," *Indiana Jewish History* 28 (June 1992), 57–96; and Meyers, "'A Sturdy Core of Thinking, Fact Seeking Citizens': The Open Forum Movement and Public Learning in Terre Haute and Hammond, Indiana, in the 1920s," *Indiana Magazine of History* 99 (December 2003), 353–69. The Social Gospel perspective is explored in Meyers, "'The Striking of Mind Upon Mind': The

Open Forum and the Social Gospel," *Baptist History and Heritage* 35 (Spring 2000), 20–36. The impact of one lecture is described in Meyers, "W. E. B. Du Bois and the Open Forum: Human Relations in a "'Difficult Industrial District,'" *Journal of Negro History* 84 (Spring 1999), 192–204.

Thanks to Nancy C. Unger of Santa Clara University for very helpful comments and encouragement; many librarians, archivists and local citizens, cited in the notes, for their diligence in responding to numerous requests for information; and the staff of Russell Library, Middletown, Connecticut, for building a strong collection over the years, seeking other materials that I needed, and sharing their computer and photo expertise. Research in the Indiana Historical Society collection was aided through a Clio Grant from the Society.

Introduction

On the fifth anniversary of the Ford Hall Forum, fifteen-year-old Philip Sagerman, in a neatly hand-written four-page letter, said the speakers "infuse a new spirit . . . to do our share in bettering our social and economic conditions," adding "my enthusiasm reaches its zenith when a forceful question is asked and the speaker is in doubt how to answer it."

In 1908, a remarkable direction in community learning began in Boston: the Ford Hall Forum. It spread across the country to hundreds of cities, ultimately becoming the Open Forum lecture movement. These locally-planned, *trans-denominational* public lectures, followed by fully open question periods, were characterized as "the striking of mind upon mind."

The unique movement that once reached thousands of people, from a wide range of economic backgrounds and faiths, has been nearly lost in the historical record. This study recovers the Open Forum, and shows what can be applied to our time. It presents the movement from several perspectives, viewing it especially as a contributor to the education of adults.

The founder, George W. Coleman, brought vision, dynamism and a deep commitment to free speech in developing the movement. Beyond linking it to the Social Gospel, which aimed at improving lives on earth, he recognized the crucial role of publicity in spreading the Forum. Mary Caroline Crawford, with great skill and intelligence, was key to implementing the movement in Boston and nationally.

As the movement spread, it made a particular impact on two Indiana cities in the 1920s. During a very conservative period, when the state's Ku Klux Klan led the nation in membership, two young clergy stepped up. A

Congregational minister in Terre Haute and a Reform rabbi in Hammond, with broadly-representative planning committees and committed congregations, displayed much vision and courage. They brought forward diverse viewpoints and cultures to their largely homogeneous cities.

The impact of the lectures is highlighted in the talk by W. E. B. Du Bois in Hammond. The visit by the African American scholar-activist reveals the double perspectives of engendering social justice and human relations during a turbulent period in the nation's history, as well as in his personal life. The many lectures he gave around the country led him to conclude that "the Open Forum in America is one of the few bright and reassuring spots."

Understanding this initiative provides fresh insight into our nation's history. It broadens awareness of personal and community courage, democratic planning, and broad-based learning. It shows that what Virginia Woolf wrote about women's lives in general—"she is all but absent from history"—is *not* true about Mary Crawford.

We can regain this informed, reflective, respectful approach. We can spread the framework of the Open Forum further. The "striking of mind upon mind" can cross today's socio-economic barriers and enter local and national discussions and engage us through electronic connections.

We can achieve an America *"to be"*—a democracy in the making.

Chapter One

Perspectives

The Most Marvelous Program That Ever Existed

One photo captures people lined up in the snow outside Ford Hall in Boston, waiting to enter the building. Another image shows the attentive audience inside the packed hall, as the lecture is ready to begin. Together, they convey what led to a father's complaint in a fictional Midwest city in 1922:

> When they were not at home, . . . they were trudging off to lectures by authors and Hindu philosophers and Swedish lieutenants. 'Gosh,' Babbitt wailed to his wife, . . . 'it gets me how Rone and that fellow can be so poky. They sit there night after night, . . . and they don't know there's any fun in the world. All talk and discussion—Lord! Sitting there—sitting there—night after night—not wanting to do anything.'[1]

The story of a remarkable movement has been nearly lost in the historical record. Yet, in the early twentieth century, the Open Forum was an innovative direction in community learning. It was a decentralized, locally planned, non-partisan, non-sectarian assembly of citizens discussing matters of public interest, always under the guidance of leaders but with full audience participation. Each program consisted of a lecture by a knowledgeable person, but, uniquely among such talks at the time, it included a probing audience question period afterwards. The movement brought together a wide range of people to discuss the vital concerns and intellectual advances of the day, and the core beliefs and values in their lives. Individualistic and autonomous, the local shaping of each Forum is the forerunner of today's global dissemination of information.[2]

During its heyday, the Open Forum reached thousands of people in several hundred medium-sized and large cities, ranging from Maine to California,

Michigan to Florida. In Boston, where the method was developed, and in a number of other cities, there was an additional element of cross-class, cross-cultural fellowship. Fortunately, through scrapbooks and files not previously explored, newspaper coverage around the country, documents and writings of some of the key persons, and contemporary and later reports by participants, we can recapture this remarkable model of participatory democracy, public learning, and freedom of speech.

George W. Coleman, a Baptist publisher and lay leader, founded the movement in 1908. Combining his strong commitment to the Social Gospel and democratic discussion with great advertising skill, he developed the Forum model after observing the People's Institute at Cooper Union in New York City. There he witnessed the transforming educational power in a working class and immigrant audience that was challenged by current issues and great ideas.

Through a network of ministers and civic leaders, Coleman quickly spread the model from Ford Hall in Boston, first throughout New England, and then around the country. In a wide range of religious and secular publications, and in hundreds of speeches, he carried the message to the nation with great enthusiasm. Today's National Issues Forums, Great Decisions programs, local study circles, broadcast town meetings, and Internet discussions are direct descendants of the Open Forum.[3]

Although public lectures have a long record in American history, the Open Forum movement differed in significant ways from earlier series and can be viewed from various perspectives. First, it was more intellectual and less religious in content than the earlier Lyceum and Chautauqua movements. By meeting to seriously consider public issues, it was a form of "deliberative democracy" that was valued so highly by reformers at the time. Open Forums sought to expand the number of participants in democracy rather than just keep the floor open to discussion. The metaphor of political theorist Adolf G. Gundersen is that of a blast furnace: "The more democratic the fuel, the hotter the argument, and the better the alloy of substantive political rationality." The goal is communication rather than unanimity. "The more voices," continues Gundersen in a notion at least as old as Aristotle's *Politics*, "the wider the discourse and the wider the discourse, the more likely it is to hit on the truth." In the canon of virtues in deliberative democracy, political theorist Peter Levine lists trust, respect for other opinions, social concern, and a desire to achieve consensus where possible.[4]

In the most idealistic concept of deliberative democracy, Federal Judge Richard A. Posner writes that people are politically informed and engaged when they ask: "What is good for the society as a whole?" They begin reasoned debate, seeking to harmonize or compromise their differing concepts of the public interest. It is political democracy as the pooling of different ideas and approaches, seeking the best solution through debate and discussion.[5]

With the exception of seeking consensus and developing a plan for action, which Gundersen writes is essential in the process, the Open Forum can be seen as a form of deliberative democracy. The movement's aim, however, was not group-focused but individual public learning as an end in itself. In addition, the topics discussed were not always public policy or ethical questions but often new horizons in the arts, sciences and humanities. The goal, conveyed through the movement's communication image, was "Let There Be Light."

Political philosopher John Rawls writes that the essential elements of deliberative democracy are public reason, a framework of a constitutional democratic institution, and the desire by citizens to follow public reason and realize its ideal in their political conduct. Although Rawls does not reference the Open Forum, these three elements are present in the lecture movement. We will also find them in the lives of the two persons who conceived and implemented the initiative.[6]

A second perspective in viewing the Open Forum is the concept of secular perfectibility in American history, the historic liberal belief that adults should be educated on important public issues. Once the civic body is informed, it will be better equipped to participate in the democratic process. Problems are best solved through intelligence, and the only way to have an intelligent public opinion is through free and open discussion. Such public discussions began first on the ships coming to New England and continued in the town meetings. While the meetings were not fully democratic in participation, and the topics were mainly on local governance, the setting provided a structure for the community to come together. Citizens were seeking to improve or *perfect* themselves.[7]

French political philosopher Alexis de Tocqueville understood the concept when he observed in *Democracy in America* that in the new nation, "the image of an ideal but always fugitive perfection presents itself to the human mind," and the democratic idea reflected "the indefinite perfectibility of man." In 1907, Walter Rauschenbusch, the most prominent theologian of the Social Gospel, used the same image in his landmark *Christianity and the Social Crisis*. He wrote that "the swiftness of evolution in our own country proves the immense latent perfectibility in human nature." (Rauschenbusch's book, in fact, directly shaped the Open Forum.)[8]

A third way to view the movement is that it was trans-denominational at a time when dogma and practice generally kept faiths apart. Even though Ford Hall and the national movement were made possible initially through Baptist financial support, the record does not show any denominational leaning. Later, when the planners had to allow non-sectarian prayers at Ford Hall, the movement still appealed to a wide range of faiths as well as non-believers. They believed in this "religion of democracy." In describing the audience they were seeking, the planners specifically spoke of those without a church, "who have no place to go for mental sustenance and moral inspiration."[9]

In the first 180 Ford Hall programs, with the primary topics being religion, race, citizenship, democracy, and ethics, half of the presenters were religious leaders. Baptists gave twenty-one of the first lectures (one-ninth of the total), while Jewish leaders spoke seventeen times. A person who observed the first seven years of Ford Hall concluded that Jews were more numerous in the audience than any other group. Further, at a time of much ethnic and religious separation from the wider community, Catholics also participated in meaningful ways in Ford Hall planning, moderating and lecturing. Mary Boyle O'Reilly, a social activist, served on the Committee of Citizens which selected speakers, while Rev. Michael J. Ahern, a Jesuit educator, sometimes moderated the programs. Rev. John A. Ryan, the leading Catholic advocate for social justice in the early 20th century, spoke five times at Ford Hall as well as in other Open Forums around the country. Whenever the speaker at Ford Hall was a Catholic clergy, the opening non-denominational prayer was omitted to avoid any offense. Other speakers described their Muslim or Hindu beliefs.[10]

A fourth perspective on the Open Forum is its wider appeal than the better-known Lyceum and Chautauqua movements. In Boston, as well as other cities, the audience included recent immigrants, long-time residents, working people, union leaders, and business owners. Henry Abrahams, the Jewish secretary of Boston's Central Labor Union, was on the committee that planned the Ford Hall series and was the first speaker at the opening night in 1908. Lowell Institute, where public lectures had begun in the city in 1836, did not have such broad-based planning or audience participation.[11]

This special aspect of the Open Forum grew out of the ideal exemplified by the University of Chicago: connecting scholars and experts to the general public through lectures, with the goal an improved civic life. The direct link was Charles Zueblin, a sociology professor at Chicago, who held that the public lecturer must remain open to the opinions of the people in the audience. The extension of the university that he advocated eventually led him to resign his position in Chicago to become a full-time public lecturer. Historian Kevin Mattson describes Zueblin's belief that without a deliberating and debating public, democracy would stagnate. "Rooting a speaker in a democratic public produced a new type of intellectual dedicated to truth and criticism that could develop only out of collective deliberation."[12]

The diversity of the Ford Hall audience is shown in a 1923 survey of 674 attendees. The audience was fifty-eight percent men, with twenty-five percent under thirty years of age. One-third of the participants were foreign born, and sixty-one percent had foreign parentage. They represented one hundred thirty-four occupations and thirty-seven religions, with twenty-two percent Jewish and six percent Catholic. (In a 1928 count, these numbers rose to twenty-nine percent Jewish and fourteen percent Catholic.) With such a diverse audience, Coleman's title of his 1915 book on Ford Hall, *Democracy in the Making*, described exactly the core of the Forum in both goal and process.[13]

A fifth way in which to view the movement is to see it as a local implementation of the Social Gospel. The 1890s had brought the country to the verge of something but it was not clear what was developing. There was an increasing feeling by people in the period that they were dealing with forces beyond their control, and perhaps beyond anybody's power. Many middle-class Americans concluded they had lost the ability to direct their own lives.[14]

For the middle class, Sinclair Lewis conveys this quandary in *Babbitt* (1922), when the booster-businessman concludes "I've never done a single thing I've wanted to in my whole life!" The only thing he had accomplished was to "just get along." For the poor, it was even worse, and no voice is more eloquent than that of Jurgis Rudkus in *The Jungle* (1906) by Upton Sinclair. Beyond the oppressions and horrors his family had suffered, he realizes in the end that he had been crushed and beaten, and then submitted, and was finally forgotten and living alone in peace. It was "a thing not to be borne by a human creature, a thing of terror and madness."[15]

In response to these societal changes, the Social Gospel, a mainly white Protestant movement not spread across the denominational spectrum, called for a better life for the masses on earth. It developed at the same time that Jewish and Catholic social justice advocates were also beginning to speak out. The voices rose from the pulpit, lecture platform, seminary, print publications, and denominational and ecumenical organizations. While most Protestants during the era maintained traditional faith and practice, historian Sidney E. Ahlstrom writes that social Christianity strove to "connect the self-oriented Christian consciousness into one that was neighbor-oriented." The Open Forum, rather than being religiously based, was a secular improvement undertaking. Instead of feeding the body or saving the soul, it broadened minds and deepened understanding of social and cultural issues.[16]

A sixth perspective is that the Open Forum was more unique and community-specific than the earlier lecture movements as a cross-section of citizens shaped each local series. In Terre Haute, in the west-central part of Indiana, the pastor of First Congregational Church started that city's series in 1920, with a wide range of community leadership on the planning committee. In Hammond, in the northwest corner of the state, the program began in 1924 under the sponsorship of Temple Beth-El, the Reform Jewish congregation, but civic leaders and residents from different faiths led the series throughout its nineteen years.

A seventh way to understand the movement, especially as it spread across the country during the culturally divided post-World War I period, is as a counterpoint to the decline in religion. Despite most Americans considering themselves religious in those years, a collection of essays in 1922, *Civilization in the United States; An Inquiry By Thirty Americans*, does not show a God-fearing outlook. No essay on religion was included, the editor said, as most of the contributors felt that real faith had disappeared. The writers found a sharp dichotomy between preaching and practice in a nation that was increasingly heterogeneous, both religiously and culturally. The editor, literary critic Harold E. Stearns, wrote that the most moving and pathetic fact in the social life of America today is "emotional and aesthetic starvation."[17]

Journalist Walter Lippmann, writing at the time, similarly capsulated the period that followed the high national spirit of the war years as one of "exhaustion." He concluded that nobody will be enthusiastic about anything until the generation grows up that has forgotten "how violent we were and how unreasonable." Theologian Reinhold Niebuhr could not find religious robustness in the nation. As a pastor in Detroit and thus a witness to the effects of industrialism, he decried the moral failure of Christianity and said it was not a vital factor in contemporary life. He questioned religion's survival and became discouraged by the failure of the ministry.[18]

While the World War initially stimulated church attendance and public religiosity, Ahlstrom found that the fervor ended in the 1920s "at the lawn socials of normalcy." During the decade, the indexes of denominational vitality show "a prevailing downward trend [and] pervasive thinning out of evangelical substance." Historian Robert T. Handy characterized the mid-1920s as the beginning of a "religious depression" because of a spiritual lethargy. Protestantism was embarrassed by "too close identification with the surrounding culture." (Paradoxically, this also meant that the pronouncements of the progressive ministers and their denominational assemblies had little popular impact.)[19]

A study of small Midwestern towns found that churches at the time seldom concerned themselves with anything beyond preaching, while service clubs and community agencies carried forward the Social Gospel. Although the churches did not generally foster social Christianity, they strongly supported lay activities that arose in their place.[20]

An eighth way of conveying the Forum is the concept, and, even more crucial, the practice, of participatory democracy, as posited by two contemporaries of the Forum founders.

The first is a political theorist who is not widely known today but developed and then implemented early an important new concept for adult learning. In 1908, in Boston, Mary Parker Follett became chairman of the Women's Municipal League Committee on Extended Use of School Buildings. In that capacity, she conceived the idea of using public schools in the evening as social or community centers for adult learning. In concept, city and year, her thinking paralleled the birth of the Open Forum. In 1913, speaking at the Ford Hall Forum on "The Social Centre [spelling of the period] and the Democratic Ideal," she listed the ways in which civic and social responsibility would be developed in the evening centers:

1. Group-centered activities aimed at developing a social being—a person who is not apart from but rather a part of others.
2. Real training in self-government through the development of individual initiative, will power and self-expression.
3. Frequent discussion and direct civic teaching of political, economic and industrial questions and political and social ethics.
4. Acquaintance, association and discussion, leading to common action for community ends.[21]

In 1918, Follett brought her ideas together in a book, *The New State*. She wrote that a new method must come into being, one of "common ideas, a common purpose and a collective will." In this new undertaking, the potentialities of the individual are released by group life. Democracy, for Follett, is bringing forth a genuine collective will, with differences integrated, neither annihilated nor absorbed. Instead of shutting out what is different, it is actually differences that make a richer, more unified life. The civic activity of citizens, she maintained, creates a democratic community. But mere association is not enough; there must be a fuller and more varied life, such as is found in discussions held by neighborhood organizations, with differences in education, interests and standards. Although the Open Forum movement did not meet in school buildings, and had programs broader than political or social topics, it brought Follett's concept to the nation.[22]

In her 1913 talk at Ford Hall, Follett said that one way of creating such a community is through genuine discussion that is used constructively for the good of society. To this end, she saw how a great advantage of the "forum movement" is that we are beginning to have discussion in the nation, which is "one of the most valuable movements of our time." In the discussion process, "increasing reciprocal adjustment . . . brings out and gives form to truth." She concluded by praising "the enormous value of [the] rapidly spreading . . . forum movement." With the exception of discussion "leading to common action for community ends," Follett is on the exact page as Coleman in stepping forward into the future.[23]

A second early theorist of participatory democracy was social philosopher John Dewey. In 1927, in *The Public and Its Problems*, he identified the public's bewilderment in the post-war period. He wrote that the "prime condition of a democratically organized public is a kind of knowledge and insight which does not yet exist." No man was ever emancipated by being left alone, and a thing is fully known only when it is "published, shared, socially accessible." The essential need is the "improvement of the methods and conditions of debate, discussion and persuasion." He concluded that "democracy must begin at home, and its home is the neighborly community." The "local is the ultimate universal," and unless "local communal life can be restored, the public cannot adequately resolve its most urgent problem: to find and identify itself."[24]

Dewey also understood the crucial role of media in the new age. Not only is there an "obvious requirement" of freedom of social inquiry, but "distribution of its conclusions" is also needed. There can be no "public" without full publicity in all consequences that concern it. "Whatever obstructs and restricts publicity, limits and distorts thinking on social affairs." Nor was reading about social issues sufficient in itself. The "winged words of conversation in immediate intercourse have a vital import lacking in the fixed and frozen words of written speech." Paralleling almost exactly the words that Coleman used in founding the Open Forum two decades earlier, the philosopher said that "vision is a spectator; hearing is a participator."[25]

Although Dewey did not make a direct link to the Open Forum in his book, he provides a succinct framework for understanding the lecture movement. He described "publics" as originating when groups of people found that they shared an interest in the "indirect consequences of social action." While not talking specifically about the Forum, the movement was in fact meeting his requirement for a new machinery in America, so that "the inchoate public . . . may function democratically." He sought conditions under which the nation might become the "Great Community." Until "the Great Society is connected into a Great Community, the Public will remain in eclipse." People learn community life (i.e., democracy) through the give-and-take of communication, in face-to-face intercourse. Instead of an educated elite directing the nation, the "publics" need a high level of knowledge about social action and consequences. The Open Forum provided this structure in many cities.[26]

A year later, in 1928, Dewey made the connection of his social philosophy to the Forum movement explicit in a letter celebrating the twentieth anniversary of the Ford Hall Forum and in particular the accomplishments of Coleman. He praised the value of Forums in keeping alive "that independent and free discussion of public issues that is so indispensable in a democracy." When Ford Hall Forum began, at a time of much urban dislocation, enormous growth in immigration, and unregulated industrial expansion, the "neighbor" concept of locally-planned lectures was particularly meaningful. It is not coincidental that in Boston the core group of attendees was called the "Ford Hall Folks."[27]

At the time the movement began, the word "folks" in the United States connoted a more intimate, neighborly relationship than "people." An historical dictionary of American English defines the meaning of the word in 1874 as, "in America, neighbors especially are folks." In 1920, the letterhead of George Babbitt's real estate company included the slogan "Homes for Folks." In 1928, Shailer Mathews, Dean of the University of Chicago Divinity School and a frequent speaker at Open Forums, wrote that, "In the last analysis social progress is not a matter of systems but of folks. And folks can be made brotherly in action by an institution having such a foundation." The founders of the Forum movement had brought together philosophy and language in a concrete way.[28]

Dewey's strong belief in participatory democracy, expressed in a wide range of writings, provides a crucial framework for understanding the Forum movement. As historian Robert B. Westbrook describes the philosopher's outlook, democracy is an ethical ideal that calls on people to "build communities," so that each individual is fully able to realize his or her particular capacities. This inner growth enables the person to become a social being, and as each becomes a member of a community, the individual becomes free. "It is through association that man has acquired his individuality and it is through association that he exercises it," Dewey wrote. The record of the Open Forum, from Ford Hall to its expansion across the country, shows the strong sense of community, i.e., association, which was integral to the movement.[29]

In 1908, the same year that Coleman brought his ideas into practice, Dewey and James H. Tufts expressed concern about the stifling of freedom in modern society. In their innovative textbook, *Ethics*, they noted the necessities of a democratic society were the advancement of equality of opportunity and the fostering of individuality and self-realization. Participation in such a community was made possible through free inquiry, toleration of diverse opinion, and free communication. While they did not make an explicit link to the Forum in this early work, the elements were intrinsic to the lecture movement.[30]

In founding the Open Forum and then expanding it to other cities, the leaders of Ford Hall showed a broad participative outlook. It was a vision that Dewey found lacking in many contemporary reformers. Westbrook describes other reformers at the time as failing to engage the active interest and cooperation of others. "Middle-class benevolence" often betrayed a view of the masses as "inert material on which reformers might work their will." For Open Forum leaders, it was not talk versus action that differentiated their movement from other reform activities of the era, but *participation*, specifically democratic participation, in planning and then carrying out the lecture movement. That was the difference.[31]

But the ninth and most distinctive way to understand the Open Forum is as continuation and contributor to the nation's education of adults in a public setting. Adult education is a voluntary activity for personal improvement, in an organized group structure, with the goal to gain knowledge. As the beginning of the twentieth century, Open Forums sponsored by civic groups and congregations played an important role in bringing intellectual currents and diverse viewpoints to the public, creating learning opportunities and deliberative democracy.[32]

Dewey's concept of "associated living" is pertinent to this understanding. He found there was individual and group growth when it "contributed positively to free intercourse, to unhampered exchange of ideas, to mutual respect and friendship and love." The chief obstacles to this growth were caste and class, which isolated different segments of society. This was *not* the path of the Forum movement. Instead it became, to use his term, a "true democracy"—a society with opportunities for individual development and free communication of feeling, knowing and thinking.[33]

In Dewey's philosophy, face-to-face associations in public learning were especially important. As Westbrook notes, "The connections of the ear with vital and out-going thought and emotion are immensely closer and more varied than those of the eye." Only in the participatory context of local communities, "could the public's education be consummated." At the local level, said Dewey, deliberate planning was crucial: "banked and conducted" in his words. The philosopher was articulating a vital element in the Forum movement that Coleman had begun two decades earlier.[34]

The tradition of Americans seeking to expand their thinking as citizens, rather than for the goal of higher education or occupational training, is too often overlooked in our history. As early as 1710, discussion groups on community improvement were planned, and lectures on science and nature were held in 1726 and on public health in 1750. Colonial towns provided opportunities to talk about events and ideas, and the clergy supported a well-educated laity so they could follow theological discussions. Historian Richard D. Brown documents an eighteenth century viewpoint that a politically informed citizenry, one that was equipped to evaluate public policy, was vital for the well-being of the state and the liberty of its people. The result of this outlook was that a deeper conception of citizenship emerged.[35]

During the Revolutionary War period, the Committees of Correspondence served as channels for public opinion, in addition to spreading propaganda and coordinating the independence movement. The Revolution helped "democratize American thought," writes historian Merle Curti, as enthusiasts insisted that intellectual life must be common to all people. Those who could not read broadsides and pamphlets listened to heated discussions in the taverns. In his famous Farewell Address, George Washington said that being informed was a necessary part of citizenship and called for the "diffusion of knowledge."[36]

In the nineteenth century, the broadening of democracy brought an extraordinary development in the spread of ideas and knowledge. Common people had a desire *to know* so they could share more fully in the life of the mind. Workingmen's and People's Institutes focused on self-improvement through discussions and lectures on science, literature and morality. Lowell Institute in Boston in 1836 and Cooper Union in New York City in 1859 went further by opening their halls to the general public.[37]

The Lyceum and Chautauqua movements expanded the concept by bringing speakers to several thousand small communities. In the mid-nineteenth century, large-scale professional lecturing began when Emerson and other speakers extended their circuits to the Midwest. Commercial lecture bureaus made it easier to diffuse and popularize knowledge on a wider basis, bridging the gap between the cultural and intellectual life of urban centers and rural and small communities. Americans could choose among a wide array of information activities, including general culture at public lectures, controversial subjects presented by touring reformers and evangelists, and political rallies.[38]

Historian Donald M. Scott notes that the lecturers of the period provided the general public with a comprehensive vision, referred to as the *democratic spirit*, making knowledge readily accessible to common people. In organization and structure, intellectual form and content, and as public ritual, the speeches transcended the fracturing of the nation over slavery. Americans displayed their commitment to the idea of an informed, knowledgeable citizenry. Merle Curti writes that the Lyceum was in a genuine sense a free forum serving to broaden the minds of the people and to make them more ready to entertain new ideas.[39]

The major tenet of the Lyceum lecture movement, which began in 1826 in Salem, Massachusetts, was to provide opportunities for people with special expertise to share their knowledge through a public forum. The Salem Lyceum in fact called for "our own improvement in knowledge, the advancement of popular education, and the diffusion of useful information throughout the community generally." In some communities, two lectures were held to avoid offending people with differing religious views. After 1865, the focus of the Lyceum movement shifted to lighter topics and entertainment as people looked for ways to escape the troubling problems of the day.[40]

The Chautauqua lecture movement, which began in the 1870s in New York State, stressed the sacredness of knowledge, self-culture, the universal right to knowledge, and continued learning for adults. While Chautauqua held the home as the center of education, local study circles and huge tent gatherings brought the idea of a cultured life to 8,500 towns and 35,000,000 people by 1920. It became in many respects a "remarkable egalitarian medium for the dissemination of ideas," writes historian Andrew C. Rieser. Ultimately, however, the movement failed, note education historians Harold W. Stubblefield and Patrick Keane, because social problems required more than a cultural solution. In an increasingly changing world, with its base a religious impulse, Chautauqua could not find a dynamic secular principle. Historian C. Hartley Grattan concludes the movement was "greater on the side of thinning the cultural brew than . . . thickening or enriching it."[41]

In New York City, in 1859, public lectures began at Cooper Union, an adult education institution. It provided opportunities for questions from the audience. In 1897, the People's Institute was formed and incorporated the forum into its program that continues today. In 1891, Dr. Henry M. Leipziger, assistant superintendent of schools in New York City, planned a system of evening public lectures at school centers. From a small experiment it grew into a huge organized lecture system, eventually drawing more than a million people a year. Leipziger was eventually named supervisor of public lectures and called the system "The People's University."[42]

At the turn of the twentieth century, the tradition of general adult learning and lectures continued as clubwomen studied social issues, universities developed extension courses, and social and cultural centers, often in evening schools and congregations, held debates. Viewed in this perspective, the Open Forum is a clear descendant of the Lyceum and Chautauqua.[43]

The proponents of the Open Forum were aware that they had to distinguish between their approach and the earlier public lecture movements if they were to be as unique and successful as their predecessors. In expressing their strong feelings for the Forum, some of the early focus was on George Coleman as the crucial element in the movement's success. James L. Hill, one of the clergy leaders of the Sagamore Beach colony, a summer gathering of intellectuals and activists that Coleman founded, described him (probably to his embarrassment) in a religious/mystical construct as "the modern St. George."[44]

Hill wrote that Coleman sets forth to destroy a mighty dragon that menaces the life of the common people and is more inspirational, creative, and constructive than the presiding officer of the Lyceum. The Lyceum went not with the lecture end but with the business end, said the minister, while the Forum is not exposed to the "mercenary evil that broke the lyceum down." (In Boston, a bequest from Daniel Sharp Ford allowed free admission to the Ford Hall Forum, while programs in other cities asked for donations or charged a small fee or subscription to meet expenses.) Hill concluded that in the Lyceum's golden age, there were not as many lecturers as were now at Forums and other public platforms.[45]

In this intellectual, social and religious milieu, arising from a need for a more meaningful inner and communal life, the Forum approach of locally-planned, non-partisan, non-sectarian civic discourse in the early twentieth century resonated across the national landscape. In 1916, on the eighth anniversary of the movement, more than 100 forums were "scattered all over the country." A 1926 study by Nathaniel Peffer, who taught international relations at Columbia University, found 195 Forums in thirty-two states, and gave a "conservative" estimate that there were 300 forums operating in the country.[46]

At Ford Hall, the audience ranged from those who traced their roots to the American Revolution to recent immigrants from Eastern Europe. In Terre Haute, Indiana, leaders of the miners union came to the Forum, while in Hammond, Indiana, Jewish business owners participated. The unique characteristic of American intellectual history, suggests historian Merle Curti, is that the gulf between the learned and the common people has been less wide and deep than in the rest of the world. In concept and implementation, the Open Forum is an excellent example of Curti's point.[47]

The titles of Forum lectures in Boston, Terre Haute and Hammond also have a ring of "higher" education in the new frontiers discussed in the arts, sciences, and humanities. In the 1920s and 1930s, however, some adult educators questioned the effectiveness of the movement.

In his 1926 study, Peffer said few generalizations could be made concerning Forums as each was autonomous, determining its own content and procedures, based upon the community's socio-economic setting. With no national census of the membership, he wrote, the importance of the movement was difficult to quantify.[48]

The Open Forum National Council, a loosely organized coordinating body, headquartered in Boston, arranged speakers when requested. The lecturers were knowledgeable and effective communicators on social, economic and civic questions. Their fee was usually $25 per lecture but sometimes as high as $75. In the 1923 to 1924 period, the Council provided speakers for 400 appearances in seventeen states. More than half of the 195 locations were in the Northeast. Religious institutions sponsored 104, and of these, thirty-four were Jewish. The average attendance was 450 persons at each meeting. Peffer projected that 135,000 Americans attended Forum lectures each week for the four months of the year they were held.[49]

In studying the lectures in several cities, Peffer reported some were dull because they were so "proper" in structure, rather than free flowing. Presenters told him that they came best prepared when they knew they had an audience ready to challenge their talk. Visiting Ford Hall, Peffer noticed that although the lecture was to begin at 8:00 pm, it started unofficially before 7:00, when the audience gathered outside the building. He found an "animated" line, with most people knowing each other from past programs. A capacity audience of 1,500 was the rule, and when Peffer was present on "a pouring, clammy winter night," 1,000 were in their seats by 7:15.[50]

Peffer noted that the speaker is given an hour exactly and then the most stimulating part of the evening begins. This is no perfunctory Lyceum, he wrote, as the audience is a participant in the discussion. Coleman as the moderator allowed questions by section of the hall, beginning that night with the balcony. He directed each question to the speaker, "editing it of superfluities and bringing out its point." The questioners were sharp and practiced, and nearly all were relevant and on the issue. Lecturers were always treated politely but vigorously. The key element in the process was the chairman, who had to be fair but firm, stimulating but skillful in handling touchy subjects.[51]

Peffer, an objective outside observer, said that the dues-paying membership of 1,350 "Ford Hall Folks" were mainly factory workers, artisans and small shopkeepers. Many nationalities were represented in the audience, including "some Negroes," with nearly as many women as men. Half were Jewish and more than half of foreign parentage. Many were radicals and socialists but in the heterogeneous mass, he wrote, "a rare unity has been welded." If Ford Hall can make no other claim as an educational institution, he continued, it teaches tolerance. Although Peffer found that the Forum was neither systematic nor consecutive, had no point of focus or line of progression, and provided no preparation in advance or study afterward, he concluded that as a social institution and an instrument of democracy "it is invaluable."[52]

In 1927, novelist and essayist Dorothy Canfield Fisher wrote that attending public lectures without prior preparation and then returning to everyday life without more study is "hardly more than a meaningless episode in anybody's existence." The essential elements in real adult learning—preparation and continuation of personal effort—are missing. Fisher found that discussion was generally from a single point of view, a politically radical perspective on the organization of society. Yet, she was always moved to see the possibilities in the Forum method for "simple folks," who have no other contact with intellectual life, as she described the setting. She especially saw possibilities in the discussions for "broadening the home background and hence opening a wider world to the next generation."[53]

In 1935, Morse A. Cartwright, Director of the American Association for Adult Education, wrote that the people in charge of the Forums "erred on the side of extremism in their zeal to see every side of public questions discussed." For Cartwright, the lectures made little effort to present the conservative point of view that represents the bulk of public thinking. He did admit that the emphasis on full and free discussion of current social problems was a cardinal principle of adult education. Earlier, the movement had drawn the ire of the National Civic Federation, a high-level collaboration of labor and business. The organization was concerned about the Open Forum and Community Center movements promoting "near-bolshevik industrial programs."[54]

The criticism by Cartwright, especially his concern about the "zeal to see every side of public questions discussed," should be viewed in the context of the institutionalizing of adult education during the period and the times itself. The Association that he had led for a decade was attempting to systemize adult learning nationally, while the very core of the Open Forum was a locally determining structure. At the same time, while the progressive period brought many changes, the nation as a whole was still very conservative. This was even truer after World War I. The Forum, on the other hand, provided alternative perspectives in the lecturers and sometimes a debate between opposing viewpoints. Representative community committees rather than professional educators planned each local series, and the programs were held in public halls, churches or synagogues, instead of schools.

In 1937, adult educator Dorothy Hewitt and geologist Kirtley F. Mather observed and compared several types of adult group learning. They saw advantages in the Forum method, beginning with the opportunity the speaker is given to present material without interruption to the "thought sequence." They found much to praise in the Forum approach but also saw disadvantages in the question period. The key to success at that point is an expert moderator, but no matter the strength of the person in charge, they wrote, one fundamental disadvantage cannot be overcome, and that is the structure of the program.[55]

The question period, Hewitt and Mather wrote, is frequently divided into only two sides, for or against the speaker's position. However, most issues are many-sided, and the dynamic of question and response, regardless of a skilled moderator, does not allow shades of gray. The effective moderator, they concluded, must serve as a kind of orchestra conductor, leading the whole, sometimes drawing out one set of instruments and another, and subduing a third group which may be overbearing.[56]

Following the prepared talk, Hewitt and Mather continued, the moderator took command, keeping order by indicating which person was to ask the next question and repeating it to ensure that everyone heard it. He rephrased the question when necessary so it would be clear, concise and pertinent to the subject. The speaker's response to the question was succinct, rarely more than two minutes. The goal was a fast-moving, stimulating evening instead of a dry academic address followed by a drawn-out question and answer period. Hewitt and Mather observed that the lecturer knew a challenge was probable, and so was more likely to stick to the subject with only valid arguments, and not "to shade his thinking in favor of some conclusion which is dear to his heart."[57]

They also saw the method as better than an open discussion approach in public learning. Several persons engaged in a conversation will often go in other directions, and even a skilled moderator will have trouble bringing them back to the main focus. The presiding officer in an open discussion did not have the commanding presence as in a Forum, where a question could be ruled out of order or beside the point. Rephrasing a question, to ensure it is in "harmony" with the issue under consideration, brought a greater sense of order, even control.[58]

In 1937, Mary Ely, in a wider, more balanced examination than Cartwright for the American Association for Adult Education, visited 75 public forums (not just the Open Forum) across the country. While finding failings in the lecture/question format, she concluded that the unifying thread of democracy bound together all the locations. "Forum audiences are consciously thinking of democracy, are talking democracy, are pointing to democracy as the one bright star of hope." In 1939, Sofia Fain focused closely on public forums in Chicago (again, not just the Open Forum model) for a graduate research project. She found that they provided a stimulus to study and an opportunity to express or hear unpopular ideas. The audience gained a "near-education and a heightened awareness of the world around them." Ultimately, critics praised the desire of the audience to become informed, to participate intelligently, as Fain wrote, "in this thing called democracy."[59]

Documentation of the impact of the Open Forum can be found in many cities. In Portland, Maine, in 1917, the municipal organist wrote that every citizen of the city owes a debt of gratitude to those who are making possible the wonderfully stimulating Forum meetings. A leading lawyer in Portland found the principle of the Open Forum is essential in carrying out "the ideals of our Government, and the spirit of tolerance and co-operation forms the basis for our hoped-for national life and prosperity." In Haverhill, Massachusetts, where an Open Forum was held from 1918 to 1943, the *Haverhill Evening Gazette* praised the series. In 1933, the paper editorialized that the thousands who had attended the Forum meetings and the hundreds who were active in the programs had embedded it "solidly in the life of the community." A person attending the Beth-El Open Forum in Hammond, Indiana, recalled it sixty years later as "the most marvelous program that ever existed."[60]

On the fifth anniversary of Ford Hall in 1913, the Ford Hall Folks, spearheaded by the administrator of the movement, Mary Caroline Crawford, presented a huge, beautifully bound book of letters of appreciation to Coleman. It weighed forty-five pounds. Letters from regular attendees as well as speakers and civic and religious leaders across the country described the impact of Ford Hall on their lives personally and the nation collectively.[61]

Boston labor leader Henry Abrahams wrote that at Ford Hall "Jew and Christian, white and black, men and women from all walks of life mingle." Freda Rogolsky, a young Russian Jewish immigrant, became a model for gauging the impact of the movement. Coleman wrote that she had been so bitter against the Christians who had tortured her family in Russia, that she would express her contempt by spitting on the sidewalk when she passed a church. Now, a product of the lecture movement, she wrote that Ford Hall "could be compared to the 'melting pot,' where we all come together, forgetting all prejudices, and are brothers listening to how we may better the conditions and make this world a better place."[62]

On the Forum's twentieth anniversary in 1928, a wide range of national leaders praised the founder and the movement in a twenty-five pound bound volume of testimonial letters. President Coolidge wrote that Ford Hall was a vital influence in Boston and a good example for other communities. Cardinal William O'Connell of Boston said that he knew of the good work of the Forum and followed it with "great interest and attention." Rabbi Abba Hillel Silver of Cleveland, who had spoken at Ford Hall, wrote that "democratic institutions will remain secure as long as the channels of public opinion and discussion are kept open."[63]

African-American leader W. E. B. Du Bois, who lectured at Ford Hall and other Forums around the country, joined in the praise. In a world of dangerous propaganda, deliberate misrepresentation, and intellectual muddle, he characterized the movement as "one of the few bright and reassuring spots." A regular attendee at Ford Hall said that it was "the bridge by which I crossed the gulf that exists between foreign-born parents and their American-born children and has helped me to keep spiritually abreast of them."[64]

Through the years, Ford Hall provided an open platform to a wide variety of viewpoints. In 1930, Reuben Lurie, editor of the *Ford Hall Bulletin*, told the story of the remarkable initiative in public learning in *The Challenge of the Forum; The Story of Ford Hall and the Open Forum—A Demonstration in Adult Education.* The Ford Hall Folks expanded their relationships with a Dramatic Society, a Musical Society, discussion groups, and classes. It was a community of learning and fellowship.[65]

In 1932, 600 of the "Folks" gathered for the annual banquet. As was often the case with Coleman in public gatherings, he had arranged a unique program. The head guests were all dressed in white so they might participate in a "Clinic." The purpose was to "diagnose civilization," which was "a very sick patient." The speakers at the program reflected the diversity of the movement in their ethnicity and occupation. The motto of "Let There Be Light" was as strong as ever.[66]

In 1968, at its sixtieth anniversary, Ford Hall continued to bring forward the leading questions of the day, attracting college students and a wide public. At that point, one writer estimated, two million persons had attended 1,465 lectures. From 5,000 anti-fascists battling the Boston Police in 1933, to prevent an avowed Nazi supporter from speaking, to the appearance of Malcolm X in the 1960s, this tradition of civic dialog, free speech and public learning persevered. It carries on today, headquartered at Northeastern University for several decades but at Suffolk University since 2008. The century-long goal is still "enriching public education, fostering civic dialogue, honoring free speech." There is no charge to attend as foundations and corporate, government and individual donors provide support. It continues to actively engage audiences on key issues in American society "in settings that facilitate frank and open debate."[67]

In 1939, poet Archibald MacLeish wrote that, "America is promises." In 1940, novelist Thomas Wolfe said that, "the true discovery of America is before us." Although the Forum movement slipped off the table of history, it has been recovered. The Open Forum learning initiative called forth an America *"to be"*—a democracy in the making. Describing the concept and conveying the experience can shape civic discussion today, whether in person, through the media, or individuals interacting with each other electronically. The image evoked by the leader of the Terre Haute Open Forum nine decades ago—*the striking of mind upon mind*—can contribute to a better community. It is an ideal and a process that may be very wisely applied today.[68]

NOTES

1. Sinclair Lewis, *Babbitt* (New York: Harcourt, Brace, 1922), 230–31.
2. Dorothy Rowden, editor, *Handbook of Adult Education in the United States*, (New York: American Association for Adult Education, 1934), 63.

3. The beginning of the movement is described by George W. Coleman and other contributors in *Democracy in the Making; Ford Hall and the Open Forum Movement—A Symposium* (Boston: Little, Brown, 1915, repr. 1917). Reuben L. Lurie, editor of the brochure distributed at the Boston lectures, updated the spread of the movement in *The Challenge of the Forum; The Story of Ford Hall and the Open Forum Movement—A Demonstration in Adult Education* (Boston: Richard D. Badger, 1930).

4. Adolf G. Gundersen, *The Socratic Citizen; A Theory of Deliberative Democracy* (Lanham, Maryland: Lexington Books, 2000), 39, 280; Peter Levine, *The New Progressive Era; Toward a Fair and Deliberative Democracy* (Lanham, Maryland: Rowman & Littlefield, 2000), 242. On the Open Forum as deliberative democracy, see Joseph M. Bessette, *The Mild Voice of Reason; Deliberative Democracy and American National Government* (Chicago: University of Chicago, 1994), 35, 46, and Sidney M. Milkis, "Progressivism, Then and Now," in Sidney M. Milkis and Jerome M. Mileur, eds., *Progressivism and the New Democracy* (Amherst: University of Massachusetts, 1999), 19.

5. Richard A. Posner, *Law, Pragmatism, and Democracy* (Cambridge: Harvard University, 2003), 17, 106–107.

6. John Rawls, *The Law of Peoples; With "The Idea of Public Reason Revisited"* (Cambridge: Harvard University, 1999), 139.

7. George H. Sabine, "The Historical Position of Liberalism," in Caroline F. Ware, ed., *The Cultural Approach to History* (New York: Columbia University, 1940; repr., Port Washington, NY: Kennikat Press, 1964), 213–14.

8. Alexis de Tocqueville, *Democracy in America*, ed. Daniel J. Boorstin, 2 (New York: Vintage, 1990), 33, 34; Walter Rauschenbusch, *Christianity and the Social Crisis*, ed. Robert D. Cross (New York: Macmillan, 1907, 1964), 422.

9. Harold Marshall, "The Open Forum Movement," 51, 73, and Thomas Dreier, "The Controlling Purpose and Spirit," in Coleman, *Democracy in the Making*, 26.

10. James P. Roberts, "The Range of Speakers and Topics," in Coleman, *Democracy in the Making*, 35–36; Paula M. Kane, *Separatism and Subculture; Boston Catholicism, 1900–1920* (Chapel Hill: University of North Carolina, 1994), 22–38; Lurie, *Challenge of the Forum*, 181–205. Deleting the opening prayer if the speaker was a Catholic clergy is remarked on by Miriam Allen deFord, "The Method of Conducting the Meetings," in Coleman, *Democracy in the Making*, 45. The background of Catholic participants is noted in "Remember Jamaica Plain?" http://rememberjamaicaplain.blogspot.com/2008/03/mary-boyle-oreilly.html (accessed May 11, 2008); and in "Rev. M. J. Ahern, 74, A Jesuit Educator," *New York Times*, 6 June 1951 http://homepages.rootsweb.ancestry.com/~aherns/ahobits5.htm#06/06/1951 (accessed May 11, 2008). Rev. John A. Ryan wrote that as a frequent speaker at the Forum, his relations were "invariably and progressively pleasant." Yet, the "discussion of socio-ethical problems . . . in a democratic spirit"—within the propagation and application of *"moral* principles"—made a Catholic uneasy. "I have written thus frankly concerning Ford Hall from the Catholic view-point because I gladly recognize the sincerity and high purpose of its promoters . . . ." John A. Ryan, "By A Catholic Priest," in Coleman, *Democracy in the Making*, 118–23.

11. "Henry Abrahams," *Who Was Who in America: A Companion Volume to Who's Who in America*, 1897–1942 (Chicago: A. N. Marquis Company, 1942), 1:4; Lurie, *Challenge of the Forum*, 181; Mona Domosh, *Invented Cities; The Creation of Landscape in Nineteenth-Century New York and Boston* (New Haven: Yale University, 1996), 152.

12. Mattson, *Creating a Democratic Public*, 26–45.

13. Lurie, *Challenge of the Forum*, 60–63.

14. William R. Ferris, "How the Century Began; A Conversation with H. W. Brands," *Humanities* 19 (3) May/June 1998, 7, 9; Steven J. Diner, *A Very Different Age; Americans of the Progressive Era* (New York: Hill and Wang, 1998), 6.

15. Lewis, *Babbitt*, 401; Upton Sinclair, *The Jungle* (New York: Doubleday, Page, 1906; repr. Viking Penguin, 1986), 366–67.

16. Sidney E. Ahlstrom, *A Religious History of the American People*, (New York: Doubleday, 1975), 2:273.

17. "Harold E. Stearns," *Current Biography 1943* (New York: H. W. Wilson, 1943), 731; Harold E. Stearns, ed., *Civilization in the United States; An Inquiry By Thirty Americans* (New York: Harcourt Brace, 1922; repr., Westport, Connecticut: Greenwood Press, 1971), v–vii.

18. Walter Lippmann, "The Causes of Political Indifference To-day," *Atlantic Monthly* (February 1927), 263; Reinhold Niebuhr, "Can Christianity Survive?" *Atlantic Monthly* (January 1925), 84–88, and "A Religion Worth Fighting For," *Survey* (1 August 1927), 444–46, 480. Niebuhr was a Student Director for the Open Forum with the Midwest Council for Social Discussion. American Baptist-Samuel Colgate Historical Library, American Baptist Historical Society, Rochester, New York, Ford Hall Scrapbooks, vol. 9, 8 May 1925. For brevity in subsequent notes, references to the scrapbooks at the American Baptist Historical Society will be "Scrapbooks," followed by the volume number:

1—1908–1910
2—1910–1911
3—1912–1913
4—1913–1914
5—1915–1916
6—1916–1918
7—1918–1921
8—1921–1924
9—1924–1927

The American Baptist Historical Society collection in Rochester was transferred to the American Baptist Historical Society, located at Mercer University, Macon, Georgia, in 2008. http://www.abhsarchives.org/publications_newsletter.html (accessed August 13, 2011).

19. Ahlstrom, *Religious History of the American People*, 384; Paul A. Carter, *The Decline and Revival of the Social Gospel; Social and Political Liberalism in American Protestant Churches, 1920–1940* (Hamden, Connecticut: Shoe String Press, 1956, 1971), 13; Robert T. Handy, "The American Religious Depression, 1924–1935," *Church History*, 29 (March 1960), 3–4.

20. Lewis Atherton, *Main Street in the Middle Border* (Bloomington: Indiana University, 1954), 257–60.

21. Frederick T. Persons, "Mary Parker Follett," *Dictionary of American Biography*, edited by Harris E. Starr, suppl. 1, (New York: Charles Scribner's Sons, 1944), 21:308–309; Kevin Mattson, "Introduction," Mary Parker Follett, *The New State; Group Organization the Solution of Popular Government* (University Park: Pennsylvania State University, 1998; Longmans, Green and Company, 1918), xxxvi–xxxviii; Mary Parker Follett, "The Social Centre [spelling of the period] and the Democratic Ideal," *Ford Hall Folks*, Scrapbooks, 4, 21 December 1913, 1, 4.

22. Follett, *New State*, 4–51, 184–215.

23. Ibid., 208–10, 370.

24. John Dewey, *The Public and Its Problems* (New York: Holt, 1927; repr., Denver: Alan Swallow, 1954), 166–76, 208, 213, 216.

25. Ibid., 166–67, 217–19.

26. Ibid., 142, 218.

27. Letter, John Dewey, New York City, to Coleman, Boston, 19 March 1928, Letters of Appreciation to George W. Coleman, Ford Hall Forum 1908–1928, (Testimonial Album), Babson College Archives. The importance of the letter is shown in that it was also quoted in Lurie, *Challenge of the Forum*, 120. For brevity in Coleman materials in the Babson College Archives and Special Collections, Horn Library, Babson College, Babson Park, Massachusetts, references will be "Babson."

28. "Folks," William A. Craigie and James R. Hulbert, *A Dictionary of American English on Historical Principles*, (Chicago: University of Chicago, 1938–1944), 2:1028; Lewis, *Babbitt*, 35; Shailer Mathews, *Jesus On Social Institutions*, edited by Kenneth Cauthen (Philadelphia: Macmillan, 1928; Fortress Press, 1971), 130.

29. Robert B. Westbrook, *John Dewey and American Democracy* (Ithaca NY: Cornell University, 1991), xv, 42–44.

30. Ibid., 166, 170.

31. Ibid., 185.

32. Harold W. Stubblefield and Patrick Keane, *Adult Education in the American Experience; From the Colonial Period to the Present* (San Francisco: Jossey-Bass, 1994), 174.

33. Westbrook, *John Dewey and American Democracy*, 247, 249.

34. Ibid., 314–316; Dewey, *Public and Its Problems*, 218–19.

35. Stubblefield and Keane, *Adult Education in the American Experience*, 10–26; "Town Meetings," *Dictionary of American History*, rev. ed., (New York: Charles Scribner's Sons, 1976), 7:78–79; Merle Curti, *The Growth of American Thought*, Second Edition (New York: Harper and Brothers, 1943, 1951), 39; Richard D. Brown, *The Strength of a People; The Idea of an Informed Citizenry in America, 1650–1870* (Chapel Hill: University of North Carolina, 1996), 38, 82, 105.

36. "Committees of Correspondence," *Dictionary of American History*, 2:140; Curti, *Growth of American Thought*, 129, 135, 213.

37. Curti, ibid., 344, 358–59, 351.

38. "Lyceum Movement," *Dictionary of American History*, 4:207; "Chautauqua Movement," 2:1; Frederick E. Schortemeier, "Indianapolis Newspaper Accounts of Ralph Waldo Emerson," *Indiana Magazine of History* 49 (September 1953), 307–12.

39. Donald M. Scott, "The Popular Lecture and the Creation of a Public in Mid-Nineteenth-Century America," *Journal of American History* 66 (March 1980), 806–808; Curti, *Growth of American Thought*, 364.

40. Carl Bode, *The American Lyceum; Town Meeting of the Mind* (New York: Oxford University, 1956), 22–23; Stubblefield and Keane, *Adult Education in the American Experience*, 87; Hartley Grattan, *In Quest of Knowledge; A Historical Perspective on Adult Education* (New York: Association Press, 1955), 155–61; Curti, *Growth of American Thought*, 365–67.

41. Andrew C. Rieser, *The Chautauqua Moment; Protestants, Progressives, and the Culture of Modern Liberalism* (New York: Columbia University, 2003), 183; Stubblefield and Keane, *Adult Education in the American Experience*, 137–38; Grattan, *In Quest of Knowledge*, 175–82.

42. Mary L. Ely, *Why Forums?* (New York: American Association for Adult Education, 1937), 8–9; http://cooper.edu/about-us/the-great-hall/ (accessed August 2, 2011); "Henry M. Leipziger," *Dictionary of American Biography*, 11:154–155.

43. Joseph F. Kett, *The Pursuit of Knowledge Under Difficulties; From Self-Improvement to Adult Education in America, 1750–1990* (Stanford, CA: Stanford University, 1994), 173, 182, 346.

44. James L. Hill, "The New Forum and the Old Lyceum," *Sagamore Herald*, 31 May 1917, n.p., repr., *Biblical World*, n.d., Scrapbooks, 7.

45. Ibid.

46. *Annual Report of the Boston Baptist Social Union*, 3 April 1916, Scrapbooks, 5; Nathaniel Peffer, *New Schools For Older Students*, (New York: Macmillan, 1926), 11–14; "Nathaniel Peffer," *Who Was Who in America*, 1961–1968 (Chicago: A. N. Marquis, 1968), 4:742.

47. Mary Caroline Crawford, "A Roll of Personalities," in Coleman, *Democracy in the Making*, 149–206; Curti, *Growth of American Thought*, 593.

48. Peffer, *New Schools for Older Students*, 10.

49. Ibid., 11–13.

50. Ibid., 14–16.

51. Ibid., 17–18.

52. Ibid., 19, 29.

53. Dorothy Canfield Fisher, *Why Stop Learning?* (New York: Harcourt, Brace, 1927), 210–11.

54. "Morse Adams Cartwright," *Who Was Who in America*, 1974–1976 (Chicago: Marquis, 1976), 6:71; Morse A. Cartwright, *Ten Years of Adult Education; A Report on a Decade of Progress in the American Movement* (New York: Macmillan, 1935), 139–40; Marguerite A. Green, *The National Civic Federation and the American Labor Movement, 1900–1925* (Washington, D.C.: Catholic University of America, 1956; Westport, CT: Greenwood, 1973), 394.

55. Dorothy Hewitt and Kirtley F. Mather, *Adult Education; A Dynamic for Democracy* (New York: Appleton-Century, 1937), 151–52; "Dorothy Hewitt," Boston Center for Adult Education, http://www.bcae.org/aboutbody.html (accessed September 8, 2007); "Kirtley Fletcher Mather," *Webster's Biographical Dictionary*, (Springfield, Massachusetts: G. & C. Merriam, 1969), 988.

56. Hewitt and Mather, *Adult Education*, 153.

57. Ibid., 151–52.

58. Ibid., 152.

59. Ely, *Why Forums?*, 211–12; Sophia Fagin, *Public Forums in Chicago* (M.A. diss., University of Chicago, 1939), 214–18, 222–24. ["Dissertation" appears on the title page.]

60. "Letters of Divers [*sic*] People Concerning the Open Forum as Conducted Under the Auspices of the Congress Square Associates," re-typed letter from Will C. Macfarlane, Portland, Maine, to Willis B. Hall, February 12, 1917, Scrapbooks, 6; *Haverhill Evening Gazette*, editorial, 4 November 1933, enclosed with letter to writer, Gregory H. Laing, Haverhill Public Library, Haverhill, Massachusetts, April 4, 1995; interview by writer, Rosalyn Friedman, Calumet City, Illinois 30 May 1992.

61. *Ford Hall Folks to George W. Coleman, February 23, 1908–1913*, testimonial album, Babson College Archives.

62. *Ford Hall Folks*, 2 March 1913, 6, 7, Scrapbooks, 3; "The 'Under Dog' Lecture Theme," *Woonsocket Call* [Rhode Island], n.d., n.p., Scrapbooks, 4.

63. Karl Schriftgiesser, "Two Decades of Discussion," *Boston Transcript*, 14 April 1928, n.p., Babson.

64. Ibid.

65. Lurie, *Challenge of the Forum*, 131.

66. Rolfe Cobleigh, "What Ails Civilization; The Ford Hall Forum Seeks the Answers," *The Congregationalist and Herald of Gospel Liberty*, 28 April 1932, n.p., Babson.

67. William Worthy, "Ford Hall Forum: Boston At Its Best, 1908–1968," *Boston Sunday Globe*, 15 December 1968, 9–10, 12, Babson; brochure, "Ford Hall Forum, Spring 2011, Free Public Lectures & Discussions," Suffolk University, Boston, Massachusetts, writer's collection; letter, Alex Minier, Ford Hall Forum, to writer, 21 April 2008; "Ford Hall Forum," http://www.fordhallforum.org/about/mission (accessed July 28, 2011).

68. Archibald MacLeish, "America Was Promises," *Collected Poems, 1917–1952* (Boston: Houghton Mifflin, 1952), 333–41; Thomas Wolfe, *You Can't Go Home Again*, quoted in Henry Steele Commager, *The American Mind; An Interpretation of American Thought and Character Since the 1880's* (New Haven: Yale University, 1950, repr. 1989), 276; John W. Herring, "The Open Forum," *Adult Bible Class Monthly* (The Methodist Concern), (November 1922), 322.

Chapter Two

Beginning

We Have Plans Laid Already

On May 11, 1907, George William Coleman, publisher of the *Christian Endeavor World* magazine and a Baptist lay leader in Boston, wrote theologian Walter Rauschenbusch that he had just read his *Christianity and the Social Crisis*. He said he would place a copy in the hands of all the workers at the magazine.

> It has impressed me most deeply and I am going to read it again right away. I have bought forty copies for distribution among my friends. [It] comes pretty near being an epoch-making book. . . . We have plans laid already that look toward a dissemination of some of the truths which you teach.[1]

With these words, Coleman linked the principles of the Social Gospel, the social justice movement that was reshaping much of Protestantism, directly to the Open Forum lecture series he was developing. In Rauschenbusch's landmark blueprint for the transformation of the nation, *Christianity and the Social Crisis*, the theologian wrote that the Old Testament Prophets were the basis for understanding the economic and social revolution shaping the new century. For Rauschenbusch, the goal was very simple: Seek justice and relieve the oppressed. He perceived clearly the social crisis facing the nation, especially the plight of the powerless working class.[2]

As Professor of Church History at Rochester Theological Seminary, Rauschenbusch brought this understanding forward into a social orientation of Christianity, one that would reconstruct the nation into a society based on love, service and equality. While a number of religious leaders stood at the front of the Social Gospel movement, Rauschenbusch understood directly from his experience as a pastor in a New York City slum district that the working class had not yet found the church supportive in their struggle. To the contrary, he argued, an increasing alienation between the working class and the churches had developed. If Christianity would add its moral force to the social and economic forces working to re-order society, it would, in his words, "rechristianize the Church." Men were needed to combine religious faith, moral enthusiasm, and economic information in shaping a public morality. A spirit of fraternity would create fraternal institutions, Rauschenbusch wrote, which would then feed back into the fraternal spirit.[3]

A century later, it is almost impossible to grasp the impact of this single book at the time. In 1909, journalist Ray Stannard Baker visited church leaders in various parts of the country. In *The Spiritual Unrest*, Baker wrote that he was aware of the waning influence of the church on peoples' lives. During his trip, he asked the clergy, "What recent book, or what man, has given you the most light?" The response of Rauschenbusch's book was startling in its unanimity. No other title had a more favorable reception or wider reading among religious leaders. It received a long, favorable review in the *New York Times Saturday Review of Books* and was listed among the "Best Books of 1907." Several times reprinted, eventually selling over 50,000 copies, and translated into eight languages, the book could not have achieved such an impact, writes historian Robert Cross, had Americans thought that widespread "spiritual unrest" was the concern only of clergymen."[4]

Even before writing Rauschenbusch about the book, Coleman had been involved in a group headed by the theologian that wrestled with social problems. Beginning in 1892, the Brotherhood of the Kingdom, comprised of Baptist ministers, theologians and laymen in several cities, sought to apply the significant concepts of social Christianity to the problems of everyday life. Among the group's aims was to keep in contact with the common people, infuse the religious spirit into the efforts for social amelioration, and jealously guard the freedom of discussion for any man who is impelled by love of the truth to utter his thoughts. These were the exact principles that Coleman would use to shape the Ford Hall Forum in 1908.[5]

The financial base for Ford Hall, and eventually the impetus for the national movement, came from the estate of Daniel Sharp Ford, a Baptist businessman. In 1899, he left $350,000 to the Boston Baptist Social Union to erect a building "for the betterment of mankind." Such a "great community force" would allow for the fullest expression of the group's principles in helping workingmen. He was specific on the location and purpose of the building: It was to be as near as practicable to the center of business in the city, in an "open field for the fullest exhibition of its principles." He described the need for Christian businessmen to come into "closer personal relations with the working-man." Time is imperative because of the worker's religious indifference, "feverish unrest," and belief that business is his enemy.[6]

Ford once said to a friend, "I want to take a building in a congested district and give it over entirely to the use of the people." He didn't think he would call it a church or have a minister over it. Instead, Ford's answer to the disquiet and lack of churchgoing around him was "Christian democracy." The 325 laymen in the Baptist Social Union would have personal interest in workingmen. Use of the halls and committee rooms was given freely to all Baptist societies. Just before his death, he expressed his ideal of the organization of a city church. It would have a "spiritual pastor and preacher" as head, a leader for benevolent and educational work, a Sunday school superintendent, a "kind-hearted man" to help the poor, a "canvasser or visitor" to search out needy families, and a person in charge of an employment bureau. Ford's vision was far more than bricks and mortar.[7]

The forward-thinking outlook of Ford and the implementation of his bequest have deep roots in American Baptist history and its adult education programs. One study of the historical records of the denomination shows that the spirit of democracy led to strong adult education programs, beginning in the early nineteenth century, along with the freedom to experiment. At the turn of the twentieth century, the increasing number of immigrants from different religious heritages, coupled with declining church attendance, brought new challenges. The study notes that those years "represent a critical time of adjustment to the problems of the contemporary age." In 1907, the Northern Baptist Convention was founded. From 1900 to 1914, articles on the problems of cities began to appear in the major Baptist periodicals with greater frequency. It was natural then that the Open Forum emanated from this Baptist public learning spirit and the need to respond to the changing city.[8]

The eight-story Ford building was erected, with two stories set aside for Ford Hall, but it needed the right leader before the donor's vision could be realized. The need and the opportunity came together in Coleman.

George William Coleman was born in Boston on June 16, 1867 and died there on July 31, 1950. After graduating from English High School with honors in 1885, he went to work, as his family could not afford college. He once looked back at "vivid and painful remembrances" between the ages of fourteen to eighteen. On Saturdays, holidays, and summer vacations, he worked in his father's bindery, "standing up to a bench ten hours a day doing mechanical, monotonous work over and over again endlessly." He hated the factory, as it seemed more like a "prison." The family's modest financial circumstances would both shape his Open Forum commitment and provide a story line in his biography. Many years later, after he had served as an investigator for the Interchurch Federation study of the Great Steel Strike of 1919, one article noted "he was not born with a silver spoon in his mouth."[9]

Coleman worked his way up in publishing at the *Christian Endeavor World*, and also began extensive Baptist denominational activities, displaying impressive speaking and leadership abilities, locally and nationally. He became president of local and national advertising associations and served as president of the Massachusetts Sunday School Association and as a director of the Boston YMCA. He entered politics as a civic responsibility for a few years, which included serving on the Boston City Council and for a brief time as Council President. He was a delegate to the 1912 Republican National Convention, as a supporter of Theodore Roosevelt, and later to the Massachusetts Constitutional Convention.[10]

A block of his time each year went to the Sagamore Sociological Conference that he had founded in 1907. For several days each summer, until 1918, Coleman brought together a select group of people in a beach house near Cape Cod to discuss societal and religious topics. The sessions differed from the Open Forum, as the invited participants were not a cross-section of the public but instead leaders in civic, academic, business and religious arenas. A booklet of the speeches, resolutions and other materials from the week was produced each year and press coverage carried the discussions further. The 1915 session was also the setting for the Second Annual Meeting of the Open Forum National Council. The gatherings were suspended in 1918 because "money, time and energy that would be given to the conference will be used in the many war activities."[11]

In addition to the extensive time he gave to the Forum, Coleman had a very busy advertising career, locally and nationally. In 1912, Rauschenbusch was undoubtedly referring to Coleman in *Christianizing the Social Order*. The theologian wrote that "one of the most wonderful symptoms of the moral uplift is the fact that the publicity men of the country under the leadership of an unusual kind of Christian have undertaken to make advertising tell the truth." Coleman was then president of the Associated Advertising Clubs of America and traveling widely around the country.[12]

During his first term as president of the national organization, the convention was held in Dallas. On the Sunday morning of the convention, advertising laymen filled the pulpits of the churches. In the second year that he was president, the organization met in Baltimore and adopted the motto "TRUTH IN ADVERTISING." It was placed in electric letters on top of the tallest building in the business district.[13]

In 1891, Coleman married Alice P. Merriam. Separately and together, they were active for many years in Baptist organizations in Boston and nationally. Both rose to leadership positions, and she worked closely with him on the Open Forum. For thirty years, beginning in 1902, he chaired the Christian Work Committee of the Baptist Social Union. The lay group oversaw the Ford bequest to several churches, in addition to providing the building and support for the Forum. From 1917 to 1918, Coleman was president of the Northern Baptist Convention. In 1918, he chaired the Baptist War Commission and went to Europe for four months to investigate war conditions, representing both the Northern and Southern Baptist Conventions. In preparation for the visit, he gained "splendid introductions" from George Creel, Chairman of the Committee on Public Information, the government agency that sought to rouse public support for the war. The introductions proved very helpful in his work, which took him to the front lines, adding further to his positive image. Creel and Coleman would subsequently link up in post-war activities seeking to bring the nation together.[14]

After Coleman returned from Europe, he assisted Roger Babson, the famed statistician, who headed the Information and Education Service in the Department of Labor. Their association eventually led to a significant career change for Coleman. In 1921, he became President of the Babson Institute, the college that the statistician had begun in a nearby suburb, and held the position until 1935. He wrote and spoke extensively about business issues during this period. Beginning in 1929, Coleman also served as president of Webber College, the women's affiliate of Babson in Florida, although there was an on-site administrator. From 1935 to 1950, he was an active member of the Board of Trustees of the historically black Howard University, becoming Vice Chairman. Over the years, he received honorary degrees from Colby College, Franklin College, and Wake Forest College.[15]

Coleman's greatest contribution, though, in vision, passion and lifelong commitment, was the Open Forum, first in Boston and then as he spread it across the nation.

In 1913, one admirer described Coleman as an ordinary-sized, "teetotaling" Baptist deacon, but also an attractive man. People gathered about him to laugh, to talk, and to follow him. He had a spirit of optimism, a sense of fairness, an air of wholesomeness and good cheer. While he would seek the counsel of others, he could be enormously determined once he decided on a course of action. Through his leadership of the Ford Hall Forum (the same enthusiastic writer added), light, hope and the power to move forward "penetrated to the smoldering masses of the socially submerged." Around 1920, another person wrote that "he makes friends easily and holds them long; and has more varieties of them than Mr. Heinz has pickles."[16]

In 1923, another observer saw similar traits, particularly his marvelous skill in "pouring oil on troubled waters." His friendly demeanor, with twinkling blue eyes, blonde hair and Van Dyke beard framing a "benign countenance," won people over. Where others would frown over difficulties, he would beam and give a throaty laugh. He was patient with others and heard them through, using gentle persuasion and calm reasoning rather than bluster or "cram-it-down dogmatism." The skills that made him such an effective Forum moderator lasted throughout his life. In a description of him in 1936, an admirer praised his ability to bring people together who apparently had nothing in common. In his "all-embracing love," he was a "friend to the friendless and a fighter against economic and political injustice."[17]

If there was a single event that shaped Coleman, it was a shipwreck. In December 1889, after he had worked in educational publishing for four years, he sailed off on a "great adventure" to Buenos Aires, as the correspondent for several newspapers. A storm shattered the ship. Almost without hope, he was rescued, but while adrift, he heard an inner voice, urging him to dedicate his life to service. He decided to switch to religious publishing. In an eighteen-year career at the *Christian Endeavor World*, he rose to the head of the advertising department and then to publisher. In 1910, he became Director of Publicity for a large shoe manufacturer, W. H. McElwain Company.[18]

In 1906, returning by train from a trip to the South for his denominational responsibilities, Coleman learned about the People's Institute at Cooper Union in New York City. He stopped off in the city on a Sunday evening and heard Charles P. Fagnani of Union Theological Seminary speak on Christianity. Coleman, recently elected President of the Boston Baptist Social Union, looked around the hall and saw the transforming educational power of a working class, immigrant audience challenged by and discussing current issues and great ideas. He realized the education they were gaining. He had found what was needed for Ford Hall—*democracy in the making*—to carry out the vision of Daniel Sharp Ford in meeting the needs of the working people of Boston.[19]

With increasing immigration in those years, Boston was undergoing a significant change in population. From 360,000 in 1880 and 448,000 in 1890, the city had grown to 560,000 in 1900. By then, thirty-five percent of the residents were foreign-born and seventy-two percent wholly or in part of foreign parentage. A 1910 encyclopedia article noted that large areas of the city, "like adjoining but unmixing nations," presented a cosmopolitan mix of languages, customs and religions. With all of this change, Boston was proud of its strong shaping influence on the nation's history and its schools, libraries, literary traditions, public works, and reputation as the center of American culture.[20]

To respond to the civic and adult education challenges of the population now in the city, Coleman developed a unique public lecture model. It differed in significant ways from earlier movements. First, it was more intellectual and less religious in program content although many clergy were involved in the planning and as speakers. It was also more appealing in a large city, such as Boston with its wider range of people, but also adaptable for smaller cities. Importantly, it was more democratic with representative local committees developing their own programs, although a national speaker's bureau was available to arrange for out-of-town lecturers. Lowell Institute in Boston had served adult education needs in a limited way but it was not intended to be democratic in its planning, structure or audience participation.[21]

In the religious, ethnic and immigrant mix of central Boston, Coleman moved beyond the small town appeal of the Lyceum. Times had changed and while the Lyceum audience accepted whatever was presented from the platform, the public now wanted to ask questions. People had "divine discontent," as one article noted. Coleman's approach was also more inclusive than women's clubs. The clubs studied various topics, developed an amazing range of activities as community builders and agents of change, and were an important factor in the popularization of knowledge, mainly among white middle class women. His concept was also wider than the Chautauqua movement as the Forum was grounded in a non-sectarian base, although Baptist funds initially sustained it. A school to teach the Forum method was actually held under Chautauqua auspices for five summers. Finally, his methods went beyond the earlier movements through well-crafted publicity and extensive use of newspapers and a wide range of periodicals.[22]

Coleman's publicity acumen developed just at the time that Social Gospel clergy and progressive political leaders were becoming aware of the power of the press in the new age. In 1912, as Chairman of the Publicity Commission of the Men and Religion Forward Movement, another Social Gospel initiative, Coleman wrote that the "two great agencies of democracy" are the press and the church. In these "new and reorganizing times," he said, they should cooperate, with a new sense of a common opportunity and a common obligation. He concluded, there is no force in the world today more potent and far reaching than the force generated by rightly directed publicity.[23]

The creation of the Publicity Bureau by James Ellsworth in Boston in 1903 is an example of the increasing role of publicity in those years. The purpose of that public relations company was to place prepackaged news items in newspapers around the country. In scrapbooks of the Forum movement, newspaper articles in different cities show a marked similarity in phrasing in announcing upcoming lectures and reporting on them afterward. It suggests a strong likelihood of carefully "planted" articles.[24]

While Coleman's Forum work was divided mainly between inspiring others and spreading the method around the country, he paused two times from his activism to articulate the vision conceptually. In 1909, in an address to a Baptist Congress, he proposed a significant broad construct for society. He saw a "co-operative social order" as the desired direction and necessary outcome of our history. He concluded that nothing less than democracy in material things will satisfy the unrest of the times. Without this cooperative approach, there is hopelessness, but with it, the nation will gain the liveliest faith, utmost expectation, and tremendous activity. A nation cannot be democratic in politics at the same time it is autocratic in business. The answer is to break down barriers through universal communication and education. Mutual acquaintance and knowledge, he said, is a forerunner of cooperation.[25]

In the second instance of describing his vision, Coleman looked back in 1915 to the beginning of the movement. He wrote that "the crying need in this country is to get folks together." There can be no real democracy if people do not know each other. Solutions to the grave problems that threaten individual, political, social and economic life will only be found in "an environment of mutual understanding and good will between the races, classes, and creeds that make up our common life." The problems of the nation and the world were clearly on his mind. We cannot afford to lose a day's time, he argued, if the destructive forces of modern civilization are not to overwhelm the constructive agencies. His greatest fear was that the country will not be quick enough with a new spirit and better ways. "Revolution may blot out evolution."[26]

It took Coleman until 1908 to convince the trustees of the Baptist Social Union that the Ford bequest of 1899 should be used for an adult learning endeavor. Employing his advertising skills, he printed fliers in English, Italian and Yiddish, announcing "The People's Sunday Evenings" for six weeks, beginning February 23. The programs will be a "meeting of the people for good fellowship, for the enjoyment of good music, and for moral and intellectual stimulus, without prejudice to race, creed or class." Admission is free. Most of the speakers had appeared at the Sunday Evening Workingmen's Meetings in Cooper Union in New York City. The Committee of Arrangements for the Ford Hall series included Christians and Jews, business and labor leaders. Extensive coverage in Boston newspapers described the purpose of the meetings is to bring "workingmen" together. In addition to box ads in the newspapers welcoming everybody, especially working people, Coleman took his message to the target audience even more directly, speaking before the Central Labor Union about the series.[27]

Five years later, when Coleman considered the factors that made the Forum movement a success, he identified publicity as of crucial importance. It was the "one force" that saved it from an early death. Not only did publicity rescue the Ford Hall series from inattention, it also protected it from those who would have destroyed it because they could not understand. He wrote that fair and generous press reports saved the day at more than one critical juncture. Articles in the secular and religious press, especially the *Watchman* (a Baptist weekly) and the *Congregationalist*, made the difference.[28]

Demonstrating his exceptional marketing skills even further, Coleman selected Henry Abrahams, the Jewish secretary of the Central Labor Union, who was on the Committee of Arrangements, to talk first at the opening night about labor development in the nation. The three other lecturers that evening talked about Daniel Sharp Ford, the meaning of democracy, and cooperation. Music, including singing, began the evening and became a regular part of each Ford Hall program and in other cities, such as in Terre Haute and Hammond. Education and entertainment, inspiration and pleasure, and cross-class, cross-cultural fellowship marked the movement.[29]

While a report in one Boston newspaper noted a good-sized audience for the opening program, another said the hall was comfortably filled with members of the Baptist Social Union, "with here and there one who appeared to be a working man." Reflecting this disappointment, the person compiling the first scrapbook of newspaper and magazine articles on the Forum wrote that 150 persons were present, while the auditorium had 1,000 seats.[30]

By the second program, a talk by Charles Sprague Smith, Director of the People's Institute at Cooper Union, the number had grown to 270. Coverage of the program included, in the *Boston Journal*, the speaker's statement that it was foolish to fear socialism, as it was preferable to the "present reign of injustice." The *Congregationalist* quoted the speaker that the fundamental social fact of the present time was the growing consciousness of the brotherhood of man. The audience was judged to be a cross-section of the city but "mostly laboring men." After the address, men and women asked questions for an hour.[31]

At the third program, in which Rabbi Samuel Schulman of New York spoke on "What the Jew Has Done for the World and What the World has Done to the Jew," attendance rose to 500. When a questioner challenged Jewish patriotism, and a verbal row took place, the rabbi responded by citing Jewish loyalty and participation in the nation's wars since the Revolution. The fourth program drew 230 persons to hear Rev. Leighton Williams, a leading proponent of the Social Gospel. Discussing the unequal distribution of wealth in the country, he called for social justice rather than socialism.[32]

Some 400 persons attended the fifth program to hear another New York minister, Rev. Thomas R. Slicer, speak on the moral imperative that man alone has to do good. The final lecturer in the series was Rev. Thomas C. Hall, a socialist from Union Theological Seminary. His topic, "The Relation of Modern Christian Life to the Social Problem," focused on the need for a reign of the morality of heart, the brotherhood of man, and the fatherhood of God.[33]

In concluding coverage on the first season, the *Boston Globe* noted that attendance had been very good, the question and answer portion the liveliest part of the meetings, and many requests had been made to continue the series. (Coleman asked for feedback and received "hundreds of letters" on the impact of the meetings.) Looking back at the programs, he was pleased at the good beginning. He had found a lively way to carry out Ford's vision, beyond the Baptist Social Union. Very importantly, he had reassured Boston ministers that he was not seeking their congregants but instead envisioned the Forum as a home for people without a church. The Open Forum, and eventually its expansion across the nation, had begun.[34]

In the middle of its growth, in 1916, Coleman said that the movement was leading to more things than anyone knows. "When a disintegrated community becomes synthesized—and that is exactly what a forum does for the community—there is nothing which the community cannot accomplish." What was regarded before as impossible becomes easy. During this period, his mentor, Rauschenbusch, and many other liberal intellectuals were in despair because of the war in Europe. Coleman, though, kept his focus on the Forum. Acknowledging the division of America into groups and classes, he saw the need for a common meeting ground for people to get together and talk things over. The answer is the Open Forum—"a place where all classes can come together . . . for the consideration of problems of interest to all."[35]

As the movement spread across America, Coleman identified what he considered one of the most intriguing developments. Originally, the Forum was established to interest people unconnected with churches but now, more often than not, local series were being established by churches or held in churches. He mentioned recent letters from ministers in Pennsylvania, Indiana and Illinois, all of whom were starting Forums. For the first time, churches were becoming acquainted with how "the other half" lives. Forums were also being started by boards of trade, synagogues, boys' athletic clubs, women's clubs, civic clubs, and school centers. "There has never been anything like it before," he was quoted. Beyond bringing a community together, as will be shown in two cities in Indiana, Forums were a boon for speakers in interacting with local communities and earning additional income as lecturers.[36]

Coleman's positive view on the future of the learning movement that he started did not cloud his perception of the nation at the time. In one address on "The Under Dog," he described conditions as "heaps of powder ready to be set off." The solution to the nation's social and economic divisions was not less but *more* democracy. The schools were fulfilling their role by holding together the children of all nationalities, although admittedly the time was short before the children were thrown into the arena of "contending forces." He saw that these "underdogs," when they had the proper training, would become good citizens. He would trust these new Americans, who were "fundamentally religious," with the future of the country before he looked to people of the "cultured class."[37]

Viewing "an enormous tide of foreigners" pouring into the country, Coleman understood the anxiety of native-born Americans as the newcomers seemed to be rapidly outnumbering them, particularly on the East Coast. The ideals, environment, and customs of life of the immigrants differed materially from the new country and even among themselves. He asked if they will accept "our institutions" and become Americanized? Is the country doing everything possible to bring them into contact with American ideals and aims? In answering his own questions, he pointed to the work of Ford Hall, which was bringing all classes and thinkers into contact for their mutual benefit. They were finding where they differed and their common ground, resulting in better understanding between labor and capital, Jew and Gentile, Protestant and Catholic. In response to a question about his own religion, he felt he was now much more a "Christian" than a Baptist.[38]

For many years, the original intent of the Ford bequest and the effect of the Sunday evening lecture series on church attendance were large issues for Coleman. In a 1922 article, he described "this new instrument for democracy" as an outgrowth of religion, although it had taken some time for the church to recognize "its own child." Three decades earlier, churches felt that the effort to reach the masses was a failure and had become anxious about the future. Building on the lecture model at Cooper Union, the Forum was an attempt to bridge the widening chasm between well-meaning people within the churches and "good folks outside." The success was unmistakable, Coleman added, with many experts in social work calling the Forum method "the soundest and most successful process of Americanization."[39]

In that 1922 article, "The Contribution of the Open Forum to Democracy in Religion," Coleman said that Boston had twenty-five Forums, many sponsored by synagogues and Catholic and Protestant churches but open to all. In the Common Cause Forum, organized by the Catholic Church at Franklin Union Hall, 1,200 people on a Sunday evening listened to the pros and cons of such vital topics as religion, the church, democracy and education. Such an extraordinary spectacle was never witnessed before the coming of the Forum idea, he added, but it is commonplace at the Franklin Union after ten years of continuous operation. He said that the Common Cause Forum went even further in the democratic discussion of religious questions than Ford Hall, which was under Baptist sponsorship. Similarly, in one of the synagogue Forums, the older men looked on in amazement and some "in fear and trembling" as young people gathered by the hundreds to discuss freely and frankly everything of interest to them.[40]

For Coleman, the establishment of Forums under religious auspices was not the only mark Ford Hall made on the religious life of Boston. The greatest effect was the changed state of mind among church people. They have been "aroused and quickened, jarred and irritated, and set to thinking and reading as to the relation of religion to the whole realm of life." Forums everywhere were democratizing the discussion of religion, with the result that "one must have a very narrow conception of religion not to see that a live forum is shot through and through with a powerful religious dynamic." Believer and unbeliever, radical and conservative, rich and poor, come together in this "democracy in religion" in action.[41]

As an example, Coleman quoted Rabbi Harry Levi of Temple Israel, who saw Ford Hall as a "half-way house" to his congregation for unattached idealistic young Jews. They were saved from indifference, agnosticism or atheism, wrote Coleman. Christians were similarly influenced by forums to take a fresh evaluation of the church. Still others who would never find their way back to church membership find in Forums "inspiration, guidance and fellowship."[42]

By scheduling speakers he knew were excellent, Coleman ensured they would hold the audience. The lectures and the question periods furthered the Social Gospel, he believed, and working people were gaining exposure to a wide range of articulate thinkers, although usually to the left in the political spectrum. Finally, by involving a variety of people in the planning, including non-Christians and labor leaders, he was creating a democratic, public learning implementation of the Social Gospel. Through his efforts, social Christianity was moving beyond a Protestant, seminary-centered, Sunday morning message. He was building a bridge to the future, one that would carry social Christianity deeper into the nation.

In the second season, the series name was changed from "The People's Sunday Evenings" to "Ford Hall Meetings," the number of programs was increased to twenty-four, running from November to April, and the range of speakers was broadened. The lecturers included social welfare advocate Florence Kelley, Rabbi Stephen Wise, a strong voice for social justice and an open pulpit, attorney (later Supreme Court Justice) Louis Brandeis, who was fighting for working people and against monopolies, Rauschenbusch, and, at the last program, Coleman. Boston's newspapers expressed support for the series and covered the lectures extensively. Attendance in the second season began with 430 persons and rose to 925. At the fourth program, a panel discussion by four clergymen on socialism, 1,400 people attended and 500 more were turned away. Photographs of crowds lined up around Ford Hall and inside the completely full auditorium confirm newspaper reports on the success of the programs.[43]

As the Ford Hall series continued, Coleman reported regularly on its progress to the Baptist Social Union, which was providing the financial support. In his December 1914 report, he said that the eighth season of the Forum had "greater manifestation of vigor than ever before." The movement was spreading, in Coleman's words, with a Dallas pastor seeking to inaugurate similar meetings, a Buffalo church "having wonderful success," and the Manchester (New Hampshire) Open Forum "almost an exact duplicate of the Ford Hall Meetings." In Manchester, a city of 80,000, with a theatre that would only seat half as many as Ford Hall, the crowd was "often overflowing." An eight-page weekly, *Ford Hall Folks*, was begun in Boston, containing the lecture for the week and the questions and answers of the preceding Sunday night, together with other news on the national movement.[44]

Coleman's March 1917 report to the Baptist Social Union noted that the title of the weekly magazine had become *The Community Forum*, and was now the monthly organ of the national movement. He also mentioned the Ford Hall Town Meetings on Thursday nights, the "Foro Italiano" on Sunday evenings, and monthly meetings of the Ford Hall Folks that carry on the work. He thanked the seventy members of the Baptist Social Union who had contributed $1,900 to meet a financial emergency. He was grateful for an additional $1,000 contributed by the Ford Hall audience and $500 from other friends to continue Foro Italiano.[45]

In September 1917, Coleman expressed anxiety over the "desperately shortened" income of the Committee on Christian Work. Although the Ford Building was better rented than ever before, it was not bringing in sufficient income. They were obliged to give up the Foro Italiano, into which so much money and energy had been given. Regretfully but realistically, he wrote "you can't continue indefinitely the process of making bricks without straw." One month later, with the Baptist Social Union's annual income reduced from $30,000 to $10,000, Ford Hall began a collection for the first time. A committee canvassed the audience, distributing envelopes to those willing to take them. The Folks were asked to be cooperative, pledge as much as they can afford, and pay the pledge promptly each week: "*Let's all do our part!*"[46]

From 1908 to 1930, 373 different speakers gave 533 programs at Ford Hall. The largest groups of presenters were eighty-eight clergy and forty-five professors. Forty-three of the speakers were women. Reflecting their popularity with the audience, Margaret Slattery (an author and public lecturer) spoke eleven times, Rabbi Wise and Charles Zueblin thirteen times each, and Dr. John Haynes Holmes fourteen times. During this period, forty-four lectures were on religion, thirty-two on America's problems, and twenty or more each on democracy, labor, marriage, Europe, war, and socialism. From 1924 to 1926, the programs, including the question period, were broadcast on radio station WBZ, Boston and Springfield.[47]

In the 1915 collection of essays on the Boston series, Coleman described his delight, as the moderator on the platform, in looking out at the audience when they would talk back to the lecturer. They were a "virile, sensitive, responsive mass of human beings" who felt closely related to each other. Men outnumbered women by two or three to one, he wrote, and "bald heads and gray hairs" were rare. Young couples and "squads of young lads" were all over the hall. "Jew and Gentile, in the proportion of one to two, are as intimately mixed as if they were part and parcel of one grand mosaic." Some "unusually good representative of the colored people" and Hindus, Japanese and Chinese were not uncommon. The absence of church people, who Coleman knew "pretty well" in the city, did not concern him. Instead, he saw socialists, philosophical anarchists, employers, teachers, lawyers, merchants, politicians, and labor unionists. The agnostic and atheist were not "discomforted," and the Catholic and the Protestant "do not know which is which."[48]

Through the years, because of controversial speakers and topics, attempts were made to stop the series. It was to no avail. Coleman was determined: He had met a need and seen the future. "The only people who are not welcomed here are the church people," he wrote. (He was referring to regular church-goers whose needs were met in their own congregations.) The Forum is for "those who have no church home, who have no place to go for mental sustenance and moral inspiration." He was seeking "the folks outside the churches . . . to grow, to develop, to become better and bigger citizens." And beyond the churches, he was developing a gospel of "neighborliness." At the Forum, "no offense to race, class, or creed is tolerated." Skilled in leading meetings and armed with his democratic beliefs, Coleman didn't need a gavel. People wanted to hear the speakers and the follow-up discussions, and so he gave unlimited time to rephrase a question until it was clearly understood.[49]

Coleman and the "Ford Hall Folks" had started a movement. Through a network of ministers and civic leaders, he spread the model from Boston through New England and then around the nation. In enthusiastic writings in religious and secular publications, and in speeches across the country, he carried the Forum model to small and large cities. A "Platform of Principles" conveyed the foundation of the movement:

1. The complete development of democracy in America.
2. A common meeting-ground for all the people in the interest of truth and mutual understanding, and for the cultivation of community spirit.
3. The fullest and freest open public discussion of all vital questions affecting human welfare.

4. For free participation from the forum floor either by questions or discussion.

5. The freedom of forum management from responsibility for utterances by speakers from the platform or the floor.[50]

In forging these general principles into practice, and responding to the times, Coleman often spoke and wrote on the importance of national unity in the postwar period, such as in "Get Together in the Open Forum" and "Fighting Disintegration—How the Open Forum Does It." He described the rumblings spreading across the country, "bringing us to the verge of complete disintegration." The only salvation is getting together and the only vehicle is the several hundred Forums all over the country, where well-meaning people of every kind and degree come together to discuss serious things of mutual concern. The fellowship of toleration, respect and open-mindedness generated by the atmosphere of the Forum movement "is one of the greatest possible assets to our American citizenship."[51]

He felt deeply that the American "get-together spirit" manifesting itself through the Forum brings harmony and good will. "It isn't that we learn to think alike"—the secret is the wonderful diversity of points of view in the audience. In Boston, a cross-section of the city brings "speakers and topics attractive to all sorts and conditions of people." The program planners "will go to almost any length to bring together opposing elements in our complex American life." Over the years, through many speeches and writings, Coleman effectively intertwined the needs of the country as it underwent change, and advanced the Open Forum as the answer.[52]

The key element was the question period after the lecture. At Ford Hall, Coleman achieved equality by dividing the audience into groups, sometimes starting with the floor, sometimes with the gallery, alternating between the right-hand and left-hand sides. No further questions were allowed from a section until the next part of the audience had an opportunity. Limiting everyone to a single question, and the moderator then repeating the question before the speaker answered, ensured that the audience heard the question clearly the second time if they had not fully understood it initially. The delay also gave the lecturer a few extra moments to think about a response. The distinctive expression of the questioner, rather than written questions, ensured the audience that no issue would be dodged or suppressed. At Ford Hall, one observer noted, the questions were "surprisingly relevant; the proportion of entirely irrelevant queries is extremely small."[53]

As was true with the nation as a whole, the war affected the Forum. Many of the Ford Hall Folks entered military service and the nation experienced the disintegrating effects of rapid industrialization and urbanization. By 1916, historian Stuart I. Rochester writes, liberals had moved from their initial ignoring of the war and then being shocked by its magnitude to a new stage: they became obsessed by it as an apocalyptic event. Within a year, many came to support the war, including working for the newly formed Committee on Public Information. The agency had been formed to mobilize public opinion and to sell the war effort to those not convinced. The goal to keep the nation united continued after the war during the social and economic turmoil. Working with the Committee on Public Information, Rochester concludes, veteran reformers "could garner more glamour and excitement than they enjoyed in their finest muckraking days." For many, the war became "a vehicle that might reverse the decline" of their reform efforts. With such notable exceptions as Rauschenbusch (of German ancestry) and Holmes, the great majority of Protestant Social Gospel ministers moved from a peace to war creed. They envisioned a new world order based on democracy and social justice.[54]

By the fall of 1918, a malaise was beginning to shroud the liberal community. The new order they imagined had become a distant dream, with unrelenting repression at home, the widening application of espionage and sedition acts, a perversion of democracy in revolutionary Russia, and the disclosure of secret agreements between nations. The triumph of progressivism and the human spirit was not inevitable after all. After the Treaty of Versailles, despondency and alienation began to prevail. The road back, notes Rochester, would be led by new men with new techniques and more specific goals.[55]

While Coleman was in Europe for the Baptist War Commission, William E. Blodgett, Acting Chairman of the Ford Hall Forum, reported to the Baptist Social Union that of twenty-five lectures originally planned, six were abandoned for financial reasons, and the last two were cancelled because of the nationwide shortage of coal. Traditional structures for an orderly economic and social life were collapsing, and tensions, such as on race, spilled over into violence in the northern states. Laws were passed that aimed at stifling dissent. At the heart of the new order was a network of cooperating industrial committees, seeking to utilize manpower more fully. Business organizations were formed, writes historian Ellis Hawley, to improve the "informational and moral base of economic individualism." Through these mechanisms, the hope was that the nation would meet its social and national needs, while retaining business independence and curbs on big government.[56]

Later in 1918, Coleman described "Win-the-War Community Rallies" that Forums in New England had begun. Many of the speakers had returned from overseas service with the message to "see the thing through," whatever the cost or sacrifice. It was important to American soldiers that the fires of loyal support were kept burning at home. As important as this support was during the fighting, he wrote that it was vital after the war to unify community spirit and vitalize the national effort for better conditions.[57]

Coleman noted that industrial centers in Massachusetts were responding to this need strongly. Haverhill, with its shoe factories, Quincy, an important ship-building center, and Lawrence, scene of "the great strike," found the patriotic rallies an opportunity to support Liberty Loans for the war effort, the Red Cross, and War Saving Stamps. Italian, French and Armenian speakers were sent to communities with large populations of those heritages. Coleman always saw the benefit of tapping into the ethnic base of communities for speakers and publicity. "The attitude of America in not only encouraging," he wrote, "but promoting democracy at home while fighting for it abroad contrasts sharply with [the situation in] Germany."[58]

A particular impact of the war was that propaganda brought to the public a wider awareness about the relationship between modern communications technology and the manipulation of popular thinking. After the war, this propaganda consciousness contributed significantly to the "chastened democratic faith" of liberal intellectuals, as historian Brett Gary describes it. Although the postwar dismay shattered important beliefs of "nervous liberals" in informed discourse, a rational public, and the eventual triumph of truth, Coleman did not lose faith in the Forum learning initiative. He looked at what the movement had accomplished and what lay ahead. Democratic realists like Walter Lippmann and Harold Lasswell, writes Gary, removed the idea of a competent public from the center of democratic theory. That was not the path for Coleman; he sought to broaden the Forum's democratic potential even deeper and wider. The postwar disillusionment that many liberals felt, as described by Stuart Rochester, did not deter Coleman, because the Open Forum was not a *program* of specific changes but rather a *process* for people to discuss societal needs. The process of an open platform continued.[59]

While Coleman was part of the nation's propaganda effort, the Forum under his direction hewed to an independent balanced path. After returning from Europe, he planned a series of "Patriotic Forum Rallies," aiming at bringing people together. In asking for support for the rallies, Mary Crawford, Secretary of Ford Hall, wrote in May 1918 that Forums unite people, where other organizations separate them. "The forum is the force which puts unity into community." Rather than seeking "correct" opinion, as promoted by the Committee on Public Information, Coleman found the secret of American democracy is bringing diverse people together in an openness of thought. Historian Daniel Rodgers writes that some progressives found an unexpected loss in class relations in the postwar period, as it taught them a "skepticism about consolidated power and a new appreciation for smaller-scale, even class-related democratic arenas." Reflecting this new mood, the "neighbor concept" of the Open Forum was gaining broader national acceptance.[60]

After the war, William H. Ingersoll, Director of the Four Minute Men organization, part of the Committee on Public Information, recommended that the trained speakers offer their services to the Forum movement. Ingersoll saw how the speakers could render an important service to the country by stimulating a deeper interest in public questions through the Open Forum. Coleman agreed fully with this direction and sent to the 7,500 chairmen of the local Four Minute Men groups "A plan for the serious discussion of public matters to make democracy safe for America." The life of the nation, he wrote, depends on our understanding one another: "We need above everything else to get together."[61]

Coleman was untiring in spreading the Forum movement in which he believed so deeply. In November 1919, he reported that he had given 131 speeches in forty-three cities in seventeen states, traveling 21,000 miles. In August 1920, he counted seventy-four speeches in thirty-two communities in nine states. All of this was in addition to his extensive writings targeted to the audience. The reach of his writings in secular publications is just as impressive today. They include "The Business Man and the Open Forum" in *Current Affairs* (Boston Chamber of Commerce), "The Motion Picture and Public Discussion" in *Paramount Screen Educator*, and "Better Understanding Through Factory Forums" in *Factory Magazine*.[62]

The extension of the Forum across the country, whether as an idea or the start of an actual series, is found in newspapers in many cities. As one example, in September 1919, the *Waco News-Tribune* quoted Coleman as seeking to develop a Forum in the Texas city. Perfect democracy, he said, is a homogeneous mass of people with a likeness of ideas and religion but it is up to a community to establish a likeness of ideas and ideals. In the postwar economy, he saw a danger in nine-tenths of the riches in the hands of one-tenth of the people, and was concerned about misunderstandings between workers and directors. "Where this glass door separation would lead to no man could tell." In such expressions, he came across in words, although not necessarily in formal affiliation, as a Christian Socialist.[63]

Coleman conveyed his concerns through the religious press even more than in secular publications. In one article, he described the dramatic, unexpected impact of the Open Forum at the Winona Assembly in northern Indiana, "one of the oldest, largest and most conservative religious assemblies." The Forum received a hearty official welcome and complete popular approval at this summer series. On six afternoons in the summer, speakers such as Judge Robert H. Terrell, a "colored" jurist (in the vocabulary of the day) from Washington, DC, and Raymond Robins, a radical leader in social reform, captivated the audience. Robins' life and character were so misunderstood, Coleman wrote, that the announcement of his coming "created a storm of disapproval." The management of the Assembly held on quietly but firmly and the capacity audience of 3,200 voted unanimously to hear him again the following year. This approval, Coleman knew, spoke more strongly about the spirit, character and importance of the Forum than its presence in larger, more liberal cities.[64]

Every day, Coleman received inquiries about the movement from around the country. What a hunger there is, he wrote, for something that will draw us together, away from the bickering of partisanship, bigotry of sectarianism, and brutality of class conflict. He decried the rising international anarchy, failure of Protestantism to find a common working basis, a dying Europe torn asunder by national jealousies and hatreds, and the rumblings of our own nation's racial antagonisms. Just as in Benjamin Franklin's time, he said, if we do not hang together, we will all hang separately. The Open Forum is the one place, he maintained, where there are no majorities or minorities, no partisanship or sectarianism—"just folks in a family gathering seeking the way of life." Despite his extensive speaking and writing, not all the efforts were successful. For example, letters to and from a minister in Middletown, Connecticut in 1924 capture the difficulty in arranging a local series because of the cost.[65]

A strong interest of Coleman was the role the Open Forum could play in promoting positive industrial relations. (His entry in *Who Was Who in America* in fact lists his occupation as "impartial arbitrator.") This direction in his activities coincided with the national postwar growth in personnel work, aimed at creating a cooperative and production-oriented work force. In 1919, he served as an investigator for the Interchurch Federation report on the nationwide steel strike. In the same year, he was Director of Information for the Department of Labor. Coleman linked the Open Forum with the Four Minute Men endeavor, yet kept it apart. Rather than the national government effort capitalizing on the popularity of the Forum movement, Coleman's activities suggest that he used the government program to further public awareness of the lecture movement. For example, in October 1918, he invited George Creel, Chairman of the Committee on Public Information, to speak at Ford Hall. Creel responded that he would be "very proud" to speak from such a platform but was unable to do it until the war situation cleared up.[66]

In a 1919 article in a denominational publication, Coleman described how the Open Forum could assist in industrial relations. He understood the far-reaching changes that had begun even before the war and the need for industrial peace. Business and labor in the postwar world needed "respectful and intelligent consideration." He called for a "Christianization of business," not in a religious sense but in the construct of the industrial democracy and cooperative social order he had first advocated in 1909. Like many socially aware people during these years, he recognized that "the old Devil-take-the-hindmost methods must go to the scrap-heap." A "new industrial order" must be ushered in.[67]

With his religious audience in mind in this article, Coleman said that the postwar period could be described in various ways: industrial readjustment, industrial democracy, or, by radicals, industrial revolution. For him, however, the inclusive label was "Christianizing business," modeled after such efforts as the YMCA-organized "Foreman's Forums." An even more innovative effort—"pointed right at the heart of the whole industrial situation"—is introducing the Open Forum into the individual factory. In this approach, employees of all grades, in both shop and office, including directors and owners, use the Forum spirit and method to discuss questions of mutual concern. A large shoe manufacturer, McElwain, where Coleman was Director of Publicity, found such an approach good for business as well as for the public.[68]

Coleman continued his linking of the Open Forum to the business world in a 1923 publication of the Boston Chamber of Commerce. After describing how the Forum shapes public opinion, he turned to the "men of power" today. They are not the preachers or teachers, artists or lawyers, or statesmen, he wrote. The "uncrowned king of the modern world" is the business man, whose term of power is long, sway is wide, and power is real.[69]

Today, Coleman continued, the rule is being challenged, and business actions must be justified before an aroused public opinion. The arena for the challenge could be the Open Forum. For decades, business has allowed itself to be misrepresented by "the greedy, the lawless and the reactionary." It is time for change. The capitalist and employer can receive a fair hearing before a jury of "just plain, ordinary folks" in the Forum. "There is nothing so moving and convincing as personality expressing itself through the human voice." Business leaders need only reach out and take the opportunity of speaking before the Forum. It is the single institution that deliberately sets out and succeeds in getting the radical to listen to the conservative and vice versa.[70]

Through many writings and speeches, Coleman interwove the basic theme of "folks" or "neighbors" as the basis for people getting along, whether in the lecture hall, local community, or the nation as a whole. As founder of the inclusive movement, and with genuine gregariousness towards people from all backgrounds, he received extensive adulation. But he never sought the spotlight for himself; it was the movement that was central. He wanted people to hear and be heard. To this end, he stressed the powerful effect of the human voice in communication, insisting on audience members expressing their own questions so their personalities would be felt. It was crucial for the moderator to use his intelligence and voice to clarify questions, when necessary, but even more so to ensure that the end result of the evening was literally "democracy in the making."

In 1921, Coleman wrote in a letter to his "Forum friends" that he was becoming president of Babson Institute. He pledged to continue to lead the Ford Hall Forum and do all that he could for the spread of the Forum idea across the country. Alice H. Samson, his long-time assistant, would succeed Mary Caroline Crawford as Executive Secretary and would be in charge of the Open Forum National Council, while Mildred C. Smith would head the Speakers Bureau. He continued his affiliation with the Forum movement for many years.[71]

Coleman's move into the president's office at Babson Institute came at the same time that he had become more explicit in expressing the changing role of business in the postwar world. In his commencement address at Crozer Theological Seminary in Upland, Pennsylvania, in 1924, Coleman reviewed the changes that had been occurring in American society. The modern business leader has to think beyond profit and efficiency, he said, to the benefit of the locality of the business as well as the nation. In many writings and speeches during his years as president of Babson, he stressed the value of a business college in shaping the new age. His direction reflected the vision of a new capitalism that managers were learning at business and professional schools. The ultimate aim, writes Ellis Hawley, was a partnership of interdependent groups working together for "an enlarged vision of neighborly relations." Coleman's goal in creating the Forum in 1908 had become part of the training of the nation's business leaders.[72]

In 1928, *The Baptist* magazine invited him to write about Christianity and the business world. In "The Ministry of Business," he described the "transforming, far-reaching and blessed revolution" that was quietly taking place. Coleman began with Henry Ford, a business leader who was increasing earnings at the same time he was decreasing prices and employing "the lame, the halt, the blind and released prisoners." Very importantly, Coleman continued, Ford translates his business principles into the establishment of a school and a hospital. Another example of the new "ministry of business" was the Filene brothers, who introduced into their successful Boston department store democratic management. A third new business "prophet" was Roger Babson, who provides information and advice to businesses based on statistics he gathers. In the process, he is blazing the way toward "a more scientific and a sounder method of conducting business." Every year, wrote Coleman, Babson divides the profits of his business with his employees on a fifty-fifty basis. The school he established is training future leaders for this new approach to business. Coleman had never met a minister of the gospel more devoted to his "ministry" than Babson. We have always had the "consecrated business man" but now we can have a "consecrated business." This was what "our beloved Walter Rauschenbusch" pointed out in his *Christianizing the Social Order.*" There are scores of other such business leaders, concluded Coleman, all headed in the same direction, "toward the stabilizing, the humanizing, the sanctifying of our commercial life."[73]

An instance of Coleman reaching out to a larger audience is his article in *Kiwanis* magazine in 1926, "Are We Afraid of Ideas?" He described the far-reaching readjustments that were taking place in the postwar world, and the nation's divisions: industrial, economic, social, political, religious, and racial. With complete disintegration on the horizon, he described how the Open Forum "draws us together . . . , furnishes a safety valve, and *forms public opinion.*" [Italics in original.] He challenged Kiwanians to play their part in this great movement. "Who is big enough, brave enough, broad enough, to give the answer . . . ?"[74]

In 1936, a year after Coleman retired as President of Babson Institute, Ford Hall Forum published short essays that he had written for Babson and Webber College alumni publications. The writings were positive messages about challenges in living that the students would face. In one piece, "A Challenge to Youth," he wondered about "the effects of transportation through the air, communication by radio, co-operative enterprise, scientific management, democracy in industry" and other changes that were coming. While the essays were not particularly intellectually deep, they reflected his lifelong interest in stimulating people at an everyday level and certainly looked ahead at the fast-changing world. He urged the students and alumni to seek a more participative role in their personal and community lives, rather than a specific philosophy or ideology. *Participation* in life, whether in hearing Open Forum lectures or engaging in civic activities, was the key. In such writings, he reflected a consistent inner compass, the same goal he articulated three decades earlier when he began the Forum movement.[75]

In the early years of the Forum, the leaders conveyed the movement motto "Let There Be Light" graphically through a burning lamp. When industrial relations became an increasing concern for the nation, as well as for Coleman, both during the war and afterwards, the Forum motto became "A Safety Valve For America." Forum publicity emphasized that open discussion led to human fellowship, abolished distrust and hatred, and brought understanding that made social progress inevitable. Later, a mechanical safety valve became its graphic image, linking the movement strongly to the new economy of manufacturing and assembly line. More immediately though, Coleman saw how the Open Forum enabled democracy to be expressed through an orderly release mechanism. (A less generous interpretation of "safety valve" is to control emotion, such as during worker discontent, but that does not appear to be Coleman's intent, either in philosophy or strategy.) He worked very hard to make the movement more inclusive, to bring all sectors of society together as neighbors. The key, he concluded, was the growing number of unionized workers, especially the leaders, and the burgeoning immigrant population. He often expressed how these two sectors were crucial in expanding the base of the Forum.[76]

For example, while "The People's Open Forum" was underway at First Baptist Church in South Bend, Indiana, in 1916, Coleman spoke in the city on "Getting Together Essential in Democracy." He praised the local series but stressed its success depended on attracting immigrants to the programs, just as was done in Boston. South Bend at the time had significant numbers of foreign-born residents, primarily from Germany, Poland, Hungary and Russia.[77]

Over the years, Ford Hall Forum faced many challenges in its operation, primarily from conservative Baptists, on the use of the Ford bequest. The first challenge was whether the lectures could be used to reach the "unchurched." Growing attendance soon made the series a reality in place. However, in view of this early financial support, Coleman was soon confronted with the need to open each program with a prayer. Determined not to offend anyone's religion, or lack of belief, he began non-denominational prayers in the third season. Reading the prayers today, ninety years after they were printed in the weekly program brochures, the words and feelings show he was successful in making them universal. The diverse audience apparently accepted them as no opposition was noted. Eventually, the American Baptist Publication Society published *The People's Prayers* in a little collection, which became widely used for family devotions and in the homes of ministers.[78]

In the introduction to the published book, Rauschenbusch said Ford Hall stood for a "new democratizing of religion." The prayers sought to ennoble the lectures in a practical, ethical, undenominational, yet devout way. Coleman, describing the origin of the prayers, said that he always kept in mind the "common aspirations of his conglomerate audience." Each expression had a definite relation to the lecture for the evening. "Our common Father" and his calls for brotherhood were his way to build bridges. To avoid offending some speakers, he would sometimes use a poem, meditation or sentiment. On the fifth anniversary of Ford Hall, he said that free speech is the "constant recognition of the rights and feelings of others . . . a continually widening vision of the truth."[79]

While the Ford bequest allowed use of the hall without charge, as well as provide ongoing operating support, the Forum leaders decided early that it would be wise to ask for a voluntary "collection" as people entered. Ushers urged the audience to drop "silver" into the "yawning pans" on the collection tables. It was a way of demonstrating commitment while at the same time reducing the burden on the original bequest and gaining a measure of independence.[80]

Despite these efforts by the Forum leaders, conservative Baptist ministers were negative from the beginning, claiming the lectures had gone beyond the intent of the bequest. Fortunately, Coleman had allies in defending the movement. In addition to chairing the Christian Work Committee of the Baptist Social Union, he nurtured friendly relations with the press, which proved especially helpful. Dr. Edmund Merriam, editor of the *Watchman-Examiner*, the leading Baptist weekly at the time, answered sharp attacks from denominational critics. *The Congregationalist*, although the voice of a different denomination, noted that "anyone who studies the exact provisions of [Ford's] remarkable will, can hardly fail to conclude that not only has the spirit of the will been adhered to, but the work . . . is precisely [what was intended.]" Even more to the point, Ford's own pastor, Dr. Robert G. Seymour, spoke from personal knowledge of the businessman's "intense longing to reach those who did not come into sympathy with the Christian Church." The Forum was truly "carrying out his idea."[81]

Support also came from the secular press. Coleman praised *Boston Globe* editor Anthony Philpott for insight, sympathy and faith, that "led him straight to the core of this new kind of meeting." The *Boston Transcript*, while a conservative newspaper, was "generous in space and comment" in providing valuable publicity. A *Transcript* editorial was especially strong: "Intended to find what truths men hold in common, what ideals they can unite to support, democratic in form and in spirit, broadly religious but non-sectarian, ever constructive in purpose, the Open Forum tends to express the best that can exist in any society." The editorial continued, "it will not only define good Americans; it will help to make them." The *Boston Herald* and its afternoon edition, the *Boston Traveler*, were also supportive.[82]

On April 17, 1928, almost 800 persons, including many city and state leaders, attended the twentieth anniversary banquet of the movement. They welcomed Coleman back from a trip around the world and presented him with a huge book of testimonials on the value of the Forum. It was similar to the volume presented to him in 1913 on the fifth anniversary. Among the 1928 testimonial letters, several stand out. African-American scholar activist W. E. B. Du Bois, who had spoken many times before Forums around the country, regarded the movement "as the straightest step toward practical, intelligent

democracy that is being taken today." John Dewey, in praising its valuable
service "to the cause of enlightened and progressive thought everywhere,"
spoke of the nation's "incalculable debt."[83]

Speaking at the 1928 banquet, Harry T. Claus, the *Boston Transcript* editor, defended the freedom of speech that Ford Hall provided. The *Boston Herald* published an entire page of photographs in connection with the banquet, and the *Springfield Republican* editorialized that the lecture series "deserves a full measure of public confidence in its mission of bringing democracy to the truth and truth to democracy."[84]

Rumors concerning the possible closing of the Ford Hall Forum by the sponsors were frequent during its first two decades. The charges were radicalism, un-Americanism, disloyalty, and misuse of the bequest. Six days after the 1928 banquet, a committee of past presidents of the Boston Baptist Social Union voted to make meetings held under its auspices "Pro-Christian and Pro-American." By a vote of nineteen to three, they decided not to use funds from the bequest for the Ford Hall Forum. An agreement was worked out for the Social Union's Christian Work Committee to provide financial support until October 1928 and free use of the hall for the next season, but not under the auspices of the Baptist group. Within an hour, 1,000 letters were sent to the Ford Hall Folks that the Forum would continue under a citizens' committee.[85]

The Forum leaders decided to move to another hall and become an independent, unsubsidized organization chartered by the state. On June 22, 1928, Massachusetts issued a charter to Ford Hall Forum, Inc., represented by Coleman and several distinguished leaders, among them the Dean of Harvard University Law School and the owner of Boston's largest department store. The purpose of the organization was to provide education for intelligent, capable and responsible citizens, minister to the welfare of all, and promote understanding of civic, moral, religious and spiritual possibilities. A "common meeting ground" would provide "full, free and open public discussion of all vital questions concerning human welfare." The meetings would be like the Open Forum conducted at Ford Hall for the past twenty years. A General Council was organized, with Coleman as president.[86]

In addition to the opposition of conservative clergy, Ford Hall Forum faced challenges from the larger community. The social outlook of many of the city's leaders, enforced politically, often suppressed free speech, banned world-famous books, and interfered with serious theatrical productions. Forum supporters responded in kind. When birth control advocate Margaret Sanger was not allowed to speak at the Forum, she was invited to a banquet, dedicated "To Our Undesirables," and placed in a chair. While she sat with a gag over her mouth, Coleman read her speech. At a second banquet, dedicated "To Freedom of Expression," John Dewey threw out a broader challenge. The United States, he said, cannot develop a culture commensurate with its physical power until the people "have a great reverence for liberalism in thought and speech." The country would not have a robust intellectual life without this "respect and reverence."[87]

While Coleman remained active in the organization, David K. Niles, who would later serve as an aide to Presidents Roosevelt and Truman, took over the day-to-day operation. Despite political opposition at times, the Forum continued to provide an open platform for all opinions. No admission charge was still the rule although voluntary contributions and an annual solicitation made the series possible. When Rabbi Stephen Wise inaugurated the independent Ford Hall Forum on October 21, 1928, "thousands" were reportedly unable to enter the building. A panel of three religious leaders spoke on November 19, 1929 on "Fellowship For Understanding," and a later panel of religious leaders spoke on racial and working class prejudices.[88]

Beyond Boston, Coleman and his colleagues had made an important contribution in building a better country. In 1914, they formed the Ford Hall Foundation, with Coleman as director, which later became the Open Forum National Council. The purpose was to spread information on the meaning and value of the public forum and to assist communities in developing local forums and binding them together more closely. For five summers, the group conducted courses on forum management and organization at the Chautauqua Institute in New York State. In addition to training, the Council developed pamphlets that local communities could use in planning every aspect of a forum, aimed at achieving as much success as Ford Hall.[89]

A variety of models evolved around the country, with the Middle West and Far West "rapidly becoming forum minded." Factory or industrial forums (such as in Lawrence, Massachusetts, which had labor troubles), Protestant and Jewish-sponsored series, a radio forum, a series limited to a women's club or community organization, and a motion picture series began. However, forums sponsored by a chamber of commerce or a radical organization wore the mantle of the movement only. They were not really true to the Forum's principles as opposite points of view were not invited. As the movement spread, local Forums came together to draw from each other's experience. In 1918, New York-area groups met, and in 1919 New England Forums gathered. The Chicago Forum Council was incorporated in 1925. The true Forum, wrote Reuben Lurie, editor of the *Ford Hall Bulletin*, the brochure distributed at the Boston lectures, was courageous. The community planning committee was inclusive, scheduling speakers for whom it had no sympathy but the community should hear. The ideal series "can reflect only the courage of its leaders."[90]

In 1928, adult educator Will Durant wrote that the public discussion of vital issues made Coleman "one of the great educators of America." On Coleman's seventieth birthday in 1937, he received letters from across the country. He had retained an active interest in religious and Baptist denominational activities. Far from retiring, one article noted, he was busier than ever. In 1947, former First Lady Eleanor Roosevelt came to his eightieth birthday party. In her widely syndicated newspaper column, she praised the courageous open platform of Ford Hall, then in its fortieth year, especially the question period. She wrote that he founded it "on the principle that everyone has a right to express his ideas, no matter how they differ from those held by others, and that people have an obligation to listen and to make up their minds what they feel after hearing both sides." His lifelong goal had been heard clearly.[91]

When Coleman died in 1950, at age eighty-three, he was remembered for many civic, religious and educational activities. Holding strong to the early logo of the national movement, the Open Forum had brought "light" to Americans in many cities through the upheavals of the early years of the century.[92]

But beyond beginning the movement in Boston, and spreading it around the country, Coleman's most brilliant single decision was his selection of the first Secretary.

NOTES

1. Letter, George W. Coleman, Boston, Massachusetts, to Walter Rauschenbusch [no address], 11 May 1907, Rauschenbusch Family Papers, American Baptist-Samuel Colgate Historical Library, American Baptist Historical Society, Rochester, New York.

2. Walter Rauschenbusch, *Christianity and the Social Crisis*, (New York: Macmillan, 1907; reprint, 1913), 2, 5–6.

3. "Walter Rauschenbusch," *Who Was Who in America*, 3:172; "Walter Rauschenbusch," *Dictionary of American Biography*, 15:392–93; Rauschenbusch, *Christianity and the Social Crisis*, 70, 83, 323–24, 329, 336, 337, 357, 399.

4. Ray Stannard Baker, *The Spiritual Unrest* (New York: Frederick A. Stokes, 1910), 263; Robert D. Cross, ed., Walter Rauschenbusch, *Christianity and the Social Crisis*, (New York: Macmillan, 1907; repr., 1964), viii; James T. Kloppenberg, *Uncertain Victory; Social Democracy and Progressivism in European and American Thought* (New York: Oxford University, 1986), 210; Joseph O'Connor, "The Spirit of Discontent," *New York Times Saturday Review of Books*, 1 June 1907, BR345, "Best Books of 1907."

5. Dores R. Sharpe, *Walter Rauschenbusch* (New York: Macmillan, 1942), 120–22; Walter Rauschenbusch, *Christianizing the Social Order* (New York: Macmillan, 1912; repr., 1915), 208.

6. J. L. Harbow, "How Ford Hall Came to be Built," in Coleman, *Democracy in the Making*, 12–13; "The Boston Social Union," *Watchman-Examiner*, 11 December 1913, 487–88, Scrapbooks, 3.

7. Charles H. Watson, "Geo. W. Coleman and Ford Hall," 15 December 1925, n. p., Scrapbooks, 9; "The Boston Social Union," 487–89.

8. William H. R. Willkens, "A History of the Adult Education Programs and Agencies of the American Baptist Convention," (abstract) *Dissertation Abstracts*, 19, 4–6, 1958, 1283; Lawrence B. Davis, *Immigrants, Baptists and the Protestant Mind in America* (Urbana: University of Illinois, 1973), 2, 6, 136.

9. "George William Coleman," *Who Was Who in America,* 3:163; John F. Cowan, "Coleman and Ford Hall Forum," *The Baptist*, 16 December 1923, 1455–56, Scrapbooks, 8; A. E. Winship, "George W. Coleman," and George Perry Morris, "Men of Today—George W. Coleman," both unattributed articles, circa 1920, President's Papers, Babson.

10. Lurie, *Challenge of the Forum*, 54–55; Grace Ann Goodman, "Free Lance for God," *Young People* (American Baptist Publication Society), 5 October 1958, 5.

11. Sagamore Sociological Conference Files, American Baptist Historical Society; "No Conference at Sagamore This Year," *Boston Post*, 2 June 1918, n.p.

12. Rauschenbusch, *Christianizing the Social Order*, 208.

13. Lurie, *Challenge of the Forum*, 53–54; Cowan, "Coleman and Ford Hall Forum," Scrapbooks, 3; Peter Clark Macfarlane, "Sunshine George of Boston," *Collier's*, 14 June 1913, 7–8.

14. "Coleman," *Who Was Who in America*; "George William Coleman," *The National Cyclopedia of American Biography*, (New York: James T. White & Company, 1930), C:455; Macfarlane, "'Sunshine George' of Boston," Scrapbooks, 3; Lurie, *Challenge of the Forum*, 56; letter, Coleman, War Commission of the Northern Baptist Convention, Boston, Massachusetts, 9 January 1918, to George Creel, Records Group 63, Committee on Public Information, Box 3, Folder 128, National Archives II, College Park, Maryland.

15. "Coleman," *Who Was Who in America*; "George W. Coleman," obituary, *New York Times*, 2 August 1950, 24; letter, Ron Rybnikar, Babson, to writer, 7 December 2004; *Babson Institute Alumni News*, 15 October 1929, 14, Babson.

16. Cowan, "Coleman and Ford Hall Forum."

17. Morris, "Men of Today—George W. Coleman"; Thomas Dreier, "A Human Catalyst and Much More . . . ," in George W. Coleman, *The Business of Living* (Boston: Ford Hall Forum, 1936), 1.

18. Although Coleman and others mentioned the shipwreck in articles through the years, it was not until 1932 that he wrote a detailed description, with some of his typical good humor. "A Resurrected Shipwreck," *Bulletin of the Babson Institute Alumni Association*, April 1932, 19 (5), 3–24, Babson.

19. George B. Gallop, "The Story of the Ford Hall Sunday-Evening Meetings," in Coleman, *Democracy in the Making*, 20.

20. "Boston," *Encyclopedia Britannica*, (New York: Encyclopedia Britannica Company, 1910), 4:290–96.

21. Edward Weeks, *The Lowells and Their Institute* (Boston: Little, Brown, 1966), 109–12; Mona Domosh, *Invented Cities; The Creation of Landscape in Nineteenth-Century New York and Boston* (New Haven: Yale University, 1996), 152.

22. Theodora Penny Martin, *The Sound of Our Own Voices; Women's Study Clubs, 1860–1910* (Boston: Beacon, 1987), 1–3, 17, 31–39, 71, 86; Robin Miller Jacoby, *The British and American Women's Trade Union Leagues, 1890–1925; A Case Study of Feminism and Class* (Brooklyn, New York: Carlson Publishing, 1994), xviii; Lurie, *Challenge of the Forum*, 140–41. For African American women's clubs in Boston at the time, see "The Woman's Era Club," http://womenwriters.library.emory.edu/advocacy/content.php?level=div&id=era1_we.1.01.03.08&document=era1 (accessed August 3, 2011).

23. Coleman, *The Church and the Press*; *Messages of the Men and Religion Forward Movement* (New York: Funk & Wagnalls Co., 1912), 7:4–5, 10, 67.

24. Stuart Ewen, *PR! A Social History of Spin* (New York: Basic Books, 1996), 86.

25. Coleman, "Is the Present Tendency Toward a Co-operative Social Order Desirable?" *Twenty-Seventh Annual Session of the Baptist Congress* (Chicago: University of Chicago, 1909), 62–65.

26. Coleman, *Democracy in the Making*, xi-xiii.

27. The beginning of the movement is outlined in Gallop, "The Story of the Ford Hall Sunday-Evening Meetings," 17–25. A more engrossing, detailed portrait is found in various newspaper clippings in the first volume of the Scrapbooks, in particular describing how Coleman reached out to organized labor in a "smoke-filled" union meeting, and in the box newspaper ads for the Forum in Yiddish, Italian and English.

28. Coleman, *Democracy in the Making*, 6.

29. "Clause In Will Brings Workingmen Together In First Meeting Of Series," *Boston Journal*, n.d., n.p., Scrapbooks, 1.

30. "People's Sunday Evenings Opened" and "Few Workers in Ford Hall," unattributed articles, n.d., n.p., ibid.

31. "Says It Is Foolish to Fear Socialism," *Journal*, n.d., n.p.; "The Brotherhood of Man," *Congregationalist*, n.d., n.p., ibid.

32. "Rabbi Has Verbal Row With Hearer," *Boston Herald*, n.d., n.p.; "Patriotism Of The Jews," *Boston Globe*, n.d., n.p.; "Democratic Gospel," *Boston Herald*, n.d., n.p., ibid.

33. "Social Duties Due To Mind's Evolution," *Boston Herald*, n.d., n.p.; "Avows Belief in Socialism," *Boston Globe*, n.d., n.p., ibid.

34. "Sunday Evenings for the People," *Boston Globe*, n.d., n.p., ibid.

35. "Progress of the Forum Movement," *Christian Science Monitor*, 1 April 1916, n.p., Scrapbooks, 5.

36. Ibid.

37. "Movement For Real Brotherhood," *Springfield Union*, n.d., n.p.; "Ford Hall Speaker Takes Alarmist View," *Springfield Homestead*, n.d., n.p.; "For The 'Under Dog'"; "The Under Dog Lecture Theme," *Woonsocket Call*, n.d., n.p., Scrapbooks, 4.

38. "Ford Hall Speaker Takes Alarmist View," ibid.

39. Coleman, "The Contribution of the Open Forum to Democracy in Religion," *The Journal of Religion*, (January 1922), 2:4–5.

40. Ibid., 4.

41. Ibid., 5.

42. Ibid., 7.

43. "Ford Hall Meetings," 1908–1909, Second Season, program brochures, Scrapbooks, 1; Lurie, *Challenge of the Forum*, 181–82. For examples of Boston newspaper editorial support, see "The Ford Hall Forum, Successful Appeals To Men Who Are Outside Churches," *Boston Herald*, n.d., n.p., and "Ford Hall Meetings," n.d., n.p., *Transcript*, Scrapbooks, 1. In 1915, the *Boston Globe* editor wrote that "it became one of Boston's institutions almost in a night." A. J. Philpott, "One of Boston's Institutions," Coleman, *Democracy in the Making*, 74.

44. Coleman, "Semi-Annual Report of the Committee on Christian Work to the BBSU," *Semi-Annual Report of the Boston Baptist Social Union*, 1 December 1914, n.p., Scrapbooks, 4.

45. Coleman, *Annual Report of the Committee on Christian Work to the Baptist Social Union*, 20 March 1917, Scrapbooks, 6.

46. Coleman, "Semi-Annual Report of the Committee on Christian Work," *Boston Baptist Social Union*, 1 October 1917, Scrapbooks, 6; *Ford Hall Meetings*, Tenth Season, 1916–1917, ibid.

47. Lurie, *Challenge of the Forum*, 106; "Margaret Slattery Speaker for Immanuel Mother-Daughter Dinner," *Hartford Courant*, 22 January 1930, A11.

48. Coleman, *Democracy in the Making*, 149–50.

49. Thomas Dreier, "The Controlling Purpose and Spirit," Coleman, *Democracy in the Making*, 26–30.

50. Program booklet, Ford Hall Forum Twentieth Anniversary Banquet, 17 April 1928, Babson.

51. Coleman, "Get Together in the Open Forum," *The Public* [New York], 16 August 1919, n.p., Scrapbooks, 8.

52. Coleman, "Fighting Disintegration—How the Open Forum Does It," *Holland's Magazine*, May 1920, n.p., Scrapbooks, 8.

53. Miriam Allen DeFord, "The Method of Conducting the Meetings," in Coleman, *Democracy in the Making*, 46–47.

54. Stuart I. Rochester, *American Liberal Disillusionment in the Wake of World War I* (University Park, PA: Pennsylvania State University, 1977), 27–42.

55. Ibid., 62–110.

56. William E. Blodgett, "Annual Report of the Committee on Christian Work of the Boston Baptist Social Union," 18–19, Scrapbooks, 6; Ellis W. Hawley, *The Great War and The Search For a Modern Order; A History of the American People and Their Institutions, 1917–1933* (New York: St. Martin's, 1979), 12–53.

57. Coleman, "The Open Forum; America's Modernized Town Meeting," Committee on Public Information, Foreign Press Bureau, Ser. 3889, 2–3, Scrapbooks, 6.

58. Ibid., 3–4.

59. Brett Gary, *The Nervous Liberals; Propaganda Anxieties From World War I To the Cold War* (New York: Columbia University, 1999), 1–4.

60. Letter, Mary C. Crawford to "Dear Friend of America," 15 May 1918, Scrapbooks, 6; Daniel T. Rogers, *Atlantic Crossings; Social Politics in a Progressive Age* (Cambridge: Harvard University, 1998), 317.

61. William H. Ingersoll, "What Shall the Four Minute Men Do in the Future?" National Archives II, Records Group 63, Correspondence Speakers Bureau, Division of Four Minute Men, May 22, 1917–December 24, 1918; Coleman, "Salvaging the Four Minute Men," *The Survey*, 29 March 1919, 924, Scrapbooks, 7.

62. "Report of President to Annual Meeting of Open Forum National Council," Chautauqua, New York, 21 August 1920, Ford Hall Forum Collection, Folder 62, Boston Public Library, Boston, Massachusetts; George W. Coleman Alpha File, Rochester. For brevity, Ford Hall Forum materials in Boston Public Library in future references will be listed as "Boston."

63. "Local Forum is Planned After a Stirring Talk," *Waco News-Tribune*, 30 September 1919, n.p., Scrapbooks, 9.

64. Coleman, "The Forum Marching On; The Leader of the Movement Reports Successes," *The Congregationalist and Advance*, 23 December 1920, 819, Scrapbooks, 7.

65. Ibid.; letters from Fred Atkins Moore, Boston, to Rev. Herbert D. Rollason, Middletown, Connecticut, 7 April 1924, 13 May 1924, and 16 May 1924, and from Rollason to Moore, 13 May 1924, Boston, Box 62.

66. "George W. Coleman," *Who Was Who in America*; letters, George Creel to George W. Coleman, 7 January 1918, and 25 October 1918, National Archives II, Records Group 63, Committee on Public Information, Executive Division, General Correspondence of George Creel, Chairman, July 1917–March 1919, Box 3, Folder 128, "George W. Coleman."

67. Coleman, "The Open Forum in the Factory; Light on the Industrial Problem," *The Congregationalist and Advance*, 3 April 1919, n.p., Scrapbooks, 9.

68. Ibid.

69. Coleman, "Fifteen Years of Ford Hall," *Current Affairs* [Boston Chamber of Commerce], 12 March 1923, Scrapbooks, 8.

70. Ibid.

71. Letter, Coleman to "My Forum Friends," 15 June 1921, Scrapbooks, 8.

72. Coleman, "Commencement Address, 1924," *Bulletin of the Crozer Theological Seminary* (Upland, PA), July 1924, 16 (3), 94–95, 99; Hawley, *The Great War*, 100.

73. Coleman, "The Ministry of Business," *The Baptist*, 22 December 1923, 1485, Scrapbooks, 8.

74. Coleman, "Are We Afraid of Ideas?" *Kiwanis*, June 1926, 2 (6), 326–327, Babson.

75. Coleman, *This Business of Living*, Babson, 10.

76. "Safety Valve," *The American Heritage Dictionary of the English Language*, William Morris, ed. (Boston: Houghton Mifflin, 1969, 1979), 1142.

77. "G. W. Coleman In City," *South Bend Tribune*, 29 April 1916, 5; "Praises Public Forum For City," *South Bend News-Times*, 29 April 1916, 3; Elizabeth Dales and Katherine Edsall, *A Brief History of South Bend, Indiana, 1820–1960; Informa-*

tion About its Economic, Political, Educational, Religious, and Social Development (South Bend: South Bend Public Library, 1970), 12–15.

78. Lurie, *Challenge of the Forum*, 181–82; Coleman, *The People's Prayers; Voiced By a Layman* (Philadelphia: Griffith & Rowland, 1914), passim.

79. Walter Rauschenbusch, "An Interpretation," 1–9, and Coleman, "Why It Is Done," 45–56, Coleman, *The People's Prayers*.

80. Lurie, *Challenge of the Forum*, 17–18.

81. Ibid., 38, 41, 97–98.

82. Ibid., 97–99.

83. Ibid., 109; W. E. B. Du Bois, New York City, to Coleman, Boston, 30 March 1928, and John Dewey, New York City, to Coleman, Boston, 9 March 1928, Letters of Appreciation.

84. Lurie, *Challenge of the Forum*, 98–101.

85. Ibid., 110–16.

86. Ibid., 127–29.

87. Ibid., 134–35.

88. Ibid., 130–33.

89. Ibid., 140, 154.

90. Ibid., 141, 148–58.

91. Letter, Will Durant, New York City, to Coleman, Boston, 19 March 1928, Letters of Appreciation; Eleanor Roosevelt, "My Day," 17 May 1947, United Feature Syndicate, Inc., Eleanor Roosevelt Papers, Mount Vernon College, Washington, D.C. The phrase "busier than ever" is in a 1937 *Watchman-Examiner* clipping, George W. Coleman Alpha File, American Baptist Historical Society.

92. Obituary, "George W. Coleman," *New York Times*, 20 August 1950, 24.

Chapter Three

Structure

Helping to Mould the Boston of the Future

In addition to viewing the Open Forum from such perspectives as secular perfectibility, public learning and the Social Gospel, the movement can also be examined in a different way. This task is recovering the women who, although not leaders in early twentieth century social reform, were crucial in administering the organizations. Such secretaries and assistants at the second tier of the programs had to fully understand and strongly believe in the ideals of the movements, and then implement with exceptional administrative and organizational skills what the founders envisioned. A change movement that does not have good management and communication, no matter the grand conception, will flounder.

Unfortunately, the secretaries and assistants were often too busy, too tired, or not focused on their inner lives, and so did not leave their own stories. People who record their lives are in a sense expressing a feeling of significance, and women in the past usually had difficulty in making such claims. What Virginia Woolf wrote about women's lives in general is even truer for these low-paid secretaries and assistants: "She is all but absent from history."[1]

Mary Caroline Crawford, Secretary of the Ford Hall Forum from 1908 to 1921, and afterwards manager of the Old South Meeting House Forum in Boston until her death in 1932, came close to being lost in the historical record. As she listened to the audience waiting to attend the Ford Hall Forum, she wrote that the sounds she heard were democracy, "many times in broken English [of] the new immigrant just coming to feel the responsibilities and problems of his adopted country." The spread of the "compact sociological institution," as the Ford Hall Forum was described in Boston, would have been impossible without her idealism, ability to develop strong interpersonal relationships, and exceptional communication and organizational skills.[2]

George Coleman early acknowledged Crawford's contributions to the growth of the lecture series. He said that without her "untiring energy, clever initiative and unswerving faithfulness," the growth of the movement would have been very much slower and might have failed altogether. He recognized the importance of her college training, special "instruction" in social questions, thorough knowledge of the ways of the press, and experience in trade unions. He credited her "first-class executive ability" for a large share of the success of the movement, noting she was "indispensable in the management of our work." The praise was repeated in Reuben L. Lurie's 1930 book on Ford Hall, which noted that she "played so large a part in the success of the meetings, and [her] ingenuity and enterprise were such tremendously vital factors" in the growth and development of the movement. In her own 1915 essay on social work, Crawford showed her perceptiveness of the changing times, by writing that "this is an age of publicity whether we like it or not."[3]

Crawford was born in the Charlestown area of Boston on May 5, 1874, to James George and Mary Coburn Crawford. During this period, Charlestown was a middle-lower class district, "predominantly bourgeois," as contemporary social reformer Robert A. Woods described it. The family's economic situation is reflected in the *Boston City Directory* listing of Mr. Crawford "working" in 1876 at the Troy and St. James Laundry Company. By 1894, the *Directory* shows he owned the James G. Crawford Laundry Machine Company. Mary attended the private Girls' Latin School, shortly after it had been founded for college preparatory training, graduating in 1892.[4]

In her youth, she was active in the nearby St. John's Episcopal Church. Her commitment to social change can be traced in large part to the rector, Rev. Philo W. Sprague, who was called by other ministers a "Prophet of Social Justice." In 1887, during labor strife in the state, he sought to bring management and workers together under the framework of the Social Gospel. He also recognized "the full personality of the woman equally with that of the man."[5]

From 1894 to 1896, Crawford studied at Radcliffe College in nearby Cambridge. The school had gained its distinctive name in 1894, after having begun as the "Harvard Annex" in 1879 and then becoming the "Society for the Collegiate Instruction of Women" in 1882. Although Crawford did not have the most famous Harvard professors of the time, the intellectual climate was nevertheless powerful and bonding. The milieu in those years was not one of preoccupation with self or learning in the abstract, as in the first generation of college women, but rather learning by relating to the world outside the college. It was the transition from "culture" to "service" as the ideal of higher education for women. Unlike other women's colleges at the time, Radcliffe's leaders, both men and women, were anti-suffrage, and the students in general followed their lead. The administrators and faculty claimed that allying the

suffrage movement and women's higher education might impede the very
academic progress that they were seeking. Rather than actively seeking the
vote, the goal was to develop an "independent professional identity."[6]

Crawford was enrolled in one course in 1897 but dropped out, "because
of business reverses." Her father's health declined and he died in 1899.
Although she did not complete the undergraduate program, her classmates
always considered her a "Radcliffe '98 girl" because of her historical writings
and the Open Forum movement. Among her classmates to gain prominence
were Gertrude Stein, a major cultural figure for years, Maude Wood (Park),
suffrage leader and first president of the National League of Women Voters,
and Mary Parker Follett, founder of the Social Centers movement and a major
political theorist.[7]

An early profile of Crawford as an author describes her as a devout Epis-
copalian, living in a Charlestown flat with her mother, brother and beloved
cat. Since the death of her father, she had become "the man of the house,"
and was "stout and jolly" with a "whole-souled vitality." In many ways, she
was like other single women entering the paid labor force at the time. As they
confronted new sets of social relations and demands, they remained tied to
their families. With Crawford now the family's provider, she was also likely
the reason that her brother, twelve years younger, was able to attend college.[8]

Even before entering Radcliffe, Crawford had determined to be a writer.
While in college, her column about campus activities appeared in a well-
known society weekly. After college, she became a special features and
editorial writer for the *Boston Transcript*, serving at the same time as literary
editor of the *Boston Budget*.[9]

In 1904, she brought together her syndicated articles for New York and
Philadelphia newspapers as *The College Girl of America*. In one of them,
"After College—What?" she spoke of the career of "social secretary," where
a woman would "devote her entire time" to becoming acquainted with employees and conditions at work. Such a position "requires training, tact, intelligence, sympathy, and experience." As she would shortly demonstrate in her
own work with the Ford Hall Forum, the position was "the high ideals of life
made attractive." The goal was, simply, to do good in a community. "Woman's real interest and happiness," she wrote, "do not consist in the number of
lines that draw from the home to the outside world, but in the multitude of
avenues by which she may bring the best from the world without to illuminate
the home." Crawford was suggesting a career path other than marriage for
personal fulfillment.[10]

She also began to write a series of regional histories on old New England,
focusing first on houses, churches and inns. Three later volumes on Boston
through the nineteenth century soon earned her the title of "Boston's Social

Historian." Her *Romance of the American Theatre* (1913) was the first popular book about the history of theatre in this country. Her biography of a literary giant, *Goethe and His Woman Friends* (1911), and her last book, *Famous Families of Massachusetts* (1930), earned the praise of critics.[11]

In 1907, Crawford graduated from the recently established "School for Social Workers" in Boston. A collaboration of Simmons College and Harvard University, this pioneering program focused on the roots of social problems, emphasizing the causes and prevention of poverty rather than amelioration. Student fieldwork encompassed public assistance, probation, settlement houses, and institutional fields. Outside speakers brought to the students the ideals of the labor union movement and other contemporary topics. Shortly after her graduation, Crawford began a business, the Social Service Publicity Bureau, which she continued for many years. In later years, her firm's letterhead noted that she was a "Financial and Publicity Counselor" and, on the right side in capital letters, "PROMOTER OF WELFARE ORGANIZATIONS."[12]

For a brief period, she was Secretary of the Boston chapter of the Women's Trade Union League (WTUL). The organization had been formed in 1903 because the American Federation of Labor was unresponsive to the concerns of women workers. Working women faced discrimination, described by the WTUL in 1909, as "so strong and bitter" that it seriously handicapped them. As a member, Crawford advocated on behalf of bindery strikers, even though the work stoppage affected the production of one of her books. From 1903 to 1911, Boston witnessed sporadic outbreaks of union organizing and labor unrest. An additional complication in Boston was that the WTUL chapter had internal problems and crystallized into two factions. Crawford's affiliation was brief. She did not attend national meetings that were held in the city, or in later years when the national board met there.[13]

Crawford carried her social commitment further through articles in national publications. In 1903, she described entrepreneurial occupations that educated women were pursuing or sometimes creating on their own. Her 1909 article looked at how women workers were providing for their later years. Bearing in mind the burden of caring for dependent relatives, establishing a bank account, and purchasing life insurance, Crawford expressed clearly the most important factor in women preparing for the future: "No provision looking to old age seems to me more sensible, then, than that which women are making in demanding *equal pay for equal work*." [Emphasis added.] In 1912, she wrote about the working conditions among Boston's telephone workers. In this first national article about the unionizing workers, she argued for better conditions. She charged that night work subjected the young women to sexual harassment, as the telephone exchanges were located in unsavory neighborhoods through which they had to walk. She also claimed that the company subordinated the safety of its work force in its desire to economize on rent. The workers' complaints were overwork, poor ventilation, regimentation, and discrimination because of union activity.[14]

In September 1908, while continuing to write local and regional history, she moved in a new direction, becoming Secretary of the Ford Hall Forum. It would provide the compass for the rest of her life.

Mary Crawford was an emancipated, educated professional working woman in turn-of-the-twentieth century Boston. We can begin to recover a sense of the inner person by bringing together the facts that are known, insights found in her own writings, and an understanding of women similar to her in that time and place. Following the framework posited by historian Edward H. Carr, we "process" the biographical facts and the broader societal picture. But while seeking to ensure the facts are accurate, we cannot stop there, writes Carr. Our duty is "to bring into the picture all known or knowable facts relevant, in one sense or another, to the theme on which [we are] engaged and to the interpretation proposed." We need from history, writes political scientist Robert N. Bellah, "some idea of how we have gotten from the past to the present . . . a narrative." The life and work of Mary Crawford provides this bridge.[15]

Beginning with the larger picture, women in nineteenth century Boston, primarily of the white middle class, formed "benevolent societies" to improve their own surroundings as well as the lives of others less fortunate. Such efforts became known as "municipal housekeeping." The long existence of these improvement organizations, such as the Women's Municipal League in Boston, broadens our understanding of the context of the shift of Crawford's activism. It is similar to the change in Radcliffe's educational goal, from individual to societal efforts.[16]

In the nineteenth century, the core of the "woman movement" was a striving to improve their status in and usefulness to society. The generation that followed Susan B. Anthony and Elizabeth Cady Stanton, for the most part, found wider options for educational, occupational and professional advancement. They could campaign for equal rights, pursue community service, engage in social action, seek personal emancipation from traditional structures and attitudes, or, depending on their personal situation, combine these possibilities. Crawford brought together her quest for personal freedom and community service in a double-track career of historical writing and social commitment. In so doing, she transformed herself from dutiful daughter to emancipated professional.[17]

Many college-educated women at the time felt a "sense of uselessness" and wanted to do "something important." Social reformer Jane Addams characterized the frustrations of these young women as a "fatal want [i.e., deficiency] of harmony between their theory and their lives, a lack of co-ordination between thought and action, [and a longing] to give tangible expression to the democratic ideal." Women like Crawford frequently organized or joined groups to achieve goals that went beyond the constraints that law and society imposed on them as individuals. Working together, they learned how to conduct the business of an organization, or they contributed to the expansion of democracy, eventually through the ballot. They proved themselves tireless social researchers and publicists. Like Crawford, many also entered the paid work force, as new opportunities became available.[18]

In the late nineteenth century, most women had married by their mid-twenties. More than ninety percent of them over age thirty-five in 1890 were wives, historian Alice Kessler-Harris notes, but it was not the only path open. "More than 75 percent of the generation of college women who graduated before 1900 remained single." Thanks to the activism of the forerunners, the century had seen a remarkable growth in female schooling, with the thirst for learning promoted in many cultural forms, including public lectures. As with many educated men and women of the time, Crawford likely read, or was familiar with, Ralph Waldo Emerson's admonition to "go alone." He said most of us have bound our eyes and attached ourselves to one of the "communities of opinion." There is an alternative, suggests Emerson: All history "resolves itself very easily into the biography of a few stout and earnest persons." This new individualism spurred the educated woman to be independent in seeking her own course. Most young women received, at best, ambivalent approval from family and society in their struggle to strike out on their own. Crawford's life demonstrates that she conceived herself in this independent yet socially committed Emersonian framework.[19]

The social and demographic changes occurring in Boston are also important in filling in Crawford's portrait. During her lifetime, from 1874 to 1932, the population grew three-fold, from 250,000 to 780,000, as the city became a magnet for new immigrants. Institutions and organizations, such as the Women's Educational and Industrial Union, developed a wide range of responses to social needs. By the 1890s, that organization had become an effective force for progressive social policies.[20]

Tackling the city's problems, activism and reform had begun to remake the political landscape, with the movement for "municipal housekeeping" providing a broader public role for women. Service for the public good grew into civic virtue, and although conflict continued, Boston became more progressive. Examples of change were the successful referendum for the eight-hour day in 1899 and early leadership for women's suffrage. By 1910, cohesive communal action had greatly improved the political environment. The entire range of "redemptive" organizations, as they were called, in which white and African American women's groups helped the working class and new immigrants, originated in Boston. Josiah Quincy, Mayor from 1895 to 1900, introduced a broad program of city services. By the second decade of the century, Boston had thirty settlement houses, dozens of public playgrounds and gyms, and twelve public baths. The city also had a rich cultural terrain, especially in the Beacon Hill area, where Ford Hall was located. The new spirit was reflected in many public lectures in the city, with Lowell Institute leading the lecture movement. As noted earlier, Mary Parker Follett had begun the Social Centers movement in the city, in which schools were used for adult education in the evening. This was the setting where Mary Crawford lived and worked.[21]

In June 1896, Elizabeth Cary Agassiz, president of Radcliffe, captured the spirit of the period in her commencement address. "We have to show that the wider scope of knowledge and the severer training of the intellect may strengthen and enrich a woman's life." Wherever the future path may turn, "[a woman's] rule and her service should be the wiser, the more steady." Through their education, the students had been trained in clear and logical methods of thinking, and their powers of concentration and observation had been highly cultivated. For Agassiz, if college did not build up character and give a more urgent sense of duty, it had failed in its most important task.[22]

The emphasis on independence through education and career commitment, expressed by the college president, resonated strongly within Crawford. At twenty-two years old, she was beginning to move from a protected family environment to a life that examined and sought to solve social problems. Rising to the challenge presented by Agassiz, and drawing on the importance of the reliance on self, articulated by Elizabeth Cady Stanton in 1892, Crawford embarked on her personal journey. Historian Richard Hoftstadter's criteria of a twentieth century intellectual fits Crawford perfectly: critically examining the meaning of the world around her, responding to the values of reason and justice, and expressing concern for the well-being of all social classes.[23]

Agassiz's words also reflect larger societal changes that were taking place. In 1904, historian George E. Howard wrote that educational equality was but one aspect of the movement for women's liberation. Other factors in "the ideal partnership of the sexes in the uplifting of society" were intellectual, political, and economic emancipation. In a 1914 essay, Howard said that educated women were not so much shunning marriage as declining to view it as a profession. In the same 1914 collection of essays, historian Mary Beard commented that, "not a single important statute has been enacted without the active support of women." Even before gaining the vote, their voices were being heard.[24]

Crawford stepped forward into this new world. Nationally, women's employment outside the home had shifted greatly from manual to clerical responsibilities but there was also growth in other professions. Between 1890 and World War I, the number of women who sought professional training mushroomed. By 1920, nearly 30,000 women had been trained as social workers. In business offices, females displaced males as private secretaries, although with a corresponding lowering of pay. A 1916 manual noted that a secretary must think independently and at the same time execute the thoughts of the supervisor. A 1910 list of women's vocations in Boston placed "social and economic service" first among careers to consider. Social critic Randolph Bourne wrote at the time that such women "are decidedly emancipated and advanced, [with an] amazing combination of wisdom and youthfulness, of humor and ability [and] of course all self-supporting and independent."[25]

In this time of new opportunities, educated and committed women like Crawford began to work through the constraints and conflicts of the period, while contributing to the reform of society. In so doing, they achieved a sense of dignity, fulfillment and productivity. Crawford's public life reflected this new era, when women, such as settlement house resident and literature professor Vida Scudder, literally and conceptually, crossed boundaries daily as they moved about Boston.[26]

For Crawford, her life became journeys that intersected, from magazine and historical writing to social work training, from Women's Trade Union League activism to arranging public lectures, from administering an office and directing volunteers, to spending time with family and friends and becoming a member of several organizations in the city. Her work choices and the way she organized her work week brought together social commitment, a sense of history, and strong administrative and interpersonal skills. The combination proved critical to the success of Ford Hall and the national movement, as well as fulfilling to her personally.

Before turning to Crawford's work in the Open Forum, it is important to explore what we know about the inner person.

A 1914 autobiographical entry notes that her recreation was canoeing. While that is not significant by itself, she goes on to say that "I know of no other [activity] that brings you immediately into such intimate touch with nature, [providing] a renewed faith in life." Coleman told the Ford Hall audience in 1914 that Crawford was always business-like. In the largely male-led lecture movement, she knew how to penetrate "the cleverest bluff of the most adept four-flusher," i.e., a bluffer. At the same time, he saw a side to her that was "ultra-feminine in its simplicity and winsomeness and no one can be with her very long without feeling its charm." He said that she was doing all she could to make the world a little better.[27]

In 1928, Crawford completed a Radcliffe alumnae form, describing herself as a "Wilsonian Democrat," deeply interested in the labor movement and international affairs. On political work, she wrote that she "heckle[s] senators etc sometimes by letter." She ranked character formation in college as more important than scholastic training and other activities. Although she had not married, some of her friends successfully combined a career and marriage. For herself, world peace was the most important forward movement in which women could be of service.[28]

In her responses, Crawford was much like her fellow Radcliffe graduates from 1883 to 1928. Historians Barbara Miller Solomon and Patricia M. Nolan found that the 3,567 alumnae in the survey generally ranked scholastic training highest, although character formation was a close second. The graduates usually joined voluntary associations and the majority belonged to more than one organization. The largest number of respondents thought that the most important way women could serve was as mothers and teachers of future generations. The second largest group said that promoting world peace was crucial.[29]

Crawford's life shows that she was an exceptionally busy and well-organized "multi-tasking" person. In addition to her research and writing, which included visiting Germany for her study of Goethe, she was a member of several clubs and active in her congregation. During these years, writes historian Sarah Deutsch, the "New Women" in Boston challenged the dominant sexual division of space and function and created a new set of relations and places. While many made a permanent break from their family, Crawford chose a different path. She decided not to live away from home. Her mother lived with her after becoming a widow, as well as her brother at various times. Such "family claim," in the contemporary phrase, was often true of unmarried middle class women. Crawford, like the women in Deutsch's study, shaped a world in which she was not marginalized, but instead played a key role as "social arbiter/social glue." More than the public face of private womanhood, notes Deutsch, they were "a new brand of middle-class womanhood."[30]

Although there is no documentation about Crawford's home life, her mother likely relieved the activist/writer of many domestic chores. Even with the invention of hundreds of cleaning and kitchen conveniences in the nineteenth century, it was still tiring and time-consuming to maintain a household. "Mrs. Middle-class Housewife," write historians Dorothy Schneider and Carl Schneider, had a huge amount of work to do, both daily and weekly. On a daily basis, she shopped, cooked, baked, cleaned the stove, and removed soot from glass globes of oil and gas lamps. Weekly, there was more extensive cleaning, laundry (boiling first), sewing, mending, and beautifying the home. Not only was a "woman's work never done," many commentators noted the exhaustion and ill health of women.[31]

Relieved of some if not most of this responsibility, Crawford had the time and determination to fuse her personal ideals and professional skills into what she described as her "typical day." She spent her mornings in history research "at the Athenaeum dealing with the Boston of the past, and the afternoons at Ford Hall helping to mould [*sic*] the Boston of the future." She probably also carried on her private business of social service publicity in the afternoon, as her office was in the same building as the Ford Hall Forum business address. An English Victorian woman writer, in describing women such as Crawford, said that they outlined their own lives, "marking out distinctly the channels in which one's energies should flow, and for which they should be reserved."[32]

One likely source of Crawford's strength was a network of friends and organizations, as was true with many single professional women during this period. This was in addition to family, work and congregation activities. For the women who sought to improve society, historians have begun to explore the crucial networks of love and support. Such founts of strength enabled the reformers to function at a high level of energy and accomplishment. But while they were building a better society, their private lives did not usually become part of the historical record. Like her counterparts, Crawford defined a new role for herself, in which she shaped the world around her. Women at the second tier in social movements, just like the prominent leaders, deserve historical recognition. They neither worked nor lived in a vacuum. They need to be seen as making decisions and sacrifices that affected their personal lives, while drawing on others for support.[33]

An exceptional strength that Crawford brought to the Ford Hall Forum was the warm interpersonal relationships she developed with the very diverse audience. In a 1914 essay, she described her connection with the core group of attendees—the "Ford Hall Folks"—in straightforward terms of love. When friends separate, she wrote, they do so without any special "pang," trusting they will meet again. "But when lovers separate the last words are, 'When am I going to see you again?'" She described the wonderful affection and zany humor of the annual dinner that provided "intimate fellowship." A clearly nurturing, family-type affiliation had developed, linking the Forum audience and leadership beyond the lectures. The core members had begun meeting in 1912 on Sunday afternoons, every three weeks, initially with fifty people, but then it grew. In March 1918, after the United States entered the war, and so many of the "Folks" went into military service, Crawford saw the interest in a "Ford Hall Reading Circle." While dubious about starting it so late in the season, she sensed a "definite desire on the part of the Folks to keep together."[34]

Another glimpse into Crawford's inner person can be drawn from her biography of the poet-playwright Goethe, particularly his relationships with women. Her well-received study shows that although Crawford had not married, she was not constrained in feeling or understanding about deep human interactions. Previous critics wrongly viewed the many women in his life as "sucked oranges from which he had taken all the sweetness." She was direct in writing about his sensual side, with his many friendships, loves and, inevitably, losses. More than one woman, she continued, "whose life touched his seems to have sincerely felt that to have been bored by *him*, if only for a little while, was enough of happiness to compensate for a childless and mateless old age." As a result, Crawford understood, that even when Goethe was seventy-four years old, a seventeen-year-old could still move him, and she quoted his own words towards the end:

"The Woman-Soul leadeth us;
Upward and on!"[35]

Further insight into Crawford as an individual can be drawn from her historical writings. In her first regional work, *The Romance of Old New England Rooftrees* (1902), she looked at old houses that had survived the years and the famous people who lived in them. In a profile of Anne Hutchinson, Crawford wrote that the seventeenth century free thinker "soon became unwisely and unpleasantly aggressive in her criticism of . . . ministers." Hutchinson spoke "more freely than was consistent with prudence and moderation . . . constantly adding fuel to the flame." In Crawford's own life and work, her balanced outlook in relating to established male leaders is shown in arranging hundreds of lectures in Boston and around the nation, mostly by men, and coordinating numerous administrative and logistical details. This is in addition to her affectionate relations with the immediate audience in Ford Hall.[36]

In her book on old New England houses, Crawford commented on mid-nineteenth century feminist Margaret Fuller, who had also written about Goethe. Fuller began a series of "Conversations" in Boston, where women and some invited men discussed women's roles in society. In this earlier time, Fuller proclaimed that "the restraints upon the sex were insuperable only to those who think them so . . . or who noisily strive to break them." A later generation "has only to look at the heroic fashion in which, after the death of her father, Margaret took up the task of educating her brothers and sisters to feel that there was much besides selfishness in this woman's makeup."[37]

Turning to the public person, Crawford's sense of history guided her administration and documentation of the Open Forum. Her goals in writing about the movement were three-fold: to inspire new communities to follow the Forum approach, to make other series as successful as Ford Hall, and to preserve the history of the learning initiative for future generations. The nine large scrapbooks of newspaper and magazine articles and Ford Hall publications, extensive office files, and two huge albums of testimonial letters attest to her preservation goal. In locating newspaper and magazine articles from around the country, she either directed volunteers or used a clipping bureau. For the first testimonial album, she solicited writings about Coleman. She knew that it is not enough to carry out a good public initiative; it must also be communicated.[38]

In a number of writings, Crawford pointed the way for other communities to succeed in following the Ford Hall Forum approach. Her 1909 article, "Getting to the Unchurched in Boston," in a Chicago Presbyterian publication, described the first year of Ford Hall. While the initial lectures were well received, she wrote, attendance was not spectacular. However, dozens of appreciative letters from the wide range of people in the audience and favorable newspaper coverage convinced the sponsoring Boston Baptist Social Union to continue the series. When she became the paid Secretary in September 1908, her immediate goal was to greatly increase attendance. In the new position, she fused together an intense interest in the social and economic advance of workers, knowledge of social work, an awareness of the power of publicity, and her recent experience in working closely with labor leaders through the WTUL. The combination was exactly what the fledgling movement needed.[39]

By the third program of the second season, Ford Hall had standing room only. At the fourth meeting, which was a discussion of socialism, five hundred persons were turned away. Each week, while the crowd waited for the doors to open, they talked about previous speakers. Crawford felt that people were beginning to understand the efforts of churches to help. Just as non-churchgoers require an understanding of Christianity, she said, Christians need to hear about social movements. She wrote that Coleman, with his sense of "brotherliness," brought together all religions in the planning committee. Who will say, she concluded, that the planning group is not doing a conspicuous service to religion in providing an unbiased and unconventional presentation of the ethical and social impulses of the time?[40]

This early article is a good example of Crawford bringing together her writing skills, resourceful use of publicity, and the ideals of the era. Coleman had these same traits but his communication was more explicitly promotional and enthusiastic, while her approach, in voice and content, was practical and at the same time inspiring. It is significant that this article was published in a Presbyterian periodical as it validated their shared conviction that the movement was religious but not denominational, despite its Baptist financial support.

A second instance of Crawford furthering the Forum as an organization and preserving its record is her lengthy 1914 essay, "The Story of the Ford Hall Meetings." In it, she traced the movement's beginnings to the People's

Institute in New York City, which Coleman observed in 1906. She caught the mix of the New York audience in "the Russian Jew, still quivering from recent persecutions . . . sitting closely by the side of the up-town youth whose interest in social questions has just been awakened." She described the difficulties Coleman had to overcome to begin a similar series in Boston, both within the sponsoring committee and the suspicious general public. Her narrative captured the smoke-heavy atmosphere of a labor meeting where Coleman urged the leaders to support the new movement.[41]

Beyond the speakers and "very tactful advertising," Crawford contended the Forum had to be developed in an organized and systematic way. This was the value of a paid Secretary, which was vital to a Forum that hoped to do important work. Many people on the planning committee did not see why a paid worker was necessary, as they had a hall and an attractive list of speakers. "The fact is," Crawford wrote, "we live in an age dominated by publicity." People do not go anywhere or do anything without having had their attention called repeatedly to a particular event. Boston was honeycombed with organizations holding free meetings on Sunday but newspapers would not cover a meeting of only a handful of people. She said that thirteen hundred people at Ford Hall meant that thirteen thousand people gained the gist of what went on the next day through news reports. She urged other Forums to concentrate on "packing your house."[42]

A very important part of a successful Forum, she continued, was the presiding officer. The moderator introduced the speaker, fielded the questions, and ensured that the evening fulfilled the goals of the movement. For Crawford, the ideal person was very much like Coleman, and contemporary accounts portray him as a master of the platform. With these ingredients, she predicted local Forums would succeed. Nearly 100 of the Ford Hall Folks met for supper at the hall every three weeks. The *Ford Hall Folks* ("our paper," in Crawford's words) was in its second successful season. The group had recently begun a "Town Meeting," where they studied civics together. Importantly for Crawford and the movement, the group was a cross-section of the city: lawyers, doctors, teachers, authors, book-peddlers, students, settlement workers, editors, shop-girls, stenographers, clerks, and day laborers. All mingled happily in "social intercourse," she wrote, content to be "the Folks."[43]

In this article, Crawford captured the cross-class essence of the Forum movement. Like many of the male Forum leaders and women reformers at the time, she was fortunate in her family's early financial situation. But her father's death, while she was in college, necessitated her becoming the breadwinner for her mother and younger brother. As with others facing this situation, it propelled her into the work world, and for the well-being of her family, she had to succeed. Drawing from her social work training and job experiences, Crawford now began to view the world from the less-advantaged side. The result, in terms of the Ford Hall Forum, was not only that she understood the ideals of the movement but she also saw that a mix of city people was needed to "pack the house." If it was to succeed, idealism was not enough. From her academic background and experience in publicity, and in practical organizational ways, she brought structure to the movement.[44]

Crawford had a further level of understanding to convey to communities that were considering an Open Forum. While the financial base of Ford Hall was Baptist and many of the early speakers were clergy, she saw that the key to a successful series was the diversity of the city's population. In the third year of Ford Hall, a Russian Jewish bookseller, a street-corner preacher, and a woman social worker spoke in successive weeks on what the meetings meant to them. In the fourth season, the Jesuit president of Boston College spoke against socialism, despite the presence of many true believers in the cause in the audience. Crawford wrote that it was all done with the utmost good will and attendance was unprecedented. In the fifth year, Rev. John A. Ryan, the foremost Catholic advocate for social justice at the time, argued for economic democracy. In the seventh season, Mary Antin, a Jewish immigrant who had recently written about her experiences, broke the attendance record.[45]

Crawford was very pleased with the diversity in class and ethnicity of the audience, and she also knew that a large number had lost touch with organized religion. This would not be a barrier. Through "intimate talks" she had with many of the people, she realized that those who had become estranged from religion were now ready to be active again. As an example, one man told her that "after five years at Ford Hall, I am more sure than ever before that man is incurably religious." Reflecting the influence of Rauschenbusch, she concluded that the Ford Hall audience cared tremendously that the Kingdom of Heaven should speedily come on earth. Like Coleman, Crawford's own strong faith allowed many paths, or indeed none.[46]

A third, more extended writing by Crawford was "A Roll of Personalities," a long section in the 1915 symposium edited by Coleman, *Democracy in the Making.* Her sketches of sixteen "typical Ford Hall Folks" captured the diverse audience that meant so much to her personally and to the success of the Forum. With such an audience, the title of the book captured the core of the Forum in concept and process.[47]

Crawford's profiles traced the power of the movement on the attendees and their families throughout the week. Her first was of an "energetic Socialist friend," who often brought her daughters to the lectures and eagerly followed up on the discussions at home with her sons. The mother had recently led a fight against high kosher meat prices, which resulted in the creation of a chain of cooperative butcher stores. With a husband on the City Council and two sons in college, she had come a long way from her Russian immigrant garment worker background. Like many in the audience, she also gave back to the community, serving as a translator for new immigrants and helping them financially. To those who did not know the meaning of poverty and injustice, she helped them understand "the hopes and fears, the struggles and aspirations, the prejudices and passions of the poor."[48]

Crawford's next profile was of an Irish-born newspaper letter writer, who was similarly committed to building a better community. In addition to his work and a full family life, he volunteered in a soup kitchen with other "Folks." Another regular was a Jewish antique shop owner and music lover. It was not lost on Crawford's sense of history that his synagogue was the birthplace of the first anti-slavery society in the country.[49]

Other sketches captured further the diversity of the audience. One suburban woman, she wrote, "proves that one does not need to be a Socialist, an Anarchist, or a Single Taxer" to find the lectures valuable. For this Ford Hall regular, who had been coming by a one-hour train ride for five years, the lectures were not a substitute for her devout Methodism. Able to trace her family to the American Revolution, her church work was planning the travels of women missionaries from New England. While Crawford pointed with pride to the many free-thinking people and secularists in the audience, she was just as pleased for "the good sense and unprejudiced conservatism [of such] housewives."[50]

Regular attendees at the lectures brought additional diversity, such as strong Baptist and Catholic backgrounds. One woman was active in floral and patriotic activities in the community. A distinguished "colored" lawyer (in the contemporary language) shared his knowledge and insights, including why African Americans were for the most part in their churches on Sunday evening instead of at Ford Hall. A man who had been blinded in a mine explosion in Mexico brought a special understanding of the cross-border conflict during the period. In four years of coming to the lectures, he had missed only two programs. "You were joyously talking here," he said, "what I had long been silently and sadly thinking." An advertiser who traced his family to the Puritans, and whose interests ranged from poetry to city planning, was another person seeking a better world. Crawford wrote that his vision kindled the imagination of citizens and had borne fruit in actual civic improvement.[51]

The sixteen portraits Crawford painted in "A Roll of Personalities" convey the wide range of interests and backgrounds of the audience. With a similar mix of people in all cities, Crawford (and Coleman in a mentor role) was telling communities not only what they should expect but also to seek in this experiment in democracy. While some people proudly traced their family back to the Revolution, others grasped the opportunity to rise from immigrant roots with little formal education. Just as surely, with the large number of clergy involved in the Forum, and Coleman and his wife long active in Baptist activities, many in the audience were committed to their own religious tradition. But as the Social Gospel and the progressive era were changing the inner landscape of America, an even larger number in the audience were free thinkers religiously and politically, ready for social change. Crawford valued deeply such diversity. She recognized and embraced how the "Folks" and the changing times were coming together through Forums around the country. Reviewers praised Coleman's book, taking special note of Crawford's portraits, which showed "representative men and women of various nationalities profoundly affected by the meetings."[52]

Crawford also wrote about the national movement beyond Ford Hall, particularly in relationship to individual-focused democracy. The Forum's locally planned "neighbor" structure was a partial implementation of the group theory of Mary Parker Follett, founder of the Social Centers movement. The true group process, Follett argued, is a continual acting and reacting that brings out differences and integrates them into larger unities, becoming "the preeminent social process in a democracy." However, the independent thinking approach of the Open Forum, articulated by Crawford, did not equate with Follett's philosophy that "we . . . are free only when we are obeying the group."[53]

The focus on the individual in the Forum is shown strongly in Crawford's report on the Fifth Annual Meeting of the Open Forum National Council, in November 1918, at Cooper Union in New York City. It captured the spirit of "reconstruction" that the country was heading into at war's end. In the twenty years since the People's Institute began, Coleman had spread the Forum idea to nearly three hundred groups around the country.[54]

Paraphrasing Coleman's talk at the New York meeting, Crawford saw the movement as representing everything for which democracy stood. The goal was not to build a great institution but to propagate a method. As the speaker after Coleman said, "the war is over: the war is only just begun." The "democratic development of the war," according to that speaker, had to be carried back into everyday life, and the Forum was the place where individuals could meet and grapple with societal problems. Having made the world safe for democracy, democracy had to be made safe for itself.[55]

America's internationalism of the war period, however, did not carry over into peace. Disillusionment and an anti-immigrant atmosphere set in and the overwhelming majority of the Progressives were done with Wilsonian internationalism, writes historian Eric Goldman. For some of them, war and post-war reconstruction fervor provided an unexpected lesson in class relations. It taught skepticism about consolidated power and an appreciation for smaller-scale, even class-related democratic arenas. The result was that the "neighbor" concept of the Forum continued to be powerful, carrying over into the next decade. In the 1930s, John Studebaker, Superintendent of Schools in Des Moines, and later Commissioner of the U. S. Office of Education in the Roosevelt administration, spread the Forum method around the country through public affairs forums.[56]

In reporting on the 1918 New York meeting, Crawford did not shy away from controversy. One of the speakers at the gathering was John Haynes Holmes, the national voice for interfaith dialogue and civil liberties. He had neither closed the lecture series at his church nor "jumped on the band wagon" of patriotism during the war. At the New York meeting, he was reassured by one of the participants that a Forum continuing during the period is much more useful than one that closes down. Crawford wrote that many Forum leaders were perplexed during the war on the best way to hold fast to the Forum motto, "Let There Be Light." Looking ahead, she saw how the Liberty Halls, which were public meeting houses under construction in many cities, would be an immediate means of education along reconstruction lines, for both returning soldiers and the general public.[57]

In a report on the 1919 meeting of the New England Congress of Forums, Crawford quoted a leader of one local series on the national unifying value of the lectures. More than any other institution, the speaker asserted, it eliminates race prejudice. At the same meeting, another leader felt the movement "keeps all races and classes . . . interested" as it unifies the country. A third speaker saw its value in preventing strikes. Whether or not the motive of such assertions was to dampen radical or racial agitation or the growth of unions, the speakers looked to the lecture movement as "the last great hope for the orderly settlement of the problems which the World War has left us to solve."[58]

Spurred by the patriotic fervor of the war years, such public addresses were frequently heard around the country, and Ford Hall reflected it. Local Forums supported the construction of Liberty Halls. Crawford reported factually, rather than with patriotic fervor, what was said at the 1919 meeting. She also conveyed how the Open Forum's ideals could strengthen local series. The letters of Crawford and Coleman during and after the war show their concern that radical speakers could cause financial or public relations problems. There was also the risk of a question period in a foreign language following a lecture. She warned one speaker "not to let herself go on the matter of the war!" Critics in and out of the Baptist Social Union were also a worry, as "however rational any Ford Hall Meeting talk may *attempt* to be it will be made more or less hectic by questions and queries on Russia." Bearing in mind what was occurring in the United States after the war, Crawford became anxious: "My own feeling is that Ford Hall and its activities are being carefully observed now and that something might be precipitated at a foreign language meeting which would just wreck the work."[59]

Despite the dangers in this period of intolerance, Crawford maintained the integrity and open platform of the Forum. Among the controversial lecture topics in the postwar period were a look at the "new spirit" in Russia, lessons of the British Labor Party, how the nation should handle victory (by Socialist Norman Thomas), state control of ideas, how to (and how not to) Americanize, the power of prejudice, and race problems in America and around the world. Other topics broadened the audience on contemporary changes in society and the economic order in the United States and other lands. The list of speakers and the subjects do not show any wavering in the basic principles of the movement since it began a decade earlier.[60]

In a 1920 article, Crawford reviewed the January meeting of the New England Forums. She quoted Coleman, who spoke at the meeting, that the Forum model was "the one outstanding instrument of our time which can bring the discordant elements together in an educational way." He said that the postwar problem was not so much the clash between political ideologies, but "disintegration," with capital against labor, wealth over poverty, and whites pulling against "negroes." [*sic*] Crawford also summarized the other speakers who came from different Forums, such as one in a New Hampshire shoe factory where workers, company representatives and foremen came together to hear discussions. Such workplace lectures clearly resonated strongly with her, because of her labor union links, "identifying the place where a man works with free speech."[61]

Crawford's extensive Forum work, publicity business, memberships in local organizations, and historical writing were not her only activities. She had one further Forum-type commitment. For a decade, she assisted Coleman in the administration of the Sagamore Sociological Conference. In reporting on the lectures and discussions, she was once again carrying the Forum ideals to a wider audience. Her article on the 1910 Conference, published in a denominational periodical, focused on the role of the church in social work. She briefly mentioned one talk, where a speaker said that a race-based "dual civilization" in the South is best. While she surely disagreed with the speaker, she recognized that her role was just reporting what was said. In the open marketplace of ideas, she would not always agree with comments of others.[62]

But Crawford's main point in the article was the discussion on child labor and the changes taking place in the church. She saw that the church as a whole is "fairly awake at last to the great work of social reconstruction." Her ability to stay focused on what was really important was a vital ingredient in her daily interactions and writings. Open-minded as she was, she continually reflected in her outlook and communication the impact of the Social Gospel. While she placed a separate report on the meeting in a secular periodical, the denominational publication ensured the message went directly to churchgoers. It was another instance of Crawford targeting her audience.[63]

In her 1917 report on the Sagamore sessions, in a leading Unitarian Weekly, Crawford noted that a minority report was submitted for the first time. The "militant pacifists" at the meeting, she wrote, were unwilling to pledge unstinted support for the war effort that had just begun. At the same session, the organizers recognized, belatedly, the need to broaden the composition of the meetings. They pledged to pay for working-people to attend future sessions. Money and a special invitation would not deter gaining the broader base that was crucial in considering social issues.[64]

Crawford found a two-fold effect in broadening participation at the Sagamore discussions. On the one hand, it deepened the respect of employers and intellectuals for the working class. At the same time, it showed workers that in a seemingly selfish world, people of privilege cared for those who made a living with their hands. Her 1917 report captured the idealism of the Forum movement. Her description about the planned change was factual, illuminating and lively. As in her other writings, she was comfortable and consistent on the levels of both reporting and personal belief. With all the other activities taking place, the Sagamore Conferences came to an end in 1918.

From 1919 to 1920, Crawford helped her own denomination by bringing her skills to the Episcopal Diocese of Massachusetts in a national campaign to raise awareness of the church. Applying the same mass media and multi-format techniques which drew people to Ford Hall, she wrote, once again, "Whether we like it or not, we live in an age of advertising."[65]

The challenge in writing the history of women, suggests historian Kathryn Kish Sklar, is to do more than reconstruct the past in new ways. The possibilities in women's present and future need to be *transformed* into an expanded understanding. Recovering the secretaries and assistants of early twentieth century social movements furthers this understanding. Historians have been recording the lives of women reform leaders but more attention is needed at the second tier, however sparse the personal stories. A century later, we can do no less.[66]

Mary Crawford played a vital role in beginning and then spreading the Forum movement. Thanks to the feminists who blazed the path, she entered the world of paid work at a time of growing opportunities and lived in an era of idealism, optimism and activism. As with many forgotten women in social and cultural movements, she enlarged the role of Secretary to "Administrator" or "Administrative Assistant" and made ideals concrete. In the process, she strengthened her own multi-layered career. She was changed by the period and, in turn, contributed to change, through an application of the Social Gospel and new ideals that reached across religious, race and class lines.[67]

Like nationally-known reformer Jane Addams, Crawford had a sense of genuine kinship with the "other half" of humanity. This was shown through her warm relationships with the "Ford Hall Folks" and her awareness of what the lecture movement was accomplishing nationally. She exemplified the progressive intellectual ideal, as proposed by historian Christopher Lasch, in going beyond an intellectual search for knowledge. Instead, she pursued the *application* of reform in education and culture.[68]

Crawford's work was also part of the broader development of a new "national class," as posited by historian Robert Wiebe, which reshaped the nineteenth century two-class structure into a three-class system. In the process, the new national class, with its emphasis on "Knowledge" and "Experts," led the nation's transformation into an urban-industrial society. Crawford's people-centered outlook and outstanding accomplishments place her in this class that transcended local attachments and boundaries. Using Wiebe's construct, Crawford is seen as a component of the "interdependent national scheme of things." She knew the crucial importance of helping ordinary people make a "rational fit with reality." She sensed that without such firm moorings, they would be confused, resentful and ill-equipped for modern life. She concluded that the Open Forum offered the best path.[69]

When Mary Crawford died on November 15, 1932, one obituary noted that "large delegations" from the clubs to which she belonged attended her funeral service. Another notice recounted her contributions to building a better city and nation and her writings that brought history alive. A quarter of a century earlier, she had written of poet/playwright Friedrich Schiller words that can stand as her own epitaph: "high ideals are their own reward for being."[70]

She understood clearly the ideals of the Open Forum movement, but went beyond what Coleman developed with strong administrative, organizational, interpersonal, and communication skills. Thanks to her sense of history, she also looked to the future in saving office files, compiling scrapbooks on the national reach of the movement, and preparing huge testimonial albums. As is true with many women, she was too busy, too tired, or not focused on herself to leave her personal story but it is a loss to American history if it is not reconstructed. It is time to ensure that other secretaries and assistants, who were crucial in shaping a better local and national community, are not "absent from history."

NOTES

1. Patricia Meyer Spacks, "Selves in History," 112–32, in Estelle C. Jelinek, ed., *Women's Autobiography; Essays in Criticism* (Bloomington: Indiana University Press, 1980), 112; Virginia Woolf, "A Room of One's Own," *Identity and Respect* (Chicago: Great Books Foundation, 1997), 140.

2. Obituary, "Mary C. Crawford, Boston Author, Dies," *The New York Times*, 16 November 1932, 17; *The Ford Hall Forum Magazine*, n.d, Scrapbooks, 8. The phrase "compact sociological institution" is in "Mary Caroline Crawford," Thomas W. Herringshaw, *Herringshaw's National Library of American Biography* (Chicago: American Publishers' Association, 1909–1914), fiche 370.29.

3. Coleman, "What Mary C. Crawford Has Done," *Ford Hall Folks*, 19 April 1914, 4, Scrapbooks, 9; Lurie, *Challenge of the Forum*, 87; Crawford, "One Way We Might Help the School," *Graduate Bulletin*, Boston School for Social Workers (October 1915), 5–6, Simmons College Archives, Boston, Massachusetts.

4. *Boston City Directory* (Boston: Sampson, 1876), 228; *Boston City Directory* (Boston: Sampson-Murdoch, 1894), 338; obituary, "Mary Caroline Crawford," *Boston Evening Transcript*, 16 November 1932, 16; Harold Ashton Crawford, "Mary Caroline Crawford," 1941, Radcliffe College Archives, Arthur and Elizabeth Schlesinger Library, Radcliffe Institute for Advanced Study, Harvard University, Cambridge, Massachusetts; Robert A. Woods and Albert J. Kennedy, *The Zone of Emergence; Observations of the Lower Middle and Upper Working Class Communities of Boston, 1905–1914*, abr. and ed. by Sam Bass Warner, Jr., 2nd ed. (Cambridge: Massachusetts Institute of Technology, 1962, 1969), 44–52; "Mary Caroline Crawford," Radcliffe Alumnae Information, 1928, Radcliffe College Archives.

5. *Pastoral Records of St. John's Church*, St. John's Episcopal Church Archives, Charlestown, Massachusetts; Norman B. Nash, "A Prophet of Social Justice," *Philo Woodruff Sprague; The Collected Essays of Eight Intimate Associates* (Charlestown: St. John's Church, 1927), 42–51.

6. Letter to writer, with Crawford college transcript, Jane Knowles, College Archivist, Radcliffe College, 14 November 1997; "Mary Caroline Crawford," *Woman's Who's Who of America; A Biographical Dictionary of Contemporary Women of the United States and Canada, 1914–1915*, John W. Leonard, ed., (New York: American Commonwealth, 1914), 215; Sarah Eisenstein, *Give Us Bread But Give Us Roses; Working Women's Consciousness in the United States, 1890 to the First World War* (Boston: Routledge and Kegan Paul, 1983), 120; Dorothy Ella Howells, *A Century to Celebrate: Radcliffe College, 1879–1979* (Cambridge: Radcliffe College, 1978), 3–14, 105–14; Joyce Antler, *The Educated Woman and Professionalization; The Struggle for a New Feminine Identity, 1890–1920* (New York: Garland Publishing, 1987), 72–73; Joyce Antler, *Lucy Sprague Mitchell; The Making of a Modern Woman* (New Haven: Yale University Press, 1987), xiv.

7. Letter to writer, Katherine Kraft, Acting College Archivist, Radcliffe College, 4 May 2000; "Gertrude Stein," 20:621–22; "Maud Park (Wood)," 17:3–4, "Mary Parker Follett," 8:174–77, *American National Biography* (New York: Oxford University, 1999).

8. "Miss Mary Caroline Crawford," *Boston Budget*, undated article pasted into author's copy of *The Romance of Old New England Rooftrees* (Boston: L. C. Page, 1902); Herringshaw, 370.22–33. Information on her brother, Harold Ashton Crawford, is from the Kautz Family YMCA Archives, University of Minnesota, Minneapolis, Minnesota, and American Relief Administration, European Operations Collections, Hoover Institution Archives, Stanford University, Stanford, California.

9. Herringshaw, 370.31; *Who Was Who in America*, 275.

10. Mary C. Crawford, *The College Girl of America; And the Institutions Which Make Her What She Is* (Boston: L.C. Page & Company, 1905), 300–13.

11. Herringshaw, 370.24–30; newspaper clipping, "Mary C. Crawford, Business Woman, Author, Idealist," *Femina*, n.d., Scrapbooks, 4.

12. Letter to writer, Claire Goodwin, Simmons College Archivist, 17 November 1998, *75th Anniversary Simmons College School of Social Work; A Retrospective on the Occasion of the Diamond Jubilee: An Historical Monograph*, March 1980, 5–9, Simmons College Archives. Crawford's business letterhead still noted in 1922: "Social Service Advertising—Welfare Organizations and Social Movements Promoted Through Planned Publicity." Letterhead on letter from Crawford to William E. B. Du Bois, 1 May 1922, *The Papers of W. E. B. Du Bois* (Sanford, NC: Microfilming Corporation of America, 1980), reel 10; Mary C. Crawford, Boston, letter to David K. Niles, Associate Director, Ford Hall Forum, 9 April 1928, Letters of Appreciation to George W. Coleman. (For brevity, subsequent references will be "Du Bois *Papers*.")

13. "Mary Caroline Crawford," *Who Was Who in America*, 275. Almost no records remain, manuscript or printed, of the Boston chapter of the Women's Trade Union League. Letter to writer, Ellen M. Shea, Arthur and Elizabeth Schlesinger Library on the History of Women, 24 November 1997. Sarah Deutsch, *Women and the City; Gender, Space, and Power in Boston, 1870–1940* (New York: Oxford University, 2000), 192–93; Edward T. James, editor, *Papers of the Women's Trade Union League and Its Principal Leaders; Guide to the Microfilm Edition* (Woodbridge, CT: Research Publications, 1981), 270; *Papers of The Women's Trade Union League*, Collection I, Reel 8, and Collection II, Reel 1. The phrase "strong and bitter" is in Nancy Schrom Dye, *As Equals and Sisters; Feminism, The Labor Movement, and The Women's Trade Union League of New York City* (Columbia: University of Missouri, 1980), 6.

14. Crawford, "New Occupations for Educated Women," *The Outlook*, 27 June 1903, 74: 517–22; Crawford, "How Our Women Workers Are Providing For Old Age," *The Survey*, 10 April 1909, 22: 95–99; Stephen H. Norwood, *Labor's Flaming Youth; Telephone Operators and Worker Militancy, 1878–1923* (Urbana: University of Illinois, 1990), 61, 106.

15. Edward H. Carr, *What Is History?* (New York: Viking, 1964), 16, 28; Robert N. Bellah, et al, *Habits of the Heart; Individualism and Commitment in American Life* (Berkeley: University of California Press, 1985; New York: Harper & Row, 1986), 302.

16. Nancy F. Cott, *The Grounding of Modern Feminism* (New Haven: Yale University, 1987), 16–22; Anne F. Scott, *Natural Allies; Women's Associations in American History* (Urbana: University of Illinois, 1993), 13–141; Dorothy Worrell, *The Women's Municipal League of Boston; A History of Thirty-five Years of Civic Endeavor* (Boston: Women's Municipal League Committees, Inc., 1943), 60–65.

17. Cott, *Grounding of Modern Feminism*, 16; Allen F. Davis, *Spearheads For Reform; The Social Settlements in the Progressive Movement, 1890–1914* (New York: Oxford University, 1967), 37; Scott, *Natural Allies*, 2; Robyn Muncy, *Creating a Female Dominion in American Reform, 1890–1935* (New York: Oxford University, 1991), 37.

18. Davis, *Spearheads For Reform*, 26–37; Jane Addams, "The Subjective Necessity for Social Settlements," http://www.infed.org/archives/e-texts/addams6.htm (accessed May 11, 2008); Barbara M. Solomon, *In the Company of Educated Women; A History of Women and Higher Education in America* (New Haven: Yale University, 1985), 14, 30.

19. Margaret G. Wilson, *The American Woman in Transition; The Urban Influence, 1879–1920* (Westport CT: Greenwood Press, 1979), 92; Alice Kessler-Harris, *Out to Work; A History of Wage-Earning Women in the United States* (New York: Oxford University, 1982), 109–14; Ralph Waldo Emerson, "Self-Reliance" in *Essays* (New York: Franklin Watts, 1987), 56, 44, 49; Solomon, *In the Company of Educated Women*, 30.

20. "Boston Population History," http://physics.bu.edu/~redner/cities/boston:html; (accessed May 11, 2008); "A Short History of the Women's Educational and Industrial Union," Women's Educational and Industrial Union, Boston, Massachusetts, n.d.; James J. Connolly, *The Triumph of Ethnic Progressivism; Urban Political Culture in Boston, 1900–1925* (Cambridge: Harvard University, 1998), 5–106; National Women's Trade Union League of America, *Proceedings of the Second Biennial Convention 1909*, 53, quoted in Dye, *As Equals and Sisters*, 6.

21. Martin Green, *The Problem of Boston; Some Readings in Cultural History* (New York: W. W. Norton, 1966), 53; Daphne Spain, *How Women Saved the City* (Minneapolis: University of Minnesota, 2001), 24, 174–75, 178; Rodgers, *Atlantic Crossings*, 135–36.

22. Lucy Allen Paton, *Elizabeth Cary Agassiz; A Biography* (Boston: Houghton Mifflin, 1919), 280, 358.

23. Elizabeth Cady Stanton, "The Solitude of Self," quoted in Linda K. Kerber, "Can a Woman be an Individual? The Discourse of Self-Reliance," in *Toward an Intellectual History of Women; Essays*, Linda K. Kerber, ed., (Chapel Hill: University of North Carolina, 1997), 201; Richard Hofstadter, *Anti-Intellectualism in American Life* (New York: Knopf, 1963), 24, 29.

24. George E. Howard, *A History of Matrimonial Institutions*, (Chicago: University of Chicago, 1904; repr. Humanities Press, 1964), 3:239–45; George E. Howard, "Changed Ideals and Status of the Family and the Public Activities of Women," 33, and Mary Beard, "The Legislative Influence of Unenfranchised Women," 58, 60, in *Women in Public Life*, James P. Lichtenberger, ed., 55 (Philadelphia: American Academy of Political and Social Science, 1914); Wilson, *American Woman in Transition*, 95.

25. Kessler-Harris, *Out to Work*, 116; Ellen L. Spencer, *The Efficient Secretary* (New York: Frederick A. Stokes, 1916), 4, quoted in Margery W. Davies, *Woman's Place Is At the Typewriter; Office Work and Office Workers, 1870–1930* (Philadelphia: Temple University, 1982), 129–30; Kane, *Separatism and Subculture*, 245;

Agnes F. Perkins, ed., *Vocations for the Trained Woman; Opportunities Other Than Teaching* (Boston: Women's Educational and Industrial Union, 1910), vii-ix; Bourne quoted in Cott, *Grounding of Modern Feminism*, 34–35.

26. Lee Chambers-Schiller, "The Single Woman: Family and Vocation Among Nineteenth-Century Reformers," in Mary Kelley, ed., *Woman's Being, Woman's Place; Female Identity and Vocation in American History* (Boston: G. K. Hall, 1979), 347; Sarah Deutsch, "Reconceiving the City: Women, Space, and Power in Boston, 1870–1910," *Gender and History*, 6, August 1994 (2), 209.

27. Herringshaw, 370.31; "Mary Caroline Crawford," *Woman's Who's Who of America*; Coleman, "What Mary Caroline Crawford Has Done." "Four-flusher" is in *The New Shorter Oxford English Dictionary on Historical Principles*, edited by Lesley Brown, (Oxford: Clarendon Press, 1933; repr. and rev., 1993), 1:1015.

28. Crawford, *Radcliffe Alumnae Information.*

29. Barbara Miller Solomon with Patricia M. Nolan, "Education, Work, Family, and Public Commitment in the Lives of Radcliffe Alumna, 1883–1928," 139–55, in Joyce Antler and Sari Knopp Birklen, eds., *Changing Education; Women as Radicals and Conservatives* (Albany: State University of New York, 1990), 140–55.

30. Herringshaw, 370.30; Deutsch, *Women and the City*, 4–104; Lynn D. Gordon, *Gender and Higher Education in the Progressive Era* (New Haven: Yale University, 1990), 20.

31. Ruth Schwartz Cowan, *More Work For Mother; The Ironies of Household Technology From the Open Hearth to the Microwave* (New York: Basic Books, 1983), 44–66; Dorothy Schneider and Carl J. Schneider, *American Women in the Progressive Era, 1900–1920* (New York: Facts On File, 1993), 32–53.

32. Herringshaw; Caroline Emilia Stephen, *Light Arising: Thoughts on the Central Radiance* (Cambridge, England: Heffer, 1908), 116–17, quoted in Martha Vicinus, *Independent Women; Work and Community for Single Women, 1900–1920* (Chicago: University of Chicago, 1985), 37.

33. Blanche Wiesen Cook, "Female Support Networks and Political Activism: Lillian Wald, Crystal Eastman, Emma Goldman," originally published in *Chryalis* 3 (1977): 43–61, repr. Linda K. Kerber and Jane S. DeHart, eds., *Women's America; Refocusing the Past,* 3rd edition (New York: Oxford University, 1991), 309–11; Susan Ware, "Unlocking the Porter-Dewson Partnership: A Challenge for the Feminist Biographer," 51–64, in Sara Alpern, et al, *The Challenge of Feminist Biography; Writing the Lives of Modern American Women* (Urbana: University of Illinois, 1992), 61.

34. "The Ford Hall Folks," *Ford Hall Folks; A Magazine of Neighborliness*, 2, 26 April 1914: 4, Scrapbooks, 4; letter, Mary C. Crawford to George W. Coleman, 11 March 1918, Scrapbooks, 3; *Semi-Annual Report of the Boston Baptist Social Union*, 2 December 1912, n.p., Scrapbooks, 3.

35. Crawford, *Goethe and His Woman Friends* (Boston: Little, Brown, 1911), v, 43, 46, 56, 71, 106–107, 428.

36. Crawford, *The Romance of Old New England Rooftrees* (Boston: L. C. Page, 1902), 218–19.

37. Ibid., 315–18.

38. Letter, Bart Moynahan, Brooklyn, New York, addressed to "Miss Crawford," 17 January 1913, Ford Hall Folks to George William Coleman, February 23, 1908–1913, (Testimonial Album), Babson.

39. Crawford, "Getting to the Unchurched in Boston," *The Interior*, 21 January 1909, 71–72, Scrapbooks, 1.

40. Ibid.

41. Crawford, "The Story of the Ford Hall Meetings," *Ford Hall Folks*, 15 March 1914, Scrapbooks, 4, 4.

42. Ibid., 5–7.

43. Ibid., 7–9.

44. On the economic background of the families of many reformers, see Kathryn Kish Sklar, "Hull House in the 1890s: A Community of Women Reformers," *Signs: Journal of Women in Culture and Society*, 1985, 10 (Summer 1985): 662–63; Davis, *Spearheads of Reform*, 33–37.

45. Crawford, "The Story of the Ford Hall Meetings," 9–16.

46. Ibid., 15.

47. Coleman, "Introduction to Part III," *Democracy in the Making*, 149–52.

48. Crawford, "A Roll of Personalities," Coleman, ibid., 153–56.

49. Ibid., 157–63.

50. Ibid., 170–72.

51. Ibid., 164–69, 173–206.

52. "Democracy in the Making," unattributed review, Scrapbooks, 5.

53. "Mary Parker Follett," 176, American National Biography, 8:176.

54. Crawford, "The Story of the Fifth Annual Meeting," n.d., Scrapbooks, 6.

55. Ibid.

56. Eric F. Goldman, *Rendezvous With Destiny* (New York: Alfred A. Knopf, 1953), 261–82; Rodgers, *Atlantic Crossings*, 317, 460; Leonard P. Oliver, *Study Circles; Coming Together For Personal Growth and Social Change* (Washington, DC: Seven Locks Press, 1987), 92.

57. Crawford, "The Story of the Fifth Annual Meeting."

58. Crawford, "New England Forum Leaders in Session," n.d., Scrapbooks, 7.

59. "Committee on Public Information," *Dictionary of American History*, 2:139; letter, Crawford to Coleman, 11 March 1918, and telegram, Coleman to Crawford and her letter to him, both dated 17 November 1919, Scrapbooks, 7.

60. Lurie, *Challenge of the Forum*, 192–205.

61. Crawford, "New England Forums in Session."

62. "Invitation to Attend a Conference on Sociology, June 18–20, 1907," Sagamore Sociological Conference Files; Crawford, "The Church in Social Work," *Zion's Herald*, n.d.

63. Crawford, "The Church in Social Work;" "The Sagamore Conference," *Survey*, n.d., Sagamore Sociological Conference Files, 1910.

64. "Business and Democracy the Theme at Sagamore," *Christian Register*, 19 July 1917, n.p., Sagamore Sociological Conference Files, 1917.

65. Letter to writer, Sandra Sudak, Diocesan Archivist, Episcopal Diocese of Massachusetts, Boston, Massachusetts, 4 February 2002; Mary C. Crawford, "'The

Church's Call'—The Campaign to Date," *The Church Militant*, March 1920, 6–7, 15–16, Episcopal Diocese of Massachusetts Archives.

66. Kathryn Kish Sklar, "Coming to Terms with Florence Kelly: The Tale of a Reluctant Biographer," in Alpern, *The Challenge of Feminist Biography*, 21.

67. The impact of the Forum was recounted by Crawford in "Dramatic Incidents" in Coleman, *Democracy in the Making*, 84–94, particularly the story of Freda Rogolsky, a Jewish immigrant teenager who became devoted to the Ford Hall Forum. Coleman often pointed to the young woman as an example of how the movement's ideals broke through barriers of class or religion.

68. Christopher Lasch, *The New Radicalism in America, 1889–1963* (New York: Knopf, 1965), xiv-xv.

69. Robert H. Wiebe, *Self-Rule; A Cultural History of American Democracy* (Chicago: University of Chicago, 1995), 141–44.

70. Mary C. Crawford, Certificate of Death, Massachusetts Department of Public Health, 15 November 1932; Obituary, *Boston Evening Transcript*, 18 November 1932, Part 2, 11; *The Radcliffe Quarterly* (January 1933), 40; Crawford, "The Schiller Centenary," *The Critic*, vol. 45, May 1905, 437.

Audience lined up outside Ford Hall Forum in Boston before a lecture. (c. 1920) Courtesy of the Trustees of the Boston Public Library/Rare Books.

Audience inside Ford Hall before a lecture. (c. 1921) Courtesy of the Trustees of the Boston Public Library/Rare Books.

George W. Coleman, founder of Ford Hall Forum in 1908 and the Open Forum national movement that developed from it. Courtesy of the Trustees of the Boston Public Library/ Rare Books.

Mary Caroline Crawford, Secretary of Ford Hall Forum, who implemented the movement across the nation. The Schlesinger Library, Radcliffe Institute, Harvard University.

Rev. John W. Herring, First Congregational Church, who brought the Open Forum to Terre Haute in 1920. (1915, while a student at Oberlin College) Oberlin College Archives, Oberlin, Ohio.

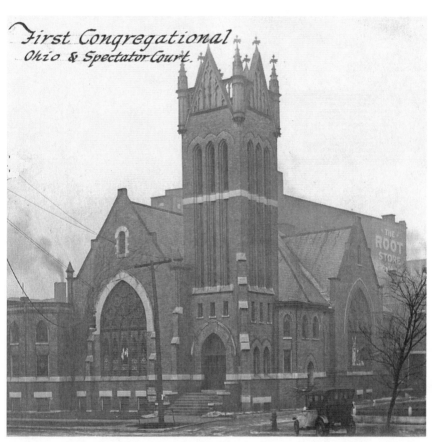

First Congregational Church, Terre Haute, where the Open Forum was held. Community Archives, Vigo County Public Library.

Rabbi Max Bretton, Temple Beth-El, who brought the Open Forum to Hammond in 1924. (c. 1925) Temple Beth-El of Munster, Indiana.

Temple Beth-El, Hammond, where the Open Forum was held. Courtesy: Hammond Public Library.

Beth-El Social Center
Open Forum Course

FIRST SEASON

Program 1924-25

Lecture every Tuesday Evening at
8:15 o'clock

at

Beth-El Social Center

916 Hohman Street
HAMMOND, IND.

TICKETS
Membership, admitting one to the
entire course of 16 lectures............$6.00

Program brochure of first year of Beth-El Open Forum in 1924.

Rev., later Monsignor, John A. Ryan, first speaker at the Beth-El Open Forum. The American Catholic History Research Center and University Archives, The Catholic University of America, Washington, DC.

Dr. William E. B. Du Bois, who spoke at the Beth-El Open Forum in 1926. Fisk University Franklin Library's Special Collections.

1513 9th Ave,
Huntington, W.Va.
Jan. 10, 1926.

Dr. W.E.B. Du Bois,
New York City.

Dear Sir:

We have just been listening by radio to your talk in Ford Hall Boston and enjoyed very much what we heard of it. When you were about half through a nearer station overwhelmed WBZ and we had no more satisfaction from it.

We are glad you had the opportunity of using the radio to bring facts to so many you could not reach otherwise.

My wife did not just appreciate the description of you to the radio audience, but of course the man who presided had to be humorous.

We appreciate very much what you are doing for the race.

Yours truly,
Walter A. Smith.

Letter to Dr. Du Bois in New York on January 10, 1926, from Walter A. Smith, a building contractor in Huntington, West Virginia, after hearing his Ford Hall Forum talk on the radio—800 miles away. W.E.B. Du Bois Library Special Collections & University Archives, University of Massachusetts, Amherst.

Chapter Four

Terre Haute

The Striking of Mind Upon Mind

Through the extensive speaking and writing of George Coleman, and the exceptional organizational skills of Mary Crawford, the Open Forum spread across the country. In 1917, in recognition of the movement's growth in the Midwest and Great Lakes states, the fourth annual meeting of the Open Forum National Council was held in Chicago. Fifty-five delegates, representing 300 local forums, came to the convention.[1]

The diversity in participation that the movement attracted in the Midwest is shown in a 1919 list of speakers available to speak at local Forums. It included the Grand Rapids, Michigan, supervisor of recreation, a Sioux City, Iowa, activist rabbi, a Detroit high school principal and civic worker, and a leader in the Chicago chapter of the Women's Trade Union League.[2]

In 1925, responding to the spread of the movement, the Midwest Council for Social Discussion, in cooperation with the Open Forum Speakers Bureau, held its first meeting in Chicago. The purpose was to direct the "spiritual force" in public education into new usefulness, establish Forums where there was a need, and strengthen existing groups. The goal was to "raise the level of public discourse" by helping all people weigh fact and opinion without prejudice and distrust, "as one faith and one fraternity on the common ground of a search for truth." The Council's president was from Indianapolis, while the secretary, who also served as field director, had led the Terre Haute Open Forum from 1920 to 1924.[3]

The movement began in many communities but more local research is needed to learn if it continued. In 1918, First Congregational Church of Jacksonville, Illinois began planning a "Community Forum" on social and economic problems of democracy. In 1919, in Jacksonville, according to a national Congregational publication, "Roman Catholics and Christian Scientists were among the most regular attendants but there were also people of no faith and those of foreign extraction as well as representatives of trades unions." The local press documented the lectures from 1921 through 1923. In 1919, Coleman spoke in Grand Rapids, Michigan. In the 1920s, Fountain Street Baptist Church in the city planned Sunday evening lectures, but these may not have evolved into the broader principles of the Open Forum. Similar series were held in Appleton and Oshkosh in Wisconsin.[4]

In Ironton, Ohio, in 1922, the *Daily Register* reported the Forum movement had a "brilliant and successful inauguration," noting the inclusiveness of the audience. "Working men, professional men and women, teachers, preachers, lawyers, doctors, readers, thinkers, all were there." The first speaker, Raymond Robins, a social economist, had spoken in Dayton the previous evening, and Jane Addams was scheduled to speak two weeks later. In 1934, a national report on adult education listed for the Peoria (Illinois) Forum an average attendance of 400 people at twelve sessions. In 1936, the Community Forum in Riverside, Illinois, was in its third successful year, drawing 100 people for the monthly sessions. According to one report, "it attempts to be a catalyzer of ideas and offers an opportunity for the expression of as many divergent points of view as can exist in a small village of seven thousand."[5]

In the 1926 study of the national movement by Peffer, sixteen Forums were listed for Ohio, nine in Illinois, four each in Michigan and Wisconsin, and smaller numbers for other states in the region. Although the two Indiana communities were not named, they were most likely Terre Haute and Hammond as their series began before 1926. In that year, the Indianapolis Jewish Community Center started non-sectarian programs with "Open Forum" in the title. A year later, Evansville adopted the Forum model but named the series "Washington Avenue Temple Men's Club Lectures," as it was sponsored by the Reform Jewish congregation in the city.[6]

Some documentation exists for other public lecture series in Indiana, both before and after the war, but these also may not have continued. The first reference to the state in the records of the Open Forum National Council notes that Rev. Elijah A. Hanley of Franklin was present at the Council meeting in Boston in July 1914. From 1907 to 1911, he was pastor of First Baptist Church in Providence, Rhode Island, the oldest Baptist church in the country. Like many other forward-thinking New England clergy at the time, he would have been familiar with the Forum movement. In Providence, the minister was considered "vigorous" and "imaginative" for recognizing that demographic changes in the city were transforming First Baptist Church. Hanley concluded that a more accessible, open "institutional" church was needed, one that expanded its services to meet the physical and social needs of a changing city. As president of Franklin College in Indiana from 1911 to 1917, he was described as a broad-minded, scholarly and enterprising educator.[7]

The second mention of the Open Forum in Indiana, found in the national records, appears in the March 1916 report of the Committee on Christian Work to the Boston Baptist Social Union. It notes that Rev. Charles A. Decker of First Baptist Church of South Bend credited "the hearty endorsement and support of his church officials" for a Forum. The minister had attended Rochester Theological Seminary, where Rauschenbusch taught, graduating in 1907, the same year that *Christianity and the Social Crisis* was published. After serving briefly in two other communities, he came in 1910 to South Bend, a growing, ethnically diverse city of 67,000.[8]

In the spring of 1916, on five consecutive Sunday evenings, "The People's Open Forum" took place at First Baptist Church. The brochure announcing the "Non-Partisan and Non-Sectarian" series said the Forum was:

1. A Community Institution.
2. A School for the Theory and Practice of Democracy.
3. A Free Platform for the Discussion of the Vital Questions Relating to Our Common Life.
4. An Institution for the Promotion of Acquaintance, Understanding and Good-Will with respect to the Social, Economic, Political and Religious Problems of the Day.[9]

The Forum, the brochure asserted, stands "squarely for the free discussion of what is common and vital to all." The whole purpose "is to serve as a means for educating the public mind and spirit on the . . . many social problems and the proposed programs." The question period after the address enables the audience to "expose weak points or to draw out further development." The series is not a church but a community organization backed by the church in which it meets, standing "squarely for the free discussion of what is common and vital to all." A local planning committee was not listed.[10]

The first speaker in the series was Mrs. George Bass, president of the Chicago Women's Club and a leader in the suffrage movement. Before a large audience, she pointed out the new role women were taking. They were instrumental in a range of social justice activities from conditions in "insane asylums" to homes for the "feebleminded" and in juvenile courts. When they are able to vote, she promised, they will elect people who will focus on children's interests.[11]

The second week's lecturer, Stoughton Cooley, editor of *The Public* magazine and contributing editor of the *Chicago Herald* newspaper, called for a change in the tax system to decrease the high cost of living and to increase workers' wages. If workers demanded the proper salary due them, the nation would move forward in solving the wage problem. The extensive local press reports are a good example of the emphasis the Forum movement gave to publicity.[12]

The following week, Edward E. Carr, secretary of the Christian Social Fellowship, advocated forcefully for Christian Socialism. He stated unequivocally that "it is impossible to barter and sell for profit and obey the 10th commandment." Carr was not condemning the individual for the wrongs of the competitive system of profit but the evils of the system itself.[13]

In the fourth week, John L. Whitman, superintendent of the Chicago House of Correction, discussed the modern treatment of criminals. The old method of suppressing the better instincts of the criminal, embittering him further, was declining. In the modern day, Whitman asserted, criminal laws were enacted for the protection of society, first by imprisonment but second by reform of the criminal. After the sentence was completed, the person was then able to take his place in society.[14]

Jenkin L. Jones was to be the final lecturer in the series on "The Ford Peace Expedition." Because he became ill, Herbert S. Bigelow, former president of the Ohio state constitutional convention, spoke in his place. His discussion of poverty in Ohio drew from his own experience as well as from statistics. Recognizing unemployment, sickness and old age as the greatest causes of poverty, Ohio had begun a farsighted initiative, a precursor to the Social Security revolution two decades later. The state planned to pay every person over 65 years of age a certain amount, so they could support themselves. Not surprisingly, Bigelow's talk received the largest press coverage of the series, including on the front page of the *South Bend News-Times*.[15]

While the lecture series was taking place, Coleman came to speak in the city. The title of his talk, similar to other speeches he gave around the country, was "Getting Together Essential to Democracy." He described Ford Hall Forum as a unique place, where no feeling of prejudice was found and everybody was equal. The Jew found himself on the same footing as others, while Socialists "thrash out many questions between themselves and . . . other political beliefs." He said there were more than 150 Forums in the country, and their success depended on the number of foreign-born residents participating in the discussion. Coleman urged communities to have every nationality represented as they discuss the future of the country.[16]

During this period, South Bend newspapers also reported on three of Decker's Sunday morning sermons, as well as a Sunday afternoon talk on a local housing campaign. The minister called the battle for housing and the progressive work of the city's organizations "a real awakening[,]" resulting in "better babies, better homes, better schools, and in fact, better conditions for general humanity in South Bend." In 1918, the minister left the city for religious work in the Army, and later served congregations in Pennsylvania and

Connecticut. Although initial research could not determine if the People's Open Forum continued after the minister left, the fact that such provocative talks and far-sighted ideas were brought to the city is a tribute to the power of the Forum approach and the courage of the pastor and congregation.[17]

A third instance of an Indiana community in the Forum movement was recorded in June 1917. An advertisement for the Open Forum National Council in a Boston religious publication listed Anderson as among the "larger forums which have secured speakers through the [Open Forum Speakers] Bureau." As no local records have been found, this may be an instance in which the Forum did not develop after initial planning and publicity.[18]

A fourth example of Hoosier participation in the movement was recorded at the Open Forum National Council meeting in Chicago, in April 1917. One of the delegates was Walter G. Greeson of Howard County. The *Kokomo Daily Tribune* reported that Greeson, as secretary of the Howard County New Constitution Forum and special representative of the Citizens League of Indiana to the Open Forum Council, would attend the meeting. The purpose of the Citizens League, which began in 1914, was to work for a non-partisan constitutional convention. Operating primarily from Fort Wayne, the organization published a monthly magazine and issued a number of statements from 1914 to 1916. Greeson had recently organized the New Constitution Forum in twenty-three counties in as many days. According to the *Tribune*, "many consider the forum movement the most significant popular movement in America today[,]" adding that even in time of war and great national distress, "forums in every community of the nation would prove of immeasurable benefit in bringing about the fullest possible cooperation of the people."[19]

From April to June 1917, Greeson organized several discussion groups in Kokomo. The meetings were identified by their specific location, such as Fourth Ward Community Forum or Howard Township Forum. The *Tribune* called the groups an "Open Forum," and a principal commented "it was the only occasion that the [school] building had been open for a public meeting in the evening in seven years." The newspaper described the movement as "a fine friendly gathering of neighbors, who were unanimous in the belief that there were great social possibilities in making the school a center of neighborhood life." Among the topics discussed were popular control of government, franchise and elections, and efficient administration and legislation. (In this time period, "franchise" didn't refer to municipal ownership of a public utility or transportation, but to women gaining the right to vote and impediments in voting.)[20]

The sole focus of the Kokomo series was the statewide effort to amend the constitution, which ultimately proved unsuccessful. However, it is an excellent example of the community-specific nature of the Open Forum: a series developed by a local planning committee within the structure of the Citizens League.

Such locally planned discussions reflect the long tradition of Americans coming together to consider issues of concern to the immediate community. The topics also illustrate how the Kokomo series differed from the national movement and the Forums in Terre Haute and Hammond, which would begin a few years later. Those programs considered societal concerns and intellectual advances beyond the state's borders.

During these years, Indiana residents rejected progressive changes in government at the state level, such as the initiative, referendum, recall, state income tax, short ballot, municipal home rule, and voting rights for women. Social and legislative change was coming, although not to the extent as experienced in other states. From 1890 to 1920, industrialization had shifted the state's work force from agriculture to manufacturing and mechanical industries. The result was a significant increase in the number of women working outside the home and a growing awareness of abuses in child labor. Although the organized labor movement was not strong overall in the state, a wide variety of industrial disturbances took place.[21]

Within this background, the Social Gospel message was prominently disseminated in two instances. In 1906, Rauschenbusch addressed the Baptist state convention. In 1914, a special Baptist committee in the state called for "industrial co-operation." However, as historian Clifton Phillips notes of this era, "there is little evidence . . . to indicate that many Hoosier clergymen paid much attention to the industrial problems of the age."[22]

The state's generally conservative social atmosphere continued in the 1920s. Hoosiers continued to represent "what was difficult and perhaps even best about America," writes historian James H. Madison. The mainly white Protestant and Catholic population from Western Europe avoided extremes and clung to past traditions. "It was nearly impossible to find in Indiana a public place, institution, or group where whites accorded blacks an equal and open reception." Local "Sundown Laws" discouraged African American workers or travelers from living or stopping in southern areas of the state, or even in industrial cities such as Hammond. The state was characterized by a hardening pattern of residential segregation, a declining percentage of foreign-born residents, sedition laws to stifle radical voices, and an emphasis on American history and citizenship training in the schools. A growing urban and declining rural population contributed to tensions and conflicts.[23]

In this setting, a large number of Hoosiers joined the Ku Klux Klan, with the organization strongest in areas most affected by industrial development.

"Not only farmers and factory workers but also some merchants, small busi-
nessmen, and Protestant ministers donned the white robe and hood," writes
Madison. An Indiana Klanswoman recalled later that, "everyone was in the
Klan." A Jewish merchant in the Terre Haute area recognized some parading
Klan members by the shoes they had purchased from his store.[24]

The Klan became a deeply troubling force in the state's politics, with
members crossing party lines in the spring primaries and again at the state
conventions. Indiana led the entire country in the number of Klan members.
It was the largest organization of any kind in the state, with more members
than the veterans' organizations and even more than Methodism, the leading
Protestant denomination.[25]

However, rather than the Klan representing a threat to the state's public
safety, historian Leonard J. Moore suggests that it should be viewed as a popular response to social conditions, expressing concerns that could be traced
to an array of social pressures and changes. Klan members had witnessed
in their communities what they were feeling within themselves. Against the
fundamental altering of society, with crime and political corruption all around
them, Indiana Klansmen sought to regain traditional religious and moral
values and a sense of social and civic unity. Only in 1925, with the murder
conviction of their powerful Grand Dragon, D. C. Stephenson, following a
vicious rape, did the deeply troubling effect of the organization become clear.
At that point, the state's newspapers began to criticize the Klan and public
attitudes shifted.[26]

In 1920, in Terre Haute, in the west central part of the state, native-born
whites made up three-fourths of the 66,000 population. Moore's study shows
Klan membership was particularly strong among that group. In 1925, 8,200
residents of Vigo County (Terre Haute was the county seat) were Klan members. The Exalted Cyclops operated an auto repair shop. Other officers represented a wide range of the community: two grocers, physician, bank teller,
insurance agent, tinner, carpenter, truck driver, blacksmith, pastor, clothing
store owner, and coal miner. The Klan was the largest community organization in the city. In spite of that, community archivist Susan Dehler notes, the
city had "a rich history of radical thought juxtaposed with more mainstream
conservative business influences." It was the home of Eugene Debs, the
national leader in railroad unions and the Socialist Party, and Presidential
candidate while in prison. In the nineteenth century, abolitionist Frederick
Douglass and women's suffrage leader Susan B. Anthony lectured in the
city, and there were many local champions for the "radical" goal of universal
suffrage. Clubs were established for the "improvement of the mind and self."
Although some of the organizations were mainstream in thought, others embraced innovation and the era's progressive reforms.[27]

A close examination of the city by historian Gary Bailey finds that the 1902 street railway strike and boycott, "possibly the most bitter labor conflict in Terre Haute's history[,] . . . shaped labor relations in the city for years to come." While the industrial base had enlarged and diversified since the turn of the century, outside anti-labor conglomerates often owned the factories and did not identify with the community.[28]

The outcome in the 1910s was larger, longer, more militant strikes. Political corruption was rampant, with witnesses reporting intimidation and assaults on voters that were aided and abetted by the police. Among 116 public officials found guilty were the mayor, who was a candidate for governor, the police chief, circuit court judge, city controller, and city judge. The *Indianapolis News* described "a corrupt and rotten system," one that was bringing the city "to the verge of anarchy." Regardless of the corruption during these pre-war years, writes Bailey, the positive "industrial development, consumerism, urbanization [and] professionalization . . . produced social change."[29]

Like much of the nation during the war years, anti-radicalism in the city was as virulent as ever and better organized. Local opinion leaders preached Americanism and industrial peace. As the community became obsessed with growth, the business class drew further away from the working class. Bailey finds that "Boosterism"—the engine of civic consciousness—"excluded workers from playing an active part in . . . the community." Yet, by the early 1920s, businessmen, as well as other boosters and public officials, had reshaped the city's image, disassociating it from labor militancy, machine politics, corruption, and constant investigations.[30]

A young clergyman came into this setting. John W. Herring, son of a national Congregational leader, received his A. B. degree from progressive Oberlin College in Ohio in 1914. The college president, Henry C. King, had a profound influence on the students, speaking forthrightly on "the sacred right of individuals to think for themselves." During the winter of 1910, in six chapel lectures on "The College and Democracy," he spoke out strongly against racial discrimination. Social Gospel leaders Washington Gladden and Rauschenbusch, who frequently visited the campus while Herring was a student, also likely shaped the students' thinking on social issues.[31]

From 1914 to 1918, Herring attended Chicago Theological Seminary, which was particularly strong in Christian sociology and social action. Graham Taylor, head of the Department of Christian Sociology at the seminary, had begun the Chicago Commons Social Settlement in 1895. Under this program, students were required to engage in supervised field work in social agencies. One of the agencies where the students could work was the People's

Institute, which was similar to Cooper Union in New York City in its focus on public learning, the model Coleman used to develop Ford Hall Forum.[32]

While he was a seminary student, Herring was disqualified from military service because of vision problems. He gained "clergy exemption" when he applied to become a chaplain. In 1925, responding to a survey of Oberlin alumni, he regretted that "I didn't have conscience and courage enuf [*sic*] to be a pacifist."[33]

In October 1918, Herring was ordained at the Congregational church in Woodstock, Illinois. He had served at that church a year earlier while a student and became the pastor after his ordination. From this background, in 1920, he came to the 205–member First Congregational Church in Terre Haute. Among his predecessors was Lyman Abbott, pastor from 1860 to 1865, one of the ministers who later shaped the Social Gospel movement. In Terre Haute, Rev. Abbott was "allowed a freedom of utterance somewhat unusual in those days."[34]

In this open tradition, Rev. Herring began his ministry and the Terre Haute Open Forum. In December 1920, a month after the series began, Coleman described it as "a beacon light for all the surrounding territory." It was launched "with a courage of initiative, a thoughtfulness of preparation, and a success of accomplishment that reminds me of the great qualities of his lamented father, who by the way gave me the right hand of fellowship in all my forum work."[35]

The young minister's spearheading of the series is an example of the trans-denominational, open-minded character of the Forum movement. Congregationalism, particularly in the Northeast and in urban churches, was proving a fertile soil for liberalism. The *Terre Haute Tribune* reported the Forum was created by "men and women interested in public questions" and hailed its "auspicious opening." The praise was typical of the descriptions of many local Forums, carefully preserved in the movement's scrapbooks.[36]

When Coleman spoke at the inaugural program in November 1920, the newspaper reported that 500 persons, "representative of the entire community," greeted him. "Business and professional men, toilers in shops and factories, men and women from stores and offices and school rooms were in the audience and their close attention to the speaker indicated their interest in the forum and the subjects to be discussed at future sessions." Coleman congratulated the local promoters and said that, "in all his experience in similar work he had not seen an opening so auspicious." An editorial the same day hailed the opening as even a greater success than expected. "Labor leaders were on hand to see if they could sense any signs of enmity in the deliberations [and others were present] to see if the forum was not a menace in disguise."[37]

Shortly after the series began in Terre Haute, Coleman described in the *Detroit Open Forum; A Journal of News and Views* the "extraordinary vigor

and great promise" of the effort. The planners had arranged twenty-two consecutive Sunday evening programs, securing commitments from two-thirds
of the speakers. "Every element in the city is co-operating," Coleman wrote.
In another publication, he said that "it has been my privilege to inaugurate
many forums in various parts of the country [but] never have I seen one
started under such favorable auspices."[38]

Following Coleman's opening talk, the Terre Haute *Open Forum News
Service* brochure noted that a "community non-sectarian committee" would
conduct the meetings. Although held on Sunday evenings, the intent of the
Forum was not to "injure church services." It was primarily for people who
have no "church home," just as Coleman had described the appeal of the Ford
Hall Forum. The planning committee used the Open Forum Speakers Bureau
in Boston in scheduling half the lecturers, although not all the speakers listed
in the Terre Haute brochure appeared.[39]

The "Rules for Open Discussion" in the Terre Haute brochure were direct
and emphatic:

1. Questions—not Speeches.
2. Principles—not Personalities.
3. A Question from each—not a Catechism by a Few.
4. A strict Taboo on anything that savours [*sic*] of Propaganda.
5. Honesty of speeches and honesty of questions.[40]

In January 1921, the *Tribune* announced that Warren S. Blauvelt of Indiana Coke and Gas Company and Vigo Mining Company was the Forum's
permanent chairman. Ten months later, the newspaper listed the speakers'
committee. In addition to Herring and Blauvelt, the group comprised John
Peck as its new chairman, Rabbi Joseph L. Fink of Temple Israel (the Reform
congregation), President Phillip A. Woodworth of Rose Polytechnic Institute,
Secretary-Treasurer William Mitch of District 11 of United Mine Workers of
America, John Dailey (a Catholic), who was Secretary of the Central Labor
Union and Editor of the union newspaper, *Terre Haute Advocate*, Professor
Frank C. Wagner of Rose Polytechnic Institute, and President Linnaeus N.
Hines of Indiana State Normal College. Hines spoke at the Forum in its first
season when he was State Superintendent of Public Instruction.[41]

Except for the lack of women and racial minorities, the committee reflected
the city's religious, educational, business and union leadership. Accounts
of the first year's programs, from November 1920 through April 1921, frequently mention a large audience. Newspaper reports do not describe the
composition of the audience, and no separate documents have been found,
but a good portion would likely have been from the groups represented on

the planning committee: Congregationalists, Reform Jews, unions, and the business and education communities. In December 1920, the *Tribune* noted that labor representatives on the Forum's board of directors were reported to be "intensely interested" in the next lecture on organized labor.[42]

At the first program, in November 1920, Flavel Shurtleff, a city planning expert, said Terre Haute was the only city west of the Appalachian Mountains in which he had spoken three times on planning. Each time, he told his listeners, "the increasing enthusiasm and audience have proved the growth of your civic interest and aspirations." While planning was not a panacea for all civic evils, he defined the process as putting in order the physical factors needed for better service. The goal was to create a "city orderly," producing maximum health and comfort for the residents, the greatest amount of industry and efficiency, contented labor, good homes, adequate transportation, and low taxes. Shurtleff called Terre Haute, with a population of 70,000 and great agricultural, mineral and commercial resources, an ideal size for effective planning. The newspaper report on the program included several of the questions and answers that followed the address.[43]

In December, Frank A. Morgan, a Christian Church minister and a founder of the Bryn Mawr Community Church in Chicago, called for the organization of congregations along lines of class and interest rather than creed. Conveying the principles of social progressive Christianity, he said the duty of the church begins only when it looks after the spiritual life of the community. Its larger responsibilities consist of caring for the material and physical welfare of the congregants. The "primary duty of the church is not to give preachers opportunity to make a living" but rather to serve the congregants. He urged "more politics, more amusement, more athletics and more human nature" in a church that serves not itself but the community.[44]

The following week, "the edifice was entirely filled, with practically all standing room taken." Thomas M. Osborne, a New York prison warden, described the humane treatment program he had begun in several correctional institutions. A prisoners' mutual welfare league sought to rehabilitate the prisoners spiritually. Reflecting the period's reform spirit, the warden said "most prisoners are exactly where they belong [but the] only successful way to rebuild them is to help them rebuild themselves."[45]

The *Tribune* noted that local labor organizations were represented on the board of directors of the Forum. The link between unions and the Open Forum, particularly in Terre Haute with its strong labor presence, is another instance of the broad base of the movement. William A. Brown, a national leader in social Christianity, wrote in 1922 that the Open Forum was an experiment in bridging the gap between religion and organized labor.[46]

At the next program, Robert N. Buck, editor of a Chicago labor publication, urged adoption of the Farmer-Labor Party creed. The party's platform comprised government ownership of public utilities, help for farmers, and improved labor conditions. "The struggle is on," he said, "between the vast poor majority and the few wealthy 2 per cent." In a political system, Buck said, labor unions had to enter politics.[47]

The following week's speaker, Charles Zueblin, a native Hoosier and former professor of sociology at the University of Chicago, was strongly involved in extending civic awareness. In his Terre Haute address, he advocated government ownership of railroads, free from control and interference by Congress or Wall Street, and operated by expert managers and government employees. Fifty questions followed his talk, with the majority opposing his position. The speaker congratulated the community on maintaining the Open Forum. In the same issue of the newspaper, the editorial praised Zueblin's speech and the "free and untrammeled nature of the public forum" in exploring such high-interest topics.[48]

The first speaker in January 1921, Linnaeus N. Hines, Indiana Superintendent of Public Instruction, decried the lack of support for education in the state. The greatest problems existed in the rural areas, where "selfish and short-sighted interests . . . fight bitterly" against financial aid. The following week, Rabbi Leon Harrison of St. Louis spoke on unhappiness in many American marriages. Before a "capacity audience," he advocated for increased legal and social difficulties in contracting a marriage and securing a divorce.[49]

At the next program, George I. Christie, who headed agricultural extension at Purdue University, described the farm crisis affecting Indiana and the nation. The *Tribune* report concluded that the discussion after his lecture was one of the most lively and interesting of any held. The selection of Rabbi Fink as vice chairman is another example of the non-sectarian nature of the movement. Ordained at Hebrew Union College, the Reform seminary in Cincinnati, in 1919, Fink had arrived in Terre Haute in May, just as the mayor and entire city council were heading to prison. The city's Jewish population during the period was less than 1,000. The rabbi became active in civic affairs and drew close to Eugene Debs, the socialist leader.[50]

At the next week's program, Dr. Harry F. Ward of Union Theological Seminary in New York City spoke on civil liberties. He had helped found the Methodist Federation for Social Service in 1907. In Methodism, Sidney Ahlstrom writes, "the liberal cause became almost as persuasive [as in Congregationalism], and in Northern Methodism as nowhere in the nation it penetrated to the grass roots."[51]

Ward's 1919 book, *The New Social Order*, called for "fundamental changes in the organization of life." Historian Donald B. Meyer describes the book as "perhaps the most sweeping announcement of Christian duty." During the 1920s, writes historian Paul A. Carter, Ward was "feeling his way toward a synthesis of Marxism and Christianity." In Terre Haute, according to the newspaper, his talk created more interest than any of the previous lectures. Ward proposed a restoration of pre-war liberties and freedom for wartime prisoners. "[When] a community dares not listen to the opinions of its discontented members it becomes enslaved by fear." The topic reflected his lifelong personal commitment as he served as chairman of the American Civil Liberties Union from 1920 to 1940.[52]

The following week, Alfred Sheldon, director of a school of commerce and business administration in Chicago, and a widely known speaker on business and industrial problems, urged cooperation between labor and capital. The newspaper called Sheldon's address "one of the most interesting and constructive of any delivered at the open forum."[53]

While these first programs focused on domestic concerns, the series broadened in February with Dr. Toyokichi Iyenaga. He had served as secretary of foreign affairs in Japan, received his Ph.D. from Johns Hopkins University, and taught at the University of Chicago for twelve years. At the time of his address, he was managing director of the East and West News Bureau in New York City and a popular lecturer in the United States. During the war, Japan occupied part of the Shantung province in northeast China. Before "one of the largest crowds yet," the speaker condemned Japan's annexation of the province and predicted its early return to China. He described the prejudices confronting the Japanese in California, the need for Washington and Tokyo to solve these problems, and the close trading relationship between the two nations.[54]

The next address was by Tsianina, a Native American opera singer, who had appeared overseas in front of soldiers convalescing from their war wounds. Her talk covered the wartime patriotism of her people at the very time they were denied both the right to vote and equal access to jobs. Native Americans had subscribed to $2,500,000 in war bonds and sent 27,000 men into the military, 10,000 of them serving overseas. A packed auditorium was expected for the evening. Dressed in a "beautifully tanned gown of buckskin, trimmed with beads, which [she had] designed and arranged," her words and her presence would have certainly broadened horizons. As in the Ford Hall model, community singing was part of each program in Terre Haute, and so Tsianina sang several Indian songs. The audience also saw a motion picture, "From the Land of the Sky Blue Waters," in its initial release. The previous week's program had been enriched by Japanese songs; a week before that, African American spirituals "received much applause."[55]

A week after Tsianina's talk, Beatrice Forbes-Robertson Hale, widely identified with the women's movement both in England and America, was the speaker. The actress, writer and rights advocate had worked in the U. S. Food Administration from 1918 to 1919, then studied post-war reconstruction and labor conditions in England afterwards. (She would also speak in the first year of the Open Forum in Hammond.) In Terre Haute, addressing "one of the largest audiences which has attended the open forum," she criticized the way business was pushed ahead of the arts in the United States, claiming that there has been no real American drama. The nation's Puritan ancestors prohibited it and the focus on commerce and industry has remained paramount. Such remarks by a woman of accomplishment, following on the Native American speaker of the previous week, further enlarged the understanding of the city's residents. The dissemination of the talks through the newspaper each week carried the ideas still deeper into the community.[56]

The next week's lecturer, George H. Allen of the Bureau of University Travel in Boston, examined political, social and economic conditions before and after the war. A large problem was "whether or not Russia is penetrable to western ideas." In March, one of the speakers was Maud Wood Park, Radcliffe class of '98. She had campaigned across the country for women's suffrage and served as first president of the National League of Women Voters from 1920 to 1924. In Terre Haute, she described how women would create a better government when they could vote. Many League members were veterans of the social justice movement and Park brought to the organization keen political skills. Once again, through a local Forum and press coverage, the lecture movement was broadening the understanding of a community to the changing national landscape.[57]

Towards the end of the inaugural year, three programs were of immediate concern to Terre Haute residents. First, Harry F. Atwood of Chicago presented the business argument for allowing workers and employers to make individual agreements, the "open shop," where workers were employed without regard to union membership. The *Tribune* said that the lecture "provided one of the most interesting subjects for discussion" in the series, and noted how mine union leaders in the audience disputed Atwood's assertions. In the following week, John H. Walker, president of the Illinois Federation of Labor, called for the "closed shop," which required employees to be members of a union, as protection from diseases and accidents in manufacturing. Concluding the series, Robert B. Wolf of New York urged a spirit of cooperation, as both employers and workers lost by failing to recognize each other's rights. He said "the trouble has been caused by the employer pulling one way while the employes [*sic*] were pulling the other. Neither has made much advancement, or at least not nearly so much as could have been made had they pulled together." Wolf's talk was wise advice for a community that had witnessed a large amount of labor strife in the first two decades of the century.[58]

The final program of the 1920–1921 season was a panel of the six candidates for Mayor that included an independent and a Socialist. The event received the most extended news coverage of the series and was on the front page for the first time. According to the report, when the Socialist candidate, Phil K. Reinbold, painted the Soviet Union "with his gayest colors, two 'bloated plutocrats' gott [*sic*] up and yawned and walked out." They returned when he finished speaking but their seats had been taken. The speaker saw the incident as a perfect example of how the wealthy will lose their reserved places "should the 'capitalistic system' be scotched."[59]

The lead editorial in the newspaper reviewed the many promises made by the candidates. It also raised the question "as to how public a public forum should be," and suggested that First Congregational Church had been transformed into a "pulpit for soviet'sm." For the public, "it is a large question and we merely drop this hint to start the discussion. Subsequent opinion should be broadly universal and intensely 'progressive.'" Ironically, four months earlier, the newspaper had praised the "free and untrammeled nature of the public forum."[60]

It was an exhilarating first year. The extensive schedule was as comprehensive a range of Open Forum lectures as may be found, enriched by a wide selection of music. The talks encompassed city planning, social Christianity, prison reform, labor-management relations, political reform, education, marriage, the farm crisis, civil liberties, foreign affairs, equal rights, and local political issues. The variety of topics and the carefully planned approach of the representative committee broadened the community's knowledge and awareness of social concerns. It was a notable achievement for the young clergyman and planning committee. It is not a surprise that George Coleman was enthusiastic in his praise. In the nation's heartland, at a time and in a place of much provincialism, his vision of "democracy in the making" was taking root.

In announcing the schedule for the second year in the fall of 1921, the planning committee said it had made "a careful and conscientious effort to maintain an even balance of radical and conservative presentations." The committee believed that "truth will eventually come out through free discussion." There would be no solicitation as people had their own churches to support. The Forum is "for the man without a Sunday evening connection [and draws] no sectarian [or] race lines [and] has no axe to grind." Probably in response to criticism of the first year's programs, Herring added that "the organization will steer clear of politics and sectarian religion." The minister's words were similar to those of Coleman, soon after he began the Ford Hall Forum, when he reassured Boston ministers that he was not seeking their congregants.[61]

The Terre Haute announcement reflects another strong element in the Open Forum approach. Local committees learned, as the Ford Hall planners recognized in 1908, how to express the non-denominational, impartial openness of their ideals. The secret was to speak the language of the congregations and clergy who were the main backers of each local series, while at the same time not alienating people of other faiths or non-believers. This sensible democratic approach and balanced expression also appeared in the Hammond program.

When the Terre Haute series resumed in the fall, the first lecturer was originally to be the Minister of Labor of China. Instead, it was Dean Shailer Mathews of the University of Chicago Divinity School. (A few years later, he would open the third year of the Open Forum in Hammond.) In Terre Haute, he discussed America's leadership at the Washington Disarmament Conference and how the aims of the United States in the Conference were "extremely democratic in nature." He saw the country as advancing steadily toward a more democratic government through Amendments to the Constitution.[62]

The appearance by Mathews, a national Baptist leader, is an example of the ability of the lecture movement to attract prominent figures to small and medium-sized communities. Throughout the first third of the century, writes Sidney Ahlstrom, the Baptist-founded University of Chicago Divinity School was "probably the country's most powerful center of Protestant liberalism." Mathews had been expressing the ideals of social progressive Christianity in writing and teaching for more than two decades. In 1928, he would bring together his published articles into a landmark work, *Jesus on Social Institutions*. His conclusion: "social progress is not a matter of systems but of folks."[63]

Two weeks later, Bruno Rosselli, Associate Professor of Italian at Vassar College and the first exchange professor from Italy to the United States, spoke on "Italy and Disarmament." He had served in the Italian army during the war and was an expert on his country's industrial situation, having been back for a visit during recent disturbances. He told the audience that a disarmament conference was the way to solve all international problems. Italy, of all the nations involved in the war, had reduced its army to the greatest extent. In a population of 40,000,000, it had lowered the number in its military from 5,000,000 during the war to 190,000.[64]

After the United States rejected the League of Nations, at a time of growing isolationism and concern about how to achieve world peace, Terre Haute citizens were learning the crucial importance of international affairs. When they heard (or read in the local newspaper) Rosselli's view that "we must have a return to the days of peace which will make us hate everything that suggests war," they were gaining a far greater insight into the world than were many other Americans. In 1921, in a non-cosmopolitan, non-academic part of the country, where the Ku Klux Klan was strong, ordinary people were being told that "we must learn to think as citizens of the world, daring to face big issues, even when they affect our own country, in the light of what is best for the world at large." No longer must our motto be "My country, right or wrong." Instead, we need to say: "My country! She must always be kept right." In carrying out the core principles of the lecture movement, the Terre Haute planners were bringing a new dimension in global awareness to common people. Far away from the East and West Coasts, it was an astonishing public learning.[65]

Another speaker early in the second season was Edward A. Steiner, Professor of Applied Christianity at Grinnell College, in Iowa. In the early twentieth century, he had been writing and lecturing widely on ethnicity, immigration and race relations. In researching his 1906 book, *On the Trail of the Immigrant*, Steiner had made ten trips across the Atlantic in steerage to understand the spirit and problems of immigrants. In Terre Haute, before a "completely filled" hall, he declared that "the world is suffering from a perverted nationalism." Self-determination has become "selfish determination." Everywhere in Europe, he found destruction resulting from the war. The "greatest damage it has done has not been to men, but to the human spirit." The foresight exemplified in his speech was typical of many Open Forum lecturers who brought first-hand knowledge and a combination of realism and idealism in foreign affairs to the different communities.[66]

A major lecturer in the second year was W. E. B. Du Bois. His global perspective on changes in the post-war world, "The Future of the Darker Races," was the same topic he would address four years later at the Beth-El Open Forum in Hammond. Although the newspaper report on his talk in Terre Haute was briefer than others in the series, it quoted the scholar-activist as seeing little danger of the darker races dying out or being exterminated, as they comprised by far the greater part of the world's population. Once again, the important words of Forum speakers in broadening awareness were carried deeper into the community than just the audience at the lecture.[67]

A later speaker that year was former U.S. Representative Jeanette Rankin of Montana, a leader in the suffrage movement. She had voted against America's entry into the World War and continued her social commitment afterwards, serving as a vice-chairman of the American Civil Liberties Union. (In 1940, she would be reelected to Congress and cast the single vote against entering the Second World War, and in 1968, she would lead a march against the Vietnam War.) The news report on her talk said that the audience "taxed the capacity of the church." The talk was "one of the most interesting ever presented to the public." Men and women were "enthralled" in the way she introduced the active parts women had played in making the business of the world "hum." She began by saying "no one believes that in gaining votes for women that we have more than opened the way for a larger interpretation of citizenship." Universal suffrage was just the beginning. She described the active role of women in the fight for maternal health and infant mortality legislation. The next goal was securing reasonable working hours and adequate remuneration.[68]

Rankin's talk, indeed her accomplishments, when bolstered by the newspaper report, further opened the awareness of the community to major national concerns. In this earlier period, Open Forum speakers were achieving what later investigative reporters would carry out through print and other mass media. (The Terre Haute paper objected editorially to Rankin's suggestion that citizens write Congress once a week. It would take time from "useful employment" and create a grave crisis on the farms, shops and in other walks of life. Even worse, the newspaper said, it would be "irritating" to Congress.)[69]

A week later, Samuel K. Ratcliffe, associate editor of the *Manchester Guardian*, lectured on the influence of British labor unions on social and economic legislation. Questions revealed interest in unions in England, the gathering of labor leaders under one political banner, and the increasing number of union members elected to the House of Commons. The audience also asked about British employment, unemployment insurance, medical insurance for workers, and other labor issues in Europe. Ratcliffe responded that although there is some uncertainty, British labor stood with less of the revolutionary tendencies and a greater belief in the power of its political movement. Once again, the local press provided extended coverage of the program, in this instance one of particular interest to union leaders who had helped bring the Forum to the community.[70]

Two years after the series began, Herring described the principles of the Forum movement and details on its operation in Terre Haute in a national Methodist magazine. He said that it is best defined as an agency that stirs people to think clearly, kindly and independently on the great issues and to articulate that thought into social speech. "It endeavors to help people think their own way through to right decisions." It was not a lecture course, he continued. Using the analogy of electricity, the message of the speaker was a "current" that connected with the "current" of the audience. The audience then added itself and its reactions to the talk. Through this process, the group produced a "spiritual lift" in which each person discovered individually new light on the business of living.[71]

The movement thus "extracted [men and women] from their compartments and, by means of free discussion, brought [them] into vital relationship with one another." Out of that relationship, Herring predicted, there will come slow but solid growth of social knowledge and social will, "the backbone of democratic progress, the only real progress." Through the optimism of the Forum, the most diverse group of people, opinion and interest "will ultimately rise to an intelligent and constructive social will."[72]

A series of committees operated a local Forum, Herring continued, financed by many modest subscriptions and free-will offerings. The doors of the church auditorium opened at 6:00 p.m., and the hall was "normally packed by five or ten minutes before the forum opens at 7." After twenty minutes of "only the best music," a brief invocation, and announcements, with very few people leaving, the moderator introduced the speaker at 7:30. At 8:30, the lecture concluded, the offering was collected, and the questioning began.[73]

The question period was the Forum's most important achievement—"*the striking of mind upon mind*, the airing of misunderstandings, challenges as to facts involved, questions that draw out and clarify the speaker's message, the pouring of every kind of a reaction from every class into the melting pot toward the end of a fairer and better considered outlook by all." [Emphasis added.] The audience was the most diverse group of people, "of every shade of red or blue in their opinions, of every nation under the sun in their paternity." He could only speculate what untold benefit a community would derive from this kind of inspiration, "week by week, year after year!" The enthusiasm of Boston had been transplanted to Terre Haute.[74]

The Terre Haute Open Forum was off to a strong start. In the close-minded post-war era, an ideal lecture series had been developed, with a representative planning committee, a range of topics of both immediate and wider interest, and speakers who broadened horizons and sparked controversy. Although the planning committee lacked women and racial minority members, they brought in representative speakers to bring forward the concerns of the broader population. Capacity audiences in the first two years attest to the public's interest, while extended coverage by the leading local newspaper confirms its importance to the entire community.

At a time when the city needed cohesiveness, the open platform and vigorous give-and-take question periods built bridges of understanding among people from different religious and ethnic groups, as well as labor and business. Nine decades later, the social progressivism of the minister and the planning committee is clear. George Coleman's prediction that the programs in Terre Haute would be "a beacon light" was on target.

The Open Forum in Indiana in the 1920s also included acts of personal courage. In September 1924, Herring addressed a well-advertised anti-Klan meeting of the "Protestant Committee of One Hundred of Parke County," in Rockville, near Terre Haute. The crowd estimate ranged from 1,000 to more than 4,500. The *Rockville Tribune* noted that while "the Klan is strong, and Catholics are few" in the area, there is "an intensely bitter feeling between the Klan and anti-Klan Protestants." The minister's remarks were reported on in the local newspapers and reprinted in full a week later.[75]

Herring began by saying it would be easy to condemn the Klan but it was more important to approach the problem without rancor, "as brothers in a democracy." He called for the Klansmen in the audience to come out in the open, as he believed that "a good old-fashioned honest town meeting" would clear up misunderstanding. The Klan has many commendable aims, he said, and no one would be happier than the people at this meeting to see "purity, law enforcement, civic honesty, [and] patriotism" put into effect. Rather than hiding behind masks in a mob at night, he urged Klansmen to "lay their facts before the court of public opinion in the broad daylight." He concluded that, "maybe I'm a red Russian or a pink alien, but I have been taught from the cradle to believe that true Americanism includes belief in freedom for all and equal opportunity for all."[76]

The vice-chairman of the Forum, Rabbi Fink, showed even greater physical courage. In 1923, the Klan ordered the rabbi to resign as president of the Welfare League, which was the predecessor to the Community Chest and later the United Way. He refused and they invited him to a night meeting on a deserted farm. Before 300 hooded members, he derided the cowardice of men who concealed their identities under the guise of Americanism. A few days later, without stating a reason, the Klan sent the Welfare League a check for $1,800. (The Klan did not likely realize the irony that the numeral 18 in Hebrew is "*chai,*" which means "life," but surely his personal courage had an impact.)[77]

In October 1924, Irving Fisher, an internationally known Yale University economist, opened the new season. He was welcomed in a newspaper editorial before he spoke. A second commentary praised his advocacy of the League of Nations and World Court. The account of his talk in the *Terre Haute Tribune* noted that it may have been excusable in 1910 or 1920 to misjudge what the League could become, but the organization's record in keeping world peace and a stable currency since then was clear.[78]

Following the opening program and leading up to the November election, various political viewpoints were presented at the Forum. After the election, Roger Baldwin, Director of the American Civil Liberties Union, spoke on "Free Speech and the Election." He examined the conservative election victory, which showed a fear of change in government and an "unthinking allegiance to the established order of things." He expressed hope that the civil liberties climate would improve. "The whole tendency of the past year has been more favorable to the free exercise of fre [*sic*] speech and freedom of assemblance." The American Legion post in the city criticized the Forum planners for allowing Baldwin, a conscientious objector during the war, to speak on Armistice Day.[79]

In subsequent weeks, Terre Haute residents (including newspaper readers) continued to be exposed to provocative lecturers. Dr. Rowena M. Mann, a Unitarian minister from Chicago, said the experiment of women in politics had shown no harm because they followed the same policies as men. Ohio State University sociology professor Herbert Miller spoke on race prejudice from a global perspective. He found no psychological difference between the races of the world. "We must learn not to despise others simply because they are different," and should discard the "myth of superiority." Dr. Arnold Wolfers of Switzerland, an authority on social and economic problems, said that for the next steps toward peace in Europe, it is vital that America participate in the efforts, whether through the League of Nations, World Court, or a similar agency. An editorial strongly supported "thinking along the lines of peace" with the League of Nations. Other lecture topics during the year included child labor and poverty and evolution. Du Bois returned to speak on global and national racial problems.[80]

From 1923 to1924, Herring also served as secretary and field director for the Midwest Council for Social Discussion, headquartered in Chicago. Part of the Open Forum movement, the Council brought together adult education groups from four Midwest states. In October 1924, the young minister resigned his pulpit in Terre Haute for a position with the Federal Council of Churches.[81]

His new responsibility was to plan conferences combining Christian and Jewish congregations, creating a "pooling of consciences." At a time of rising anti-Semitism in Europe, he saw "dangerous signs in our social body" and a need to challenge falsehoods. He wanted to work urgently for "profound understanding," to achieve nationally what he had begun in a divided city four years earlier. In announcing his departure, the Terre Haute newspaper praised his many contributions.[82]

Following his work with the Federal Council of Churches, he organized the National Conference of Jews and Christians, later renamed National Conference of Christians and Jews, and today the National Conference for Community and Justice. He then directed an experimental community development project and helped organize the Nashville (Tennessee) Educational Council. By 1930, he had abandoned his ministerial standing in the Congregational movement to work solely in civic activities. He directed the Chester County (Pennsylvania) Health and Welfare Council, using adult education in carrying out a "Social Plan."[83]

Planning, Herring wrote, "the most comprehensive of social tasks, should be undertaken with education, the most effective of tools." As the planning continued in Chester County, adult education activities "did not prove feasible." He then worked for a number of years in adult education in New York State, spreading the Forum approach in many communities, and later in Kansas City, Missouri. In his later years, he carried out community development projects in other lands, and then returned to the ministry in California, as a Unitarian, emphasizing again the Forum approach. His final position, appropriately, was executive secretary of the Council of National Organizations for Adult Education, seeking community education nationwide.[84]

Max Einstandig, an historian of the Jewish community, suggests several reasons why the non-denominational, broad-based Open Forum was successful in Terre Haute. First, there was a good relationship with the churches "in spite of a 'five o'clock shadow' among the Jewish and non-Jewish merchants." The Jewish community was several hundred strong (actually more) and pulled members from surrounding towns in both Indiana and Illinois. While the Klan was active, its members did business with many of the Jewish merchants. One merchant, Sid Levin, characterized many Klan members as not having hatred for anyone but belonged to the organization "as a kind of fraternal type of thing." Einstandig also attributes the Forum's success to the city's three colleges and a strong middle and upper class. Finally, despite its reputation as a strong labor town, which kept new industry from moving in, Terre Haute's immediate trading area was populated by over half a million, as it was surrounded by many small communities. It was the largest big town between Indianapolis, St. Louis, Lafayette and Evansville.[85]

Although there is no record that the Open Forum continued in Terre Haute after the 1924–1925 series, the program had just begun in another house of worship in the northwest corner of the state.

NOTES

1. "A Notable Convention of Forum Leaders, Practical Idealism in Chicago Meeting," *The Congregationalist*, 3 May 1917, Scrapbooks, 6; "Fourth Annual Gathering Open Forum Council," Chicago, Illinois, April 15–17, 1917, ibid.

2. "Partial List of Speakers Available in the Middle West, Speakers' List," Number 8, Open Forum Speakers Bureau, Scrapbooks, 7.

3. "The First Birthday of the Midwest Council for Social Discussion, May 28, 1925," Scrapbooks, 9.

4. Letter to writer, Ivor F. Yeager, First Congregational Church, Jacksonville, Illinois, 12 August 1995, and various newspaper clippings in Church Record Book #3; "Jacksonville Forum," *Congregationalist*, 17 July 1919, n. p., Scrapbooks, 7; Grand Rapids: "Church and Its Work," *Grand Rapids Press*, n.d. [but likely 22 April 1919], Ford Hall Papers; "The Open Forum National Council," *Universalist Leader* [Boston], 9 June 1917, n.p., Scrapbooks, 6; "A Notable Convention of Forum Leaders," *The Congregationalist*, 3 May 1917, Scrapbooks, 6.

5. Ironton: "Open Forum Given Magnificent Start Mon. Night," *The Daily Register*, 14 January 1922, n.p., Scrapbooks, 8; Peoria: "Open Forums," *Handbook of Adult Education in the United States* (New York: American Association for Adult Education, 1934), 65; Riverside: A. E. Dooley, "A Forum in a Village," in Mary L. Ely, editor, *Adult Education in Action* (New York: American Association for Adult Education, 1936), 278–80.

6. Peffer, *New Schools For Older Students*, 10–11; Jewish Community Center Records, M 349, and Jewish Welfare Federation Papers, M 463, Indiana Historical Society, Indianapolis, Indiana; Washington Avenue Temple Men's Club Lectures, Historic Clipping File, Evansville-Vanderburgh County Public Library, Evansville, Indiana.

7. Minutes, Open Forum Council, July 3, 1914, Ford Hall Papers; J. Stanley Lemons, *The First Baptist Church in America* (East Greenwich, Rhode Island: Charitable Baptist Society, 1988), 97–101; Elba L. Branigan, *History of Johnson County Indiana* (Indianapolis: B. F. Bowen, 1913), 600–603; letter to writer, Mary A. Medlicott, Archivist, Franklin College Library, Franklin, Indiana, 10 December 1997.

8. *Annual Report of the Committee on Christian Work to the Boston Baptist Social Union*, March 1916, Scrapbooks, 5:17; letter to writer, Dana Martin, Acting Director, American Baptist-Samuel Colgate Historical Library, 18 December 1997; "Walter Rauschenbusch," Bill J. Leonard, ed. *Dictionary of Baptists in America*, (Downers Grove, Illinois: InterVarsity Press, 1994), 231; *South Bend Today*, IV (South Bend Chamber of Commerce, May 1916 and November 1916), unpaged; Elizabeth Dales and Katherine Edsall, *A Brief History of South Bend, Indiana, 1820–1960; Information About Its Economic, Political, Educational, Religious, and Social Development* (South Bend: South Bend Public Library, 1970), 12–15, with enclosed unpaged handwritten census chart.

9. Brochure, "The People's Open Forum," Clippings File, Local History and Genealogy Room, St. Joseph County Public Library, South Bend, Indiana; letters to writer, John F. Palmer, Local History and Genealogy Room, St. Joseph County Public Library, 27 and 28 December 1997.

10. Brochure, "The People's Open Forum," ibid.

11. "Urges Women To Seek Vote," *South Bend News-Times*, 10 April 1916, 2.

12. "Land Tax Would Solve the H. C. L. [High Cost of Living]," *South Bend News-Times*, 17 April 1916, 2.

13. "Christianity and Business Clash," *South Bend News-Times*, 24 April 1916, 2; "Dr. E. E. Carr Speaks," *South Bend Tribune*, 24 April 1916, 9.

14. "Says Spirit of Law Observed," *South Bend News-Times*, 1 May 1916, 2; "John L. Whitman Talks," *South Bend Tribune*, 1 May 1916, 2, 5.

15. "Tells How To Abolish Poverty," *South Bend News-Times*, 8 May 1916, 1, 3; "Poverty Subject of H. S. Bigelow," *South Bend Tribune*, 8 May 1916, 7.

16. "G. W. Coleman In City," *South Bend Tribune*, 29 April 1916, 5; "Praises Public Forum For City," *South Bend News-Times*, 29 April 1916, 3.

17. "Pastor Praises Housing Fight," *South Bend News-Times*, 8 May 1916, 1; "Sermon By C. A. Decker," *South Bend Tribune*, 1 May 1916, 5; "Do Not Blame Eve Too Much—Decker," 15 May 1916, 2, *South Bend News-Times*; "Asserts Bible Great Civilizer," 22 May 1916, 5, *South Bend News-Times*; letter to writer, Dana Martin, American Baptist Historical Society, 18 December 1997; "Former Pastor Here Dies In Connecticut," *South Bend Tribune*, 3 January 1926, 2; letters to writer, John F. Palmer, Local History and Genealogy Room, St. Joseph County Public Library, 4 December 1997 and 28 December 1997.

18. "The Open Forum National Council," *Universalist Leader*, 9 June 1917, n.p., Scrapbooks, 6; letter to writer, Indiana Room Librarian, Anderson Public Library, Anderson, Indiana, 16 June 1997.

19. "National Meetings Of Open Forum Of Great Importance," *Boston Globe*, 10 April 1917, n.p., Scrapbooks, 6; "Greeson A Delegate," *Kokomo Daily Tribune*, 14 April 1917, 2; letter to writer, Martha E. Wright, Reference Librarian, Indiana Division, Indiana State Library, Indianapolis, Indiana, 9 December 1997; "Reorganizes To Work For New Constitution," *Indianapolis News*, 30 November 1916, 4; brochure, "Plan of Organization of the Citizen's League of Indiana," 30 June 1914, Indiana Division, Indiana State Library; brochure, "Fourth Annual Gathering, Open Forum Council," April 15–17, 1917, Chicago, Scrapbooks, 6; "A Notable Convention of Forum Leaders; Practical Idealism in Chicago Meeting," *The Congregationalist*, 3 May 1917, n.p., Scrapbooks, 6.

20. "Zoercher Will Speak Here on Constitution," *Kokomo Daily Tribune*, 7 April 1917, 7; "Expect A Large Crowd," *Kokomo Daily Tribune*, 10 April 1917, 1; "Talk On Constitution," *Kokomo Daily Tribune*, 12 April 1917, 1; "Constitutional Forum," *Kokomo Daily Tribune*, 24 April 1917, 2; "Call Made For Forum Meeting Friday Evening," *Kokomo Daily Tribune*, 26 April 1917, 7; "Forum Session Pushing Work Of Organizing," 28 April 1917, 5; "Forum Special To Tour County Middle Of May," *Kokomo Daily Tribune*, 5 May 1917, 5; "Three Wards Of City Organize Forum Bodies," *Kokomo Daily Dispatch*, 9 June 1917, 7; "Third Ward Citizens To Organize A Forum," *Kokomo Daily Dispatch*, 15 June 1917, 1; "Community Forum Meetings Scheduled For This Week," *Kokomo Daily Dispatch*, 26 June 1917, 5; "franchise" is in *Dictionary of American English on Historical Principles*, 1058.

21. Clifton J. Phillips, *Indiana in Transition; The Emergence of an Industrial Commonwealth, 1880–1920* (Indianapolis: Indiana Historical Bureau, 1968), 127, 323–31, 350–58.

22. Ibid., 442–44

23. James H. Madison, *Indiana Through Tradition and Change; A History of the Hoosier State and Its People, 1920–1945* (Indianapolis: Indiana Historical Society,

1982), 6–22. A recent study of "sundown towns" nationally is James W. Loewen, *Sundown Towns; A Hidden Dimension of American Racism* (New York: New Press, 2005).

24. Madison, *Indiana Through Tradition and Change*, 45; Leonard J. Moore, *Citizen Klansmen; The Ku Klux Klan in Indiana, 1921–1928* (Chapel Hill: University of North Carolina, 1991), 57; Katherine M. Blee, *Women of the Klan; Racism and Gender in the 1920s* (Berkeley: University of California, 1991), 168; Sid Levin, 16 June 1981, Oral History Transcript SpC 977.245 L, Community Archives, Vigo County Public Library, Terre Haute, Indiana; letter to writer, Max R. Einstandig, Terre Haute, Indiana, 5 September 2001.

25. Madison, *Indiana Through Tradition and Change*, 57; "Indiana Klan Leads the Entire Country In Membership," *Lake County Times*, 16 June 1924, 1.

26. Moore, *Citizen Klansmen*, 6–11, 152, 184.

27. "Terre Haute Population" http://www.2.census.gov/prod2/decennial/documents/41084484v1ch4.pdf. (accessed May 11, 2008); Moore, *Citizen Klansmen*, 49, 60–61; letter to writer, Susan Dehler, Community Archives, Vigo County Public Library, 28 August 2001.

28. Gary L. Bailey, *Losing Ground; Workers and Community in Terre Haute, Indiana, 1875–1935*, (Ph.D. diss., Indiana University, Bloomington, Indiana, 1989), 395, 335.

29. Bailey, *Losing Ground*, 435, 486, 429; "Terre Haute's Jailed Government," *Literary Digest*, January, 16, 1915, 87–88; "Fear of God in Terre Haute," *Literary Digest*, April 24, 1915, 943–944; *Indianapolis News* quoted in "In the Indiana Belfry," 3 July 1915, 6.

30. Bailey, *Losing Ground*, 486–87, 336, 490–95.

31. Letter to writer, Roland Baumann, College Archivist, Oberlin College, Oberlin, Ohio, 19 November 1997; Oberlin College as "progressive" during this period, letter to writer, Roland Baumann, 4 April 2005; Donald M. Love, *Henry Churchill King of Oberlin* (New Haven: Yale University, 1956), 153–56.

32. Letter to writer, Joan Blocher, Assistant Librarian, Chicago Theological Seminary, Chicago, Illinois, 30 October 1997; Arthur C. McGiffert, Jr., *No Ivory Tower; The Story of the Chicago Theological Seminary* (Chicago: Chicago Theological Seminary, 1965), 92–103. "Social Gospel," "social reform," and "Christian sociology" are delineated by Susan E. Henking, "Sociological Christianity and Christian Sociology: The Paradox of Early American Sociology," *Religion and American Culture: A Journal of Interpretation*, vol. 3, no. 1 (Winter, 1993), 49–67.

33. John W. Herring File, Oberlin College Archives, Oberlin, Ohio.

34. Letter to writer, Harold F. Worthley, Executive Secretary and Archivist, Congregational Christian Historical Society, Boston, Massachusetts, 11 October 1997; Eleanore W. Nichols, ed., *The Congregational Year-Book; Statistics for 1921* (Boston: The Jordan & More Press, 1921), 142; "Lyman Abbott," *Dictionary of American Biography*, 1:24.

35. "Another State Coming," *Detroit Open Forum; A Journal of News and Views*, 6 December 1920, 7, Scrapbooks, 7; Coleman, "The Forum Marching On," *The Congregationalist and Advance*, 23 December 1920, 819.

36. Ahlstrom, *Religious History of the American People*, 238; "Forum Opens Tonight," *Terre Haute Tribune*, 14 November 1920, 7; "Forum Movement Has Auspicious Opening," *Terre Haute Tribune*, 15 November 1920, n.p., Scrapbooks, 7. Except as noted, subsequent newspaper articles are from the *Terre Haute Tribune* for the dates provided.

37. Ibid.

38. "Another State Coming;" Coleman, "The Forum Marching On."

39. *The Open Forum News Service*, 1920–1921 Season, Terre Haute, Indiana, ibid., n.p., Scrapbooks, 7.

40. "Rules For Open Discussion," ibid.

41. "Forum Speaker To Discuss Farming," 16 January 1921, 28; "Chinese Speaker Will Open Forum," 23 October 1921,11; "Deaths Reported," 24 June 1926, 2; Pearl B. Becker, "United Temple," *The Wabash Valley Remembers, 1787–1938* (Terre Haute: Terre Haute Northwest Territory Celebration Committee, [n.d.]), unpaged; "Hundreds Attend Wagner Funeral,"24 November 1928, 1, 2; "Wagner Funeral Held Saturday," 23 November 1928, 1, 2; "Noted Educator Taken by Death," 15 July 1936, 1, 2; "Hines Rites To Be Held Friday," 16 July 1936, 1; "Final Tribute Paid Dr. Hines," 17 July 1936, 1, 2; letter to writer, Dehler, 17 September 1997; "Linnaeus Neal Hines," Logan Esarey, *History of Indiana, From Its Exploration To 1922*, (Dayton, Ohio: Dayton Historical Publishing Co., 1922), 246.

42. "Forum Speaker Tells New Prison Methods," 6 December 1920, 12.

43. "City Planning Expert Makes Forum Address," 22 November 1920, 9.

44. Letter to writer, Chicago Public Library, 27 May 2008, on Frank A. Morgan; "Forum Speaker Urges New Church Methods," 29 November 1920, 7.

45. "Forum Speaker Tells New Prison Methods," 6 December 1920, 12.

46. Ibid; William A. Brown, *The Church in America; A Study of the Present Condition and Future Prospects of American Protestantism* (New York: Macmillan, 1922), 90.

47. "Labor In Politics Discussed At Forum," 13 December 1920, 12; "Farmer-Labor Party" http://www.answers.com/topic/minnesota-farmer-labor-party (accessed May 11, 2008).

48. Brochure, *Second Sagamore Sociological Conference*, 1908, 42, Sagamore Sociological Conference Files; Mattson, *Creating A Democratic Public*, 23, 29–30; "Plumb Plan Favored By Forum Speaker," 20 December 1920, 12; "Dr. Zueblin," 20 December 1920, 4.

49. "School Crisis Here; Speaker Tells Cure," 3 January 1921, 2; "Favors Revision of Laws of Marriage," 10 January 1921, 13.

50. "Forum Speaker To Discuss Farming," 16 January 1921, 28; "Open Forum Speaker Tells Farms Needs," 17 January 1921, 2; *25th Anniversary Program Booklet*, Temple Beth Zion, Buffalo, New York, 1949, Nearprint Box-Biographies, "Joseph L. Fink," American Jewish Archives, Hebrew Union College, Cincinnati, Ohio; Jacob R. Marcus, *To Count a People: American Jewish Population Data, 1585–1984* (Lanham, Maryland: University Press of America, 1988), 68.

51. Ahlstrom, *Religious History of the American People*, 238; "Harry Frederick Ward," *Who Was Who in America*, 4:982.

52. Donald B. Meyer, *The Protestant Search for Political Realism, 1919–1941* (Berkeley: University of California, 1961), 13; Carter, *Decline and Revival of the Social Gospel*, 126; "Urges Freedom For War Time Prisoners," 24 January 1921, 3.

53. "Sheldon Speaks Tonight," 30 January 1921, 3; "Open Forum Speaker Urges Cooperation," 31 January 1921, 3.

54. "Japanese To Speak," 6 February 1921, 10; "Talks Japanese Problem," 7 February 1921, 7; "Shantung Peninsula," *Webster's New Geographical Dictionary* (Springfield, Massachusetts: Merriam, 1972), 1100.

55. "Indian Girl To Sing," 13 February 1921, 12; "Indian Girl Tells Patriotism Of Race," 14 February 1921, 4.

56. "Forum To Hear Woman," 20 February 1921, 10; "Business Pushes Drama To Rear," 21 February 1921, 4.

57. "Problems Of Peace Discussed At Forum," 28 February 1921, 3; "Open Forum Lecture," 13 March 1921, 7; "Women In Politics Is Forum Subject," 14 March 1921, 6; "Maud Wood Park," *Who Was Who in America*, 3:664; Scott, *Natural Allies*, 173.

58. "Labor Leaders Take Forum Talker To Task," 21 March 1921, 6; "Forum Speaker Urges Closed Shop Views," 28 March 1921, 5; "Forum Speaker Tells Need of Co-operation," 4 April 1921, 5; "open shop" is in http://www.answers.com/topic/open-shop?cat=biz-fin (accessed May 11, 2008); "closed shop" is in http://www.bartleby.com/65/cl/closedsh.html (accessed May 11, 2008).

59. "Candidates At Forum Bare Their Hearts," 11 April 1921, 1, 3.

60. "Here's A Hope," 11 April 1921, 4; "Dr. Zueblin," 20 December 1920, 4.

61. "Chinese Speaker Will Open Forum," 23 October 1921, 11.

62. "Forum Program Has Auspicious Opening," 14 November 1921, 6.

63. Miles H. Krumbine, ed. *The Process of Religion; Essays in Honor of Dean Shailer Mathews* (New York: Macmillan, 1933; repr. Freeport, NY: Books for Libraries Press, 1972), 3–12; Ahlstrom, *Religious History of the American People*, 238; Shailer Mathews, *Jesus on Social Institutions* (New York: Macmillan, 1928), 130–34.

64. "Speaker At Forum," 27 November 1921, 3; "Italian Gives Views On Permanent Peace," 28 November 1921, 6.

65. "Italian Gives Views On Permanent Peace," ibid.

66. "Noted Traveler Coming," 11 December 1921, 8; "Past Lessons Fail To Impress The World," 12 December 1921, 6.

67. "Talks On Race Problem," 30 January 1922, 3.

68. "Jeannette Pickering Rankin" in Barbara Sicherman and Carol H. Green, eds., *Notable American Women; The Modern Period, A Biographical Dictionary* (Cambridge: Harvard University, 1980), 566–68; "Big Audience Hears Noted Suffragist," 20 February 1922, 5; "Miss Rankin," ibid., 4. Rankin's ACLU affiliation is on the letterhead of Roger Baldwin, Director, American Civil Liberties Union, New York, New York, to V. R. M'Millan, Commander, Fort Harrison Post No. 40, American Legion, Terre Haute, Indiana, 17 January 1925, Eugene V. Debs Papers, Cunningham Memorial Library, Indiana State University, Terre Haute, Indiana.

69. "Miss Rankin," 20 February 1922, 4.

70. Letter, James Peters, Archivist, John Rylands University Library, University of Manchester, United Kingdom, to writer, 8 December 2004; "Forum Speaker Tells About British Labor," 27 February 1922, 9.

71. Herring, "The Open Forum," 321.

72. Ibid., 322.

73. Ibid.

74. Ibid., 322, 325.

75. "Rev. Dr. Herring Ponders Klanism," *Rockville Tribune*, 20 September 1924, 1, 2; "Fifth District Snarled Up By Klan And Antis," *Rockville Tribune*, 24 September 1924, 1, 7; "'The Other Side,'" *Rockville Republican*, 24 September 1924, 1; "Greatly At Variance," *Rockville Tribune*, 17 September 1924, 1; 1 October 1924, 1, 5.

76. "Rev. Dr. Herring Ponders Klanism," ibid.; "Should Come Out In The Open To Fight," *Rockville Tribune*, 1 October 1924, 1, 5

77. *25th Anniversary Program Booklet*, Temple Beth Zion, Buffalo, New York, 1949, Nearprint Box-Biographies, "Joseph L. Fink," American Jewish Archives, Hebrew Union College, Cincinnati, Ohio; the meaning of "chai" as the number 18 in Judaism is in http://judaism.about.com/od/judaismbasics/g/chai.htm (accessed August 5, 2011).

78. Eugene V. Debs, in a letter dated 13 October 1924, wrote that the course of Open Forum lectures opened the previous week. Eugene V. Debs, *Letters of Eugene V. Debs*, J. Robert Constantine, ed., vol. 3, 1919–1926 (Urbana, IL: University of Illinois, 1990), 447; "A Matter of Interest," 25 September 1924, 4; "Dr. Fisher's Visit," 7 October 1924, 4, "Yale Man Urges League Of Nations," 7 October 1924, 20; "Dr. Fisher Talks At Forum Session," 8 October 1924, 11.

79. "Will Address Forum," 9 November 1924, 16; "Urges Free Speech," 12 November 1924, 15; "Women in Politics," 19 November 1924, 11; "Race Prejudice Hit By Forum Speaker," 26 November 1924, 5; letter, Roger Baldwin, Director, American Civil Liberties Union, New York, New York, to V. R. M'Millan, Commander, Fort Harrison Post No. 40, American Legion, Terre Haute, Indiana, 17 January 1925, Eugene V. Debs Papers, Cunningham Memorial Library, Indiana State University, Terre Haute, Indiana.

80. "Rowena Morse Mann," *Who Was Who in America*, 3:551; "Women In Politics," 19 November 1924, 11; "Race Prejudice Hit By Forum Speaker," 26 November 1924, 5; "Will Address Forum," 7 December 1924, 25; "Peace In Europe," 10 December 1924, 3; "The Large Idea," 10 December 1924, 4; 25 January 1925, 2; 31 December 1924, 3; "Discusses Race Problem," 21 January 1925, 10.

81. Herring File; "The First Birthday of the Midwest Council For Social Discussion," ibid.; "Dr. Herring Joins New Social Force," 3 October 1924, 1, 10.

82. "Dr. Herring Joins New Social Force," ibid.

83. Herring File; Harold F. Brigham, "Nashville Educational Council," *Journal of Adult Education*, 2 (June 1930), 324–25.

84. Herring, *Social Planning and Adult Education* (New York: Macmillan, 1933), v-xi, 15–25; John W. Herring and Leo T. Osmon, *Forums and a Community Forum Program* (New York: New York University, 1936), New York State Emergency Adult Education Program, Series 2, No. 3; Harold F. Worthley, Executive Secretary and Archivist, Congregational Christian Historical Society, Boston, Massachusetts, letter to writer, 16 September 1997; Herring File, ibid.

85. Einstandig, letter to writer; Sid Levin, interview.

Chapter Five

Hammond

A Sturdy Core of Thinking, Fact Seeking Citizens

Paralleling the development of the Social Gospel, some rabbis began addressing social justice issues from a Reform Jewish perspective. At a meeting in Pittsburgh in 1885, they called for social and economic justice: "We deem it our duty to participate in the great task of modern times, to solve, on the basis of justice and righteousness, the problems presented by the contrasts and evils of the present organization of society."[1]

This final paragraph in the "Pittsburgh Platform" was added at the insistence of Rabbi Emil Hirsch of Sinai Temple in Chicago. In the wake of increasingly violent strikes and riots in Chicago and the nation, he had been forcefully speaking out against laissez-faire capitalism. Through sermons, speeches and the journal he edited, *Reform Advocate*, Hirsch condemned sweatshops and argued in favor of the six-day workweek, unemployment insurance, and provisions for workers' old age.[2]

Similar to the proponents of the Social Gospel, Hirsch and others sought to change Judaism from its emphasis on individual conduct to addressing social issues. They realized that the advocates of the Social Gospel, basing their beliefs on the Old Testament Prophets, "were now drawing on common values for a common American cause," according to historian Michael Meyer. Christianity was "forsaking her historical position and enlisting under the banner of prophetic Judaism." Both movements were carrying forward the concept of secular perfectibility in American idealism.[3]

The social justice movement that the progressive rabbis called for in Pittsburgh went on to wider influence. In 1908, the Central Conference of American Rabbis, which was established by Reform rabbis in 1889, gave its support to the campaign against child labor. At the group's annual meeting in 1909, they recommended that students at Hebrew Union College, the Reform seminary, learn about industrial relations. At the group's 1914 meeting, one of the speakers was Rabbi Horace Wolf of Rochester, New York, who knew Rauschenbusch, and was to shortly lead the Reform social justice movement.[4]

These efforts came to fruition at the organization's 1918 conference, when the rabbis adopted a comprehensive, bold Declaration of Principles, "the first social justice platform of Reform Judaism," writes Meyer. It was similar to the platform that the Federal Council of Churches approved in 1912 and what Catholic bishops would express in 1919. On certain points, the rabbis went beyond the Protestant and Catholic positions, presenting specific imperatives which American society had not yet fully accepted.[5]

As with the Social Gospel leaders, the rabbis were confident that the energy and thought of an enlightened citizenry could solve the nation's social problems. However, just as Protestant ministers discovered, the rabbis' beliefs were not predominant within their national organization or in the wider Jewish community. Similar to their clergy brethren, who had lost prestige in the age of business enterprise, progressive rabbis were frequently out of step with their congregational leaders, the businessmen. The rabbis' views, writes historian Jerrold Goldstein, were often "treated as irrelevant when real problems of national Jewish interest were at stake." Their sermons on social issues were not heard, either by their members or workingmen, who were not coming to synagogues.[6]

At the 1915 rabbinical conference, Rabbi Abraham Cronbach, a very strong advocate, argued that social justice was Jewish and right—and right must be done. To the dismay of leaders in the congregations where he had served, the rabbi used the pulpit to speak out vigorously on social problems. The acrimony his positions engendered eventually forced him to withdraw as a pulpit rabbi entirely. In 1922, he became the first Professor of Jewish Social Studies at Hebrew Union College. One of his early students was Lithuanian-born Max Bretton, who would shortly assume the pulpit at Temple Beth-El in Hammond, Indiana, next to Chicago.[7]

Cronbach knew that in the brief time he had the students, he could present only a small amount of information on social problems, but he could impart compassion. In that capacity, he exercised a deep influence upon the training of Reform rabbis. Seventy years later, his impact was still felt by a fellow graduate of Bretton, Walter G. Peiser, who went on to serve in Baton Rouge, Louisiana.[8]

In 1993, at age 94, Rabbi Peiser wrote movingly about his teacher, who was also a close friend, as one who "was thoroughly sold on the Levitical precept of loving one's neighbor." Many times, in the early 1920s, Cronbach invited the seminary students to his house for dinner, as well as other guests, some of whom were African-American. Practicing what he constantly preached, he

greatly influenced the students. He particularly emboldened Peiser in the 67
years he would serve in the South.⁹

When newly–ordained twenty-six-year-old Rabbi Max Bretton came to Hammond in 1923, he found a warm welcome in the growing industrial community. The population was 36,000 in 1920 and 64,000 by the end of the decade.
In 1920, the community had 8,000 foreign-born whites, mainly from Poland,
Germany and Austria. During the decade, the African American population
rose from 168 to 715 residents. The Jewish population was 1,200 in 1927.
Looking back sixty and seventy years later, several Jewish residents recalled
a hard-working, comfortable milieu. Religious lines were crossed, with one
person remembering a grandfather playing checkers with a Catholic priest.¹⁰

Increased opportunities were developing from new construction and new
businesses, planning of a large residential addition, and enlarging of existing
industries. The city's Chamber of Commerce reorganized in late1922 and
its membership grew from 300 to 700, with the rabbi shortly becoming a
member. The group's slogan, "The Map Shows Why Hammond Grows," was
conveyed graphically.¹¹

Jewish residents were extensively involved in business and civic activities.
The co-owner of a large department store was a bank director and president
of the Chamber when it reorganized. His brother-in-law and business partner
was the director of another bank in 1922 and a director of the Hammond Kiwanis Club in 1925. Other Jewish residents and business owners, as well as
the rabbi, were members of the Chamber. Soon after the rabbi arrived in the
community, he spoke at the Chamber on "Let's Get Down To Brass Tacks."
The talk, "very well received," according to *Pep-In-Calumet*, its weekly
magazine, was on the development of Hammond, "not only along industrial
lines, but along the lines of parks, playgrounds, beautiful streets and further-
more the development of the artistic possibilities of its citizens."¹²

There was, however, another side to Hammond during those years, as
shown in the Chamber's candid "New Year Wish" for 1924. After listing
positive aspects of the community, the business organization enumerated
many drawbacks. It said that the city is lacking cooperation among people,
with selfish ambitions, special interests, jealousies and group advantages
holding back development. "I need citizenship, not partisanship; friendliness,
not offishness; sympathy not criticism; intelligent support, not indifference."
Too many people were willing to take everything they can out of the community and put back nothing out of their abundance. Too many had jawbones but
no backbones. The New Year Wish concluded: "I hope that my people will
learn the lesson of co-operation in 1925 and thus help me grow and expand

intelligently." What courageous, far-sighted leadership to speak so candidly on the front page of the very publication in which they were seeking to attract business.[13]

One reason for the community's self-criticism during the 1920s and 1930s were several instances of Ku Klux Klan activity, including well-attended parades. In 1922, as a result of a City Ordinance in nearby Gary, which prohibited masked parades, the organization moved its public meetings to other cities and towns. In April 1923, more than 5,000 regalia-clad Klansmen marched in a Hammond parade, with an additional three to four hundred in regular clothing. "Spectators lined the streets in support." In the following month, four crosses were burned in the area. The rabbi spoke of a cross burning on the Temple grounds and long-time Jewish residents recalled Klan marches. On election night in 1924, when the Klan-backed candidate for Governor swept the state, including Hammond, the *Lake County Times* headlined that "A Cross Blazed In Every Park of Hammond." Supported by the Klan, the Democratic candidate won nearly twice the number of votes as the Republican nominee.[14]

It was against this background, a week later, that the Beth-El Open Forum began. On the whole, Bretton found a comfortable Jewish community in a growing city. It was a good pulpit for the new rabbi. He understood, however, that such a situation did not necessarily ensure an invigorating congregation or genuine community health. He knew that the essence of the role of a rabbi was to not only guide congregants through ritual but also to teach and raise disturbing questions. An important first step in the process was urging the congregation to establish its own building. Previously, they had used the Orthodox synagogue, Keneseth Israel, for religious services but they now purchased a very large private home, across from a lovely city park. Importantly, in the building's basement, they established a "Social Center" for programs, with seating for 100.[15]

On June 24, 1924, Bretton wrote to Rabbi Stephen Wise, the leading national Jewish voice on social justice concerns and a strong advocate for building bridges between religions. Wise had spoken in the second season of the Ford Hall Forum and later served as first vice-president of the Open Forum National Council. Bretton wrote that "we are preparing an open forum course in Hammond, Indiana, which is just a few miles outside of Chicago, similar to that . . . of the Sinai Social Center." (Hirsch, the long-time leader in Jewish social justice, began the Sinai Temple Forum in southeast Chicago in 1914. He would have likely been an influence on the young rabbi.)[16]

A year after Bretton's arrival, the *Lake County Times* announced "an open forum . . . expected to have an educational and liberalizing effect upon the entire community." More than mere lectures, it will have "plenty of time for questions and expression of view." As in Boston and Terre Haute, musical selections would precede the lectures. This was especially important to the young rabbi as his wife was a professional classical singer. A month before beginning the Tuesday evening series, he introduced the concept of an "Open Forum" at a Friday night service, with the *Times* noting it "has proven very popular with a great majority of the congregation." It was an opportunity for "all present to ask questions and freely discuss the subject matter of the sermon." Laying the groundwork for the future lecture series was the title of one of his sermons: "The Part That the Church and the Minister Should Play in the Social, Economic, and Political Questions of the Day."[17]

In 1937, looking back at the first thirteen years of the series, the president of the re-named "Hammond Open Forum" discussed the rabbi's motives. Dr. Hedwig Stieglitz Kuhn wrote that the rabbi felt "there was a sturdy core of thinking, fact seeking citizens in this community that craved an authoritative discussion of vital problems affecting all angles of their lives." While she was instrumental in starting the series, Kuhn was not a congregant. She said that the "Beth-El Social Center Open Forum Course" was from the start a non-sectarian group. After being taught its first steps by the Beth-El leadership, it was "realigned as the Hammond Open Forum with a representative civic committee" in the 1932–1933 season.[18]

Along with the title change, a cross-section of community leaders of diverse faiths was listed as sponsors:

1. Arthur J. Weiss (realtor and temple and civic leader who served as the moderator from the beginning)
2. Mrs. Grace R. Conroy (stenographer and widow with children, Unitarian)
3. Timothy P. Galvin (Catholic attorney, considered "civic-minded")
4. Rabbi Jacob Krohngold (rabbi of the congregation at the time)
5. Lee L. Caldwell, (superintendent of schools and trustee of First United Methodist Church, remembered as being "staunchly conservative")
6. Leo Wolf (department store owner and Jewish community leader)
7. James Howard (director of Hammond Public Library, likely a Unitarian)
8. Mrs. O. C. E. Matthies (mother of two children and wife of an advertising manager, Methodist)
9. Dr. Kuhn (medical doctor and civic activist, a leader of the series from the beginning)
10. Mrs. S. H. Wightman (widow of a Chicago manufacturer)
11. Mrs. Ben Wolf (husband was a salesman at the Wolf store)
12. Edward Hackett (would shortly become secretary of the Chamber of Commerce)
13. Joseph L. Hirsch (vice president of a clothing store and another temple leader)[19]

Extensive documentation exists on the Hammond series through printed programs listing the speakers and topics, newspaper coverage on many of the lectures, several references in Hammond Chamber of Commerce publications, correspondence in the Du Bois *Papers*, and interviews with long-time residents, some who attended the lectures. The brochure for the 1932–1933 season stated the programs were presented in cooperation with the Adult Education Council of Chicago. In 1931, a list of agencies in the federated Adult Education Council included Hammond Public Schools, Hammond Open Forum, and Hammond Public Library. Kuhn was on the Council's Board of Directors.[20]

While the Terre Haute Open Forum took up a collection for expenses at the end of each lecture, season tickets were sold in Hammond. Beginning in 1924–1925 with a $6.00 membership ticket for sixteen lectures, the cost was reduced to $3.00 in the 1930s, and then increased to $4.00 for the last few years. For the final 1942–1943 season, only twelve lectures were arranged. It was more important to preserve a modest admission price over the years and to cover any increases in expenses through private contributions or congregation funds.[21]

The very first lecture demonstrated right away the non-sectarian, open platform principles of the Open Forum in action. Rev. John A. Ryan, Professor of Moral Theology and Industrial Ethics at Catholic University of America, spoke on "Industrial Democracy." Drawing from the 1894 encyclical of Pope Leo XIII, *Rerum Novarum*, the priest had early become active in moral and labor problems, uniting Catholic natural law with progressivism. His 1906 dissertation, *A Living Wage; Its Ethical and Economic Aspects*, was published in the same year, and was described by economist Richard Ely as "the first attempt in the English language to elaborate a Roman Catholic system of political economy." In 1913, he worked for minimum wage laws for women in Wisconsin and Minnesota. In 1919, he wrote the Catholic social justice statement, the Bishops' Program of Social Reconstruction. In 1920, he became head of the Department of Social Action in the National Catholic Welfare Council. Of the twelve major proposals in the Bishops' Program, eleven became Federal law during the New Deal. He became a strong advocate for a Constitutional amendment limiting child labor and was active in the American Civil Liberties Union.[22]

Clearly, he was in the forefront of social justice and the perfect person to lead off the series. Theologian Harlan Beckley, comparing Ryan with Walter Rauschenbusch and Reinhold Niebuhr, points out that the priest was "uniting Catholic natural law with similar ideas in American progressivism." With the priest's passion for justice, Beckley writes, he "exhibited courage and independence of mind in his application of Catholic moral theology to industrial problems." Several years before his Hammond talk, Ryan wrote that the concept of industrial democracy would result in a greater voice by wage earners in their workplace. After the Hammond lecture, he brought his ideas together in a book, *Industrial Democracy From a Catholic Viewpoint,* suggesting that the concept is "simply a greater degree of popular control than has . . . existed in our industrial system." The program brochure in Hammond noted that democracy is based on the idea that every human being is entitled to equal consideration, and that the speaker was one of the ablest and clearest thinkers on the topic "in a sorely vexed world."[23]

Beginning the Forum with this specific topic and speaker, at this time and place, was an act of courage. Indiana had emerged from the World War with economic problems, a determination to return to normalcy, and a growing illiberal mood. As the Klan found a hospitable climate, it was able to shape much of the state political scene. Like many Hoosier cities, Hammond was not immune from this socio-political atmosphere. Two nights after the Forum's opening lecture, thirteen robed Klansmen visited the new African Methodist Episcopal church, donated $100, and extended words of greeting to the congregation.[24]

Klan members marching into the church may not have been directly related to the Beth El lectures, as it was a frequent tactic they used to intimidate congregations. It does, however, provide important context. For the most part, writes historian Leonard Moore, "Klan politicians ignored Indiana's black and Jewish citizens." Instead, they were responding to changing social conditions, seeking to revitalize a sense of civic unity. For the black congregation, however, the motivation did not matter: robed Klansmen striding into their church made terror palpable.[25]

The visit so frightened the congregants that a delegation met with the Mayor. They asked him to keep the Klan from coming into their part of the city wearing their uniforms. They warned that a repetition of the affair was certain to bring trouble and bloodshed. The priest of the Polish Catholic church seconded their prediction, as he was expecting his church to be burned. "I have it heavily insured. You don't know what they will do. All I can do is warn my people to be ready to defend their homes. I have a gun loaded at my home and will use it if they come around my place."[26]

The second week's speaker, Syud Hossain from India, contrasted and compared Eastern and Western ideals. In the 1920s, like many advocates for social and political causes, he had been lecturing in the United States, championing the cause of independence for his native land. The program brochure for the series described him as "perhaps the Orient's most brilliant and eloquent representative in America." He was a "spiritual force of great significance" and the talk will bring forward "a culture and a civilization in the Eastern world different from our own." The increased understanding will further tolerance and lessen race and religious hatred, which is mainly due to lack of knowledge of other points of view.[27]

In selecting Hossain, the local Forum leaders were again exhibiting vision and courage. Hammond at the time had only a handful of residents from Asia. With this second speaker, the planners were bringing forward the importance of understanding other cultures. Introducing an Eastern religion to a somewhat narrow, largely homogeneous community was significant for a broader reason. It showed that non-majority, non-Western religions contained meaningful values for America and Hammond, an important point for the Jewish congregation arranging the series. This was especially noteworthy during "The Tribal Twenties," as described by historian John Higham, when nativism was sweeping the country and the gates were closing on new immigrants.[28]

The third lecture in the first year was an illustrated program on the stars. The brochure noted that the program would be a journey to the frontiers of the universe, billions of miles away in immeasurable space. This talk showed that not every Forum program would have a social action purpose. Through the years, a number of the Hammond programs enabled the audience to become more knowledgeable about science, literature and the arts. Later in the first year, Homer St. Gaudens, Director of Fine Arts at the Carnegie Institute in Pittsburgh, and son of the great sculptor, Augustus Saint-Gaudens, spoke on "The Relation of Art to Industry." The *Times* described the talk as having special appeal to the industrial Calumet area where Hammond was located. The program brochure elaborated that man cannot live by industry alone, as "a recognition of the need for art and beauty in life is equally important." Other well-known speakers over the years would include poet Carl Sandburg, sculptor Lorado Taft, journalist Anna Louise Strong, and anthropologist Melville Herskovitz.[29]

The fourth week's lecture was by George L. Scherger, Head of the Department of History at Armour Institute in Chicago. In discussing "Prejudices and Superstitions in History," he imparted an understanding of the new approach to history, drawing from research in psychology, anthropology, ethnology and other sciences. Nine decades after the first programs in Hammond, it is clear how current the planners were in intellectual ideas. It would be fifteen years before the American Historical Association would bring together these new frontiers in studying history at its annual program meeting.[30]

As in other cities, many of the programs were reported on in the local newspaper. The article on Scherger's lecture noted that it covered "race prejudice from the early Roman intolerance of Christianity to the present day

Ku Klux Klan." The historian said that a "man's religion makes no difference
to the true cosmopolitan." There is no such thing as pure American stock;
"America always has been a great melting pot [and we] are all brothers of a
great world." Scherger longed to see "every American extend a helping hand
to his brother who has just landed on these shores." Once again, these were
remarkable words, considering the anti-immigrant atmosphere in Indiana and
the country at the time.[31]

The next scheduled speaker was Clarence Darrow, the famed Chicago
lawyer, on "Crime and Punishment." He was to speak three months after he
had brilliantly fused law and psychiatry in defending Loeb and Leopold, the
murderers of a young boy. Because he was so well known, and the talk was
not reported in the newspaper, it may have been cancelled. (A year later,
his lecture in the city on the World Court did make front-page headlines.)
Continuing the first season's series into 1925 was novelist Sherwood Anderson, speaking on "America—The Storehouse of Vitality." He had already
published his masterpieces on small-town life and the destruction of a sense
of community by industrialism. In his talk, he asked whether the strongest
and richest country in the world would become the center of aesthetic and
cultural strivings.[32]

Among other lecturers in the first year were Charles Beard, nationally-
known historian, Will Durant, director of the Labor Temple School, an adult
education institute in New York City, and Norman Thomas, Executive Director of the League for Industrial Democracy, the education arm of the Socialist
Party. Beard spoke on "An Interpretation of American Politics," Durant on
"Does Man Progress?" and Thomas on "Giant Power—Master or Servant."
John H. Holmes, the nationally-known minister and leader in interfaith and
social justice causes, provided perspective in understanding the historical
importance of the 1914–1924 decade. Other talks were on the importance of
sexual knowledge for psychological and physical health, problems confronting the modern young woman, and the role of schools in Hammond for the future of America. A local minister, speaking on "Great Dramatists Who Have
Helped Me Find My Soul," continued the Forum ideal to reach further than
the familiar. That spiritual truths might be found in other than religious texts
was consistent with the humanistic framework of the movement, nationally
and in Hammond. Bretton concluded the year's programs by arguing for the
proposed constitutional amendment prohibiting child labor, a crucial national
issue at the time.[33]

As in Terre Haute, newspaper reports often carried the Hammond lectures
deeper into the community than the audience that was present in the hall.

Janet W. Pence, who attended regularly from 1930 to 1933, and was the daughter of Arthur Weiss, the Forum moderator, estimates that 100 to 150 people enjoyed the programs during that period, a good number for the size of the facility. The fact that the series continued for nineteen years on Tuesday evenings, from late fall to early spring, suggests the talks were well-received. Coupled with news articles on many of the programs, the wider educational impact of the Open Forum in Hammond can be sensed.[34]

The city's Chamber of Commerce also recognized its value, pointing out the importance of the social and esthetic development of citizens. The value cannot be measured in terms of finance but rather in "civic development." The business group noted that, after a community has established such social agencies, its growth is along a new line, enriching community culture. "This type of civic endeavor will pay a generous dividend on service—in terms of community betterment—from which those who collect receive far more joy than they ever would from dividends of any kind received from any other source." Along with the Chamber's praise for the "very best" music programs in Beth-El, as well as the organization's "New Year Wish for 1924," calling for citizenship, friendliness, sympathy and intelligent support, the statement reflects more forward thinking than would be expected among business leaders in that area at the time.[35]

What conclusions can be drawn from the first year of the Beth-El Open Forum?

First, with the speakers selected, the planners displayed much vision and laid the groundwork for future programs. In a community that saw some hatred, and without a strong intellectual tradition, Jewish leaders brought to the city Catholic and Indian theologians, espousing ideas of equality and industrial democracy and opening minds to other ways of worship. In Durant, the planners showed foresight, as he would shortly popularize the study of philosophy, religion and world history, the latter in a ten-volume, 9,000–page opus. Still other speakers enabled the community to learn the most current ideas on history, science and literature.[36]

Secondly, in the "Red Scare" that began in the World War and continued into the 1920s, the Forum planners demonstrated courage in scheduling a number of the speakers. Beard had written one of the most controversial and influential books on the Constitution. During the war, he resigned from Columbia University over the suppression of free speech. Thomas was a former Presbyterian minister who had vigorously opposed America's entry into the war and helped found the ACLU to aid conscientious objectors. He then left the church and joined the Socialist Party, embarking on his life's work in speaking forthrightly about the nation's shortcomings, as well as running six times for President as a Socialist.[37]

In Holmes, the Forum planners brought to the community a person who saw socialism as political Christianity. He was instrumental in founding the National Association for the Advancement of Colored People before the war and the ACLU afterwards. He had persuaded his congregation to change from particularistic Christianity to a religion of democracy. A leading voice against the war, the minister continued for years as a strong advocate for liberal causes. He was a supporter of striking workers and fought to spare the lives of Sacco and Vanzetti, anarchists convicted of a payroll holdup and murder in Massachusetts. He spoke several times at the Open Forum in Hammond, an indication of his popularity.[38]

Finally, the first year carried forward not only the highest ideals of Reform Judaism (thinking freely and doing justly) but the American faith in secular perfectibility, as expressed by novelist Thomas Wolfe, that "the true discovery of America is before us[;] the true fulfillment of our spirit . . . is yet to come." As in Terre Haute, the Hammond series carried forward the ideals of Ford Hall. In a period of significant narrow-mindedness and intolerance, it had become a non-denominational blending of Social Gospel and Jewish social justice principles and progressive political beliefs.[39]

At the beginning of the second season, a long editorial in the Hammond newspaper congratulated the planners on "the excellence of the program." It described in detail the background of several of the speakers and their topics. The second year's lectures did not disappoint. Irish novelist Shaw Desmond described how traditional religion had become bankrupt. The war had nothing to do with democracy, the *Times* quoted Desmond, but was a war for markets, driving millions of people into materialism and brutal living. People realized how the clergy did not have the courage to denounce war but instead turned their pulpits into recruiting stations. Another speaker in the second year was Du Bois on "The Future of the Darker Races." While the newspaper editor did not know how the lecturers were selected, they were "the cream of the field" and the entire series was "of vital interest to everyone." At a cost of $6.00 for the series, the editor called it a "good investment." Once again, considering the times and area of the country where the series was held, such community praise was remarkable.[40]

The third season began with Dean Mathews of the University of Chicago Divinity School on "The Rising Generation and Its Moral Tasks," and was followed by equally prominent speakers on vital topics. In the 1930s and continuing into the 1940s, foreign affairs became a more frequent topic, eventually dominating the series each year. But the broadening goal of the planners in the arts and humanities was always there. The 1937–1938 season concluded with lectures by historian Abram L. Sachar of the University of Illinois, in a series entitled "Historic Outlook on Life." He covered Schopenhauer, Disraeli, Michelangelo, Magellan, Spinoza, and Hitler. Speakers in later years included well-known pacifist and radical Scott Nearing, Rabbi Wise, James Weldon Johnson of the NAACP, and Roger Baldwin of the ACLU. First Lady Eleanor Roosevelt opened the 1938–1939 season, speaking on "The Individual and the Community." In her nationally syndicated column, "My Day," she wrote that the fifteen-year-old Hammond Forum had earlier "a great deal of difficulty keeping it going, but this year forums have suddenly become popular and the demand for season tickets is overwhelming."[41]

In 1926, after developing a strong foundation for the series, Bretton left Hammond and the pulpit. He briefly headed a Jewish orphanage in Hartford, Connecticut. Later, he became Executive Director of the Young Men's Hebrew Association in Kansas City, Missouri, where his cultural series "filled halls," his daughter recalled. Eventually, he opened a restaurant that Jacob R. Marcus, the father of American Jewish historiography, remembered as an enjoyable place to visit. Marcus was a contemporary of Bretton when they were students at Hebrew Union College. In 1955, the rabbi returned briefly to Hammond to participate in the dedication celebration of the new Temple Beth-El sanctuary.[42]

The Hammond lectures continued into World War II, stopping only when the gasoline shortage made private transportation too difficult. Arthur Weiss, a highly respected leader in the temple as well as the business community, worked on the Forum with Kuhn from the beginning, serving as the moderator. In the model developed at Ford Hall, the moderator was crucial in interpreting the speaker to the audience and the audience to the speaker, ensuring that each meeting fulfilled its greatest possibilities. The best forum chairman, writes Emory S. Bogardus, insists on fair play all around, shifting discussion when it becomes too heated and ensuring that no person monopolizes. Weiss probably also wrote the publicity before the programs and most news accounts afterwards, as the movement placed much emphasis on public communication.[43]

The daughter of Weiss recalled his leadership role in the local chapter of the ACLU during the 1920s. In December 1938, concerned about world events, he organized a large democracy rally in the city. Attorney Galvin and School Superintendent Caldwell, both sponsors of the Open Forum, participated in the rally. In addition to extensive coverage of their talks, the *Hammond Times* (renamed) printed their speeches in full. One month later, the three leaders, along with others, organized the Inter-Faith Association to increase group understanding among the different faiths. In 1942, Weiss was a leader of the Post-War Planning Committee of the Hammond Chamber of Commerce, reflecting his strong involvement in community and looking to the future. It is not surprising that the photo of him in the community's centennial history shows him marching his platoon through the city's streets in 1917.[44]

Dr. Kuhn continued to lead the Forum for many years. In 1933, after the Hammond chapter of the League of Women Voters had disbanded, she revived it, serving as president until 1936, and contributing actively to the chapter's activities in later years. With her husband, she pioneered industrial eye safety and was instrumental in the development of safety glasses. During World War II, the Kuhn Clinic handled thirty to fifty eye injury cases a day from the Calumet Region's war plants. She went on to broader public safety concerns in safe driving and crime prevention, receiving national recognition. While her political opinions became more conservative as she grew older, she was known as a caring physician, and many older residents remembered "Dr. Hedy" fondly.[45]

Local historian Marjorie Sohl writes that the Open Forum in Hammond was held in high regard because of the leaders who volunteered their time and talents in organizing it. While the nearness to Chicago made it easier for speakers to travel, personal friendships among the leaders were ultimately of great importance to the Forum's success. With such civic leadership and broad range of stimulating speakers, and as radio was just then entering peoples' lives, the lecture-discussions opened new vistas, raised disturbing questions, and showed the power of democracy in the industrial city.[46]

Crosses blazed in Hammond as the Beth-El Open Forum began but the lectures cast a wider, deeper and more lasting light for two decades. Thanks to a Baptist lay leader in Boston, the nation was building a bridge to the future, and the path had led to a Jewish congregation in Hammond. Sixty years later, Rosalyn Friedman, who attended the lectures, called it "the most marvelous program that ever existed," and remembered Holmes as a "dynamic speaker."[47]

The sonority of America's great orators in the first half of the nineteenth century may not have surfaced in every instance in the Hammond series or in the Open Forum nationally, but the impact was strong nevertheless. An outstanding example of the importance of the series, on both the intellectual awareness and interpersonal relationship levels, is captured in deeply moving letters between the Hammond planners and Du Bois, described in the next chapter.[48]

In view of the social, intellectual and religious currents at the time, intriguing parallels emerge in the careers of the Terre Haute minister and the Hammond rabbi. Both began activist leadership in Hoosier congregations soon after their ordinations, in 1918 and 1923, respectively. Each also linked up with fellow clergy in their communities. One Terre Haute resident remembered Herring was "good friends" with Rabbi Fink, vice-chairman of the Forum. A long-time Indianapolis rabbi wrote that Herring and Fink successfully organized a mass meeting "to protest against the rising tide of Klanism in their vicinity," and recommended a similar meeting to the Church Federation of Indianapolis.[49]

Eugene Debs, Terre Haute resident and national leader of the Socialist Party, wrote that Herring "is the most progressive preacher we have had here for years and a thoroughly fine fellow to boot." Debs said that the minister managed the Open Forum "very successfully." The feeling was mutual, as shown in a draft essay by the young minister several years earlier, when he described the high regard in which the labor leader was held in Woodstock, Illinois, the location of his first pulpit.[50]

Bretton's daughter recalled her father was "very close to an Episcopal minister" in Hammond. Rev. Peter Langendorff of St. Paul's Episcopal Church in fact spoke in the first year of the Forum on spiritual truths in great dramatic works. Langendorff joined the Chamber of Commerce several months after his friend became a member. The minister continued to speak and write on public issues after Bretton left the city, such as in a 1936 article in the Chamber's magazine on the importance of the U.S. maintaining neutrality in the world.[51]

After their trailblazing work, Herring and Bretton left their pulpits, the minister for a career in community relations and adult education, using the Forum method, and the rabbi for Jewish communal work and to operate a restaurant. The departures suggest they may not have found in their daily pastoral duties the fulfillment that the Open Forum brought them, or possibly their inner lives might have reflected what Reinhold Niebuhr and John Dewey were describing at the time about the nation's loss of faith and the need for a sense of community. Whatever the reasons, their accomplishments in the two cities are evident. They broke new ground, bringing the "light" of the Open Forum movement to their communities.

Soon after the minister and rabbi began their Forums, similar series were started in Indianapolis and Evansville. While many of the same lecturers came to the latter cities, the planning committees were not as broadly representative. In 1926, the Indianapolis Open Forum began under the auspices of the Jewish Community Center Association. The program brochure noted it was "Dedicated to the Public Discussion of Live and Interesting Subjects [,]

Free from Sectarian influence, and Open to All, Regardless of Creed." The format of speaker and question period was the same as in the other cities. JCCA membership dues were the chief support but the programs were open to non-members at a modest price. The series was part of an extensive adult education effort in the newly-built Kirshbaum Center. The JCCA was very pleased with the results. Among the first season's speakers were Holmes and Durant. As events unfolded in Nazi Germany, the focus shifted to international and American political affairs in a perspective sympathetic to Jewish concerns.[52]

In Evansville, the first date on a list of the Washington Avenue Temple Men's Club Lectures is 1927. An October 1933 newspaper article refers to the "eighth annual lecture series," which would set the first year in 1926. However, a 1974 account by one of the participants noted that the group attempted to schedule Clarence Darrow in 1926 but canceled it as a result of community objections. It was a difficult period in the city, with large parades by masked Klan members from 1923 to 1925. Race relations eventually began to improve, led in part by Jewish civic and business leaders.[53]

In 1927, at the urging of Rabbi Jack Skirball, the Men's Club of the congregation decided to bring "a prominent liberal speaker . . . to change the attitude of the community." This lecture by Will Durant drew 400 people at an admission price of 75 cents. Among other speakers in the early years were some of the same lecturers who had addressed earlier Open Forums in the state—Syud Hossain, Scott Nearing, Norman Thomas, John H. Holmes, and A. Phillip Randolph of the Brotherhood of Sleeping Car Porters and Maids. Such provocative, often radical thinkers show that the Evansville series was just as broadening as the earlier programs in Terre Haute and Hammond. Four years earlier, Hossain had spoken in Evansville on the Moslem world and Western civilization, under the auspices of the Teachers' Federation. According to the *Evansville Courier* account of the earlier talk, he left a "deep impression."[54]

In February 1928, before 200 people at the Washington Avenue Temple, Hossain called for internationalism through fostering culture and more human contacts. In February 1933, after Hitler had become Chancellor of Germany, Oswald Garrison Villard, editor of *The Nation*, lectured on his apprehension for Europe. The foresight of the planners of the series is reflected in such speakers and topics.[55]

From 1928 through 1938, sixty-two lectures drew 100 temple members and 300 of the general public to each program. "Lively and stimulating discussion by the audience" followed the addresses. Senators, journalists, diplomats, religious leaders, academics, and world leaders spoke at the series. Historian Darrel Bigham assesses the non-sectarian public lectures, which filled the temple auditorium, as "one of the most progressive aspects of river city culture at that time."[56]

We now know that, despite the largely insular-thinking atmosphere in the state, many Hoosiers came together under the Open Forum to discuss vital public issues, intellectual advances, and the core beliefs and values in their lives. The locally-developed programs brought stimulating, often controversial speakers to the communities. Through wide newspaper coverage, the talks played an important role in public learning. Activist clergy in Terre Haute and Hammond worked with representative committees to develop model programs. At a time when the Klan was strong in the state, and the public was largely intolerant of radical or even liberal viewpoints, clergy and lay leaders built bridges of racial, religious and global understanding. Lecturers of national and international renown drew capacity audiences, and local news accounts extended their words and values deeper into the public's awareness.

While Herring and Bretton each served as the catalyst in bringing this public learning to their cities, the Forums would have been impossible without the financial and moral support of their congregations and the wider communities. A deep sense of civic responsibility is shown by:

• the commitment of prominent persons in various fields and different faiths to serve on planning committees;
• the search for just the right lecturers for their particular cities, for both current and long range interests;
• making the necessary arrangements for the visits in hospitality and driving; and
• frequent newspaper accounts, before and after the visits, that both brought the learning to the public and carried forward Mary Crawford's goal to preserve the history of the learning initiative for future generations.

These factors reflect a strong local civic commitment, during a dangerous period for liberal ideas, which has been largely left out of the historical record. It is a story that awaits examination beyond Indiana for comparison and contrast. If the impact on public learning can be found in this handful of cities, a much wider narrative awaits in the several hundred other Forums in the country that were counted in 1926.

For Terre Haute, the Forum became the training ground for a Congregational pastor embarking on a long career, using the Forum method and communication between people to build better communities in the United States and abroad. The Terre Haute series can also be viewed in the broader perspective of the Social Gospel movement. Rather than the national Forum movement "Christianizing the social order," historian Donald Gorrell suggests that the church in general adapted Social Gospel ideas as situations changed.[57]

For Hammond, nineteen years of a thoughtfully-prepared lecture series, much newspaper coverage, and strong support by the business community confirm the recollection of one person who attended that it was a "marvelous program." The adult education goal was carried further through the involvement of Hammond Public Library. The 1939–1940 series included a reading list, "This Troubled World," which brought to the participants (and general public) recent books on the international situation and on social and economic problems to be discussed by the lecturers. The book list in 1940–1941 was tied to the specific week's lecture. The final image of the Open Forum, as described by Herring—*the striking of mind upon mind*—is a model for a human-centered approach to public learning today, no matter the setting.

One final intriguing question is whether the two clergy ever met to exchange ideas or discuss obstacles in carrying out their lecture series, or problems in their communities or the nation in general. In 1925, the Midwest Council for Social Discussion met in Chicago, which adjoins Hammond. The group's purpose was to establish Forums where there was a need and strengthen existing groups. Herring was Secretary of the Council and Field Director. Bretton was just finishing up the first year of the series in his congregation, a short distance from where the Council was meeting. In the 1950s, in Kansas City, their paths may have crossed while the minister directed a national adult education project in the city, and the rabbi operated a popular restaurant. Recalling their experiences in Indiana in the 1920s, they would have had some conversation.

The minister and the rabbi, working with their planning committees, shared one other special act of courage. At a time when the Klan was strong in their cities, and racism was pervasive throughout the country, they each invited W. E. B. Du Bois to speak at their Forums.

NOTES

1. "Pittsburgh Platform (November 16–19, 1885)," www.jewishvirtuallibrary.org/soures/Judaism/pittsburgh_program.html (accessed May 11, 2008).

2. Michael A. Meyer, *Response to Modernity; A History of the Reform Movement in Judaism* (New York: Oxford University Press, 1988), 272, 287.

3. Meyer, 288; Leonard Judah Mervis, "The Social Justice Movement of the American Reform Rabbis, 1890–1940" (Ph.D. diss., University of Pittsburgh, 1951), 9.

4. Meyer, *Response to Modernity*, 288; Mervis, "The Social Justice Movement of the American Reform Rabbis, 1890–1940," 45; Jerrold Goldstein, "Reform Rabbis and the Progressive Movement" (MA Thesis, University of Minnesota, 1967), 87–89.

5. Meyer, *Response to Modernity*, 88.

6. Goldstein, "Reform Rabbis and the Progressive Movement," 4, 52–53, 56, 59; Richard Hofstadter, *The Age of Reform; From Bryan to F.D.R.* (New York: Alfred A. Knopf, 1955), 152.

7. Mervis, "The Social Justice Movement of the American Reform Rabbis," 52–53, 181–83.

8. Ibid., 185.

9. Letter to writer, Walter G. Peiser, 31 December 1993, Baton Rouge, Louisiana.

10. *HUC-JIR Alumni Directory*, Hebrew Union College-Jewish Institute of Religion (Cincinnati, Ohio: Rabbinic Alumni Association and HUR-JIR, April 1992), 110; "Beth-El Holds Fine Service," *Lake County Times*, 15 September 1923, 1; U.S. Department of Commerce, *Statistical Abstract of the United States, 1935* (Washington, D.C.: Government Printing Office, 1935), 22–23; *The Yearbook of the State of Indiana, 1921* (Indianapolis: William B. Burford, 1921), 1159; interviews by writer: Alexander Morris, 8 February 1991, Hammond, Indiana; Sylvia Friedman, 3 April 1991, Munster, Indiana; Ida and Arthur Friedman, 9 April 1991, Munster, Indiana.

11. "Chamber of Commerce Roster," *Pep-In-Calumet* (Hammond Chamber of Commerce, Hammond, Indiana), 27 October 1924, 1–7; "Five Million Dollars of Big Building Now Under Way," *Pep-In-Calumet Magazine*, March 1925, 21. *Pep-In-Calumet* was both a weekly publication and a monthly *Pep-In-Calumet Magazine*.

12. "Chamber of Commerce Roster;" "Brass Tack Talk," *Pep-In-Calumet*, 14 January 1924, 1; *Smith's Directory of Hammond, Indiana and West Hammond, Indiana, 1921–1922*, (Dorchester, Massachusetts: Edgar Smith, 1922), 14, 25, 32; Lance Trusty, *Hammond; A Centennial Portrait*, 2nd edition (Norfolk, Virginia: Donning Company, 1990), 26, 45.

13. "Hammond's New Year Wish," *Pep-In-Calumet*, 29 December 1924, 1.

14. Neil Betten, "Nativism and the Klan in Town and City: Valparaiso and Gary, Indiana," *Studies in History and Society*," (Bellingham, Washington: Western Washington Press, 1973), 4:6; telephone interview by writer, Deborah Bretton Granoff, 13 May 1991, Kansas City, Missouri; interview, Alex Morris, Hammond, Indiana, 8 February 1991; interview, Sylvia Friedman, Munster, Indiana, 3 April 1991; interview, Ida and Arthur Friedman, Munster, Indiana, 9 April 1991; "A Cross Blazed In Every Park of Hammond," *Lake County Times*, 5 November 1924, 1.

15. Rabbi Ulrick B. Steuer, "History of Congregation Beth-El," *Dedication of Temple Beth-El, Hammond, Indiana*, 1955, unpaged; "Beth-El Social Center Thrives," *Pep-In-Calumet*, March 1925.

16. Letter, Rabbi Max Bretton to Rabbi Stephen S. Wise, 24 June 1924, Stephen S. Wise Papers, American Jewish Historical Society, Brandeis University, Waltham, Massachusetts; letter to writer, Marc Lee Raphael, 15 July 1991, Wolfson College, Oxford University; S. D. Schwartz, "Sinai Social Center—An Expression of the New Democracy," *Reform Advocate*, 11 October 1914, 225; S. D. Schwartz, "The Sinai Public Forum," *Character* February-March 1935, 19.

17. "Jewish Congregation Meets in Church," *Lake County Times*, 2 August 1923, 1; [Subsequent newspaper articles in this note are from the *Lake County Times*.] "Bethal [*sic*] Meets at Elk's Hall," 8 September 1923, 1; "Critics in Many Cities Praise Hammond Singer," 9 December 1925, 24; telephone interview, Granoff; "Open Forum Proves Popular," 11 October 1923, 1; "Sermon at Beth El," October 18, 1923, 1 "Beth Els [*sic*] Open Forum," 20 October 1924, 1.

18. Hedwig S. Kuhn, "Time Again for Open Forum," *Hammond Business* (Hammond Chamber of Commerce), vol. 3, no. 9, September 1937, 1.

19. Sponsors of the Hammond Open Forum:

- Arthur J. Weiss: "Arthur J. Weiss," *Hammond Times*, undated article, Suzanne G. Long Local History Room, Hammond Public Library; "Civic Leaders Plan Meeting on Democracy," *Hammond Times*, 20 December 1938; Steuer, "History of Congregation Beth-El."
- Mrs. Grace R. Conroy: *Polk's Hammond City Directory, 1931* (Indianapolis, Indiana: R. L. Polk & Co., Publishers), 129; letters to writer, Suzanne Long, Hammond Public Library, 3 December 1997, and 10 March 1999; letter to writer, Richard Lytle, Hammond Public Library, 23 August 2011.
- Timothy P. Galvin: "Civic Leaders Plan Meeting on Democracy," *Hammond Times*, 20 December 1938; Long, letter to writer, 13 January 1999.
- Rabbi Jacob Krohngold: Steuer, "History of Congregation Beth-El."
- Lee L. Caldwell: "Civic Leaders Plan Meeting on Democracy," *Hammond Times*, 20 December 1938; letter to writer, Long, 18 November 1998.
- Leo Wolf: *Hammond City Directory*, 448; letters to writer, Long, 3 December 1997, 10 March 1999.
- James Howard: Long, letter to writer, 30 November 1998.
- Mrs. O. C. E. Matthies: *Hammond City Directory*, 289; letters to writer, Long,
- 3 December 1997, 30 November 1998, 10 March 1999; Letter to writer, Lytle.
- Dr. Hedwig Kuhn: "Founder of Kuhn Clinic Dies at 78," *Times*; 18 June 1973, 1.
- Mrs. S. H. Wightman: *Hammond City Directory*, 441; letters to writer, Long, 3 December 1997, and 10 March 1999.
- Edward Hackett: *Hammond City Directory, 1935*, 171; Richard M. Lytle, Hammond Public Library, letter to writer, 30 November 2004.
- Joseph L. Hirsch: *Hammond City Directory, 1931*, 214; Steuer, "History of Congregation Beth-El"; letter to writer, Long, 10 December 1997.

20. "Card of Admission for 1931–1932 Course of lectures of The Beth-El Open Forum," Hammond, Indiana; brochure, "The Adult Education Council of Chicago," October 1931, Newberry Library, Chicago.

21. Brochures, "Beth-El Social Center Open Forum Course; First Season Program, 1924–25," through "Hammond Open Forum; Nineteenth Season, 1942–1943," Suzanne G. Long Local History Room, Hammond Public Library, Hammond, Indiana.

22. "John Augustine Ryan," John J. Delaney, *Dictionary of American Catholic Biography*, (Garden City, New York: Doubleday, 1984), 501–502; Aaron I. Abell, "Monsignor John A. Ryan: An Historical Appreciation," *Review of Politics*, (1946),

8:128–34; Richard J. Purcell, "John A. Ryan, Prophet of Social Justice," *Studies; An Irish Quarterly Review*, (June 1946), 35:153–75.

23. Harlan Beckley, *Passion for Justice; Retrieving the Legacies of Walter Rauschenbusch, John A. Ryan, and Reinhold Niebuhr*, (Louisville, Kentucky: Westminster/John Knox Press, 1992), 113–14; brochure, "Beth-El Social Center Open Forum Course; First Season Program, 1924–25."

24. "Indiana Klan Leads Entire Nation in Membership," *Lake County Times*, 16 June 1924, 1, 26; "Maywood Thrown In Ferment," *Lake County Times*, 14 November 1924, 1.

25. Moore, *Citizen Klansmen*, 10.

26. "Maywood Thrown In Ferment."

27. "Syud Hossain," *New York Times Obituaries Index, 1858–1968* (New York: New York Times, 1970), 483. [Note: "Hassain" was the wrong spelling in the Beth-El program brochure.] "Beth-El Social Center Open Forum Course; First Season Program."

28. *The Yearbook of the State of Indiana, 1921*; John Higham, *Strangers In the Land; Patterns of American Nativism, 1860–1925* (New York, NY: Atheneum), 1967, 264–330. Higham's final two chapters are entitled "The Tribal Twenties" and "Closing the Gates."

29. Brochures, "Beth-El Social Center Open Forum Course" and "Hammond Open Forum," passim; "St. Gaudens Here Tonight," *Lake County Times*, 10 February 1925, 5.

30. "Beth-El Social Center Open Forum Course, First Season, Program 1924–1925"; "Lecturer Pleads For Poor Immigrant," *Lake County Times*, 3 December 1924, 3; Caroline F. Ware, editor, *The Cultural Approach to History* (Port Washington, NY: Kennikat Press, 1964), passim.

31. "Lecturer Pleads For Poor Immigrant."

32. "Clarence Seward Darrow," *Dictionary of American Biography*, Suppl. 1, 41–44; "Darrow Lambasts World's Court in Hammond," *Lake County Times*, 20 January 1926, 1; "Sherwood Anderson," *Dictionary of American Biography*, Suppl. 3, 12–15.

33. "Charles A. Beard," *Dictionary of American Biography*, Suppl. 4, 61–64; "William J. Durant," in Stanley J. Kunitz and Howard Haycraft, eds., *Twentieth Century Authors; A Biographical Dictionary of Modern Literature*, (New York: H. W. Wilson, 1942), 408; "Norman R. Thomas," in John A. Garraty, ed., *Encyclopedia of American Biography*, (New York: Harper & Row, 1974), 1086–87; "John H. Holmes," *Dictionary of American Biography*, Suppl. 7, 355–57.

34. Letter to writer, Janet W. Pence, Mill Valley, California, 3 April 1991.

35. "Beth-El Social Center Thrives," *Pep-In-Calumet*, March 1925, 18–21.

36. "William James Durant," *Twentieth Century Authors*.

37. "Charles Austin Beard," *Dictionary of American Biography*; "Norman Mattoon Thomas," *Encyclopedia of American Biography*.

38. "John Haynes Holmes," *Dictionary of American Biography*.

39. Quoted in Commager, *American Mind*, 276.

40. "The Beth-El Lecture Course," *Lake County Times*, 6 November 1925, 4; "Shaw Desmond Assails Churches, Priests and Clergymen in Lecture," *Lake County Times*, 11 November 1925, 1, 5.

41. "Mrs. Roosevelt Raps Fascism," *Hammond Times*, 19 October 1938, 1–2; Eleanor Roosevelt, "My Day," 20 October 1938, United Feature Syndicate, Inc., Eleanor Roosevelt Papers, Mount Vernon College, Washington, DC.

42. Telephone interview, Granoff, 13 May 1991; letter to writer, Jacob R. Marcus, Cincinnati, Ohio, 13 January 1995; letter, Rabbi Ulrick B. Steuer, Hammond, to Max Bretton, Kansas City, Missouri, 19 September 1955, Temple Beth-El Archives, Hammond, Indiana.

43. Emory S. Bogardus, *Democracy by Discussion* (Washington, DC: American Council on Public Affairs, 1942), 8.

44. Janet W. Pence, letter to writer, Mill Valley, California, "7 May 1991" [mistyped as 1941]. [Subsequent newspaper articles in this note are from the *Hammond Times* for the dates noted.] "Civic Leaders Plan Meeting On Democracy," 20 December 1938, 1; "Democracy Is Theme Of Big Meet Tonight," 28 December 1938, 1; "Hammond Opens Fight On Isms," 29 December 1938, 1 2; "Which Way America,"10; "Let America Speak Out" and "What Are We Here For," 30 December 1938, 10; "Three Faiths Cooperate To Kill Bigotry," 22 January 1939, 2; "Post-War Planning Proposed By Chamber Of Commerce," *Hammond Business*, February 1942, 1, Suzanne Long Local History Room; Lance Trusty, *Hammond; A Centennial Portrait* (Norfolk, Virginia: Donning Company Publishers, 1984; second edition 1990), 140.

45. "Founder of Kuhn Clinic Dies at 78," *Times*, 18 June 1973, 1, 14; Archibald McKinlay, "Tale of Two Doctors—Hedy and Hugh Kuhn," *Times*, 23 September 2001, Long Local History Room; scrapbooks, Hammond League of Women Voters, Long Local History Room; telephone interview, Millie Pilot, Hammond, Indiana, 10 October 1995.

46. Letter to writer, Marjorie Sohl, Munster, Indiana, 10 August 2001; "Radio," *Dictionary of American History*, 6:15–16.

47. R. Friedman interview, 30 May 1992.

48. Gerald W. Johnson, *America's Silver Age; The Statecraft of Clay, Webster, Calhoun* (New York: Harper, 1939), 195–97.

49. Notes from interview of Carolyn Gurman by Max Einstandig, Terre Haute, Indiana, 23 September 1997; Morris M. Feuerlicht, "A Hoosier Rabbinate," *Indiana Jewish History*, 4 (Fort Wayne: Indiana Jewish Historical Society, 1974), 48.

50. *Letters of Eugene V. Debs*, 447; John W. Herring, undated, unpublished draft essay, Eugene Debs Papers, with letter from Dennis Vetrovec, 11 November 1997, Department of Rare Books and Special Collections, Cunningham Memorial Library, Indiana State University, Terre Haute, Indiana.

51. Granoff; Margaret C. Dust, *"People of the Place of Fire," St. Paul's Episcopal Church; A Century of Progress* (Hammond, Indiana: 1988), 27–28; "Chamber of Commerce Roster," 3; Rev. Peter Langendorff, "Will the U.S. Remain Neutral?" *Hammond Business*, February 1936, 8a-8f.

52. *The First Annual Report of the Jewish Community Center Association of Indianapolis*, September 1, 1926–March 31, 1927, *The Second Annual Report*, April 1, 1927–March 31, 1928, *Three Years After—The Annual Report*, April 1, 1928–March 31, 1929, Jewish Welfare Federation Papers, M 349, Box 2, Indiana Historical Society, Indianapolis, Indiana; brochure, "The Open Forum of Indianapolis," M 463, Indi-

ana Historical Society; Judith E. Endelman, *The Jewish Community of Indianapolis; 1849 to the Present* (Bloomington, Indiana: Indiana University, 1984), 132, 177–78. [Subsequent newspaper articles in this note are from the *Indianapolis Star* for the dates noted.] "Rabbi Pleads For True Liberalism Among Creeds," 25 October 1926, 7; "Plans Kirshbaum House Exercises," November 6, 1926, 1, 10; "Kirshbaum Hope For Useful Gift Will Come Through," 26 November 1926, 10; "Center Speakers Laud Kirshbaum," 8 November 1926, 1–2; "Prejudices Are Artificial, Says Forum Speaker [Holmes]," 30 January 1927, 6; "Durant Picks 10 Greatest Sages In Forum Talk," 7 March 1927, 10. Brochures, "The Indianapolis Open Forum Program of Lectures," 1945–1946, 1946–1947, 1947–1948, Indianapolis-Marion County Public Library Reference Department, Indianapolis, Indiana.

53. List, "Washington Avenue Temple Lectures," vertical file, "Evansville. Jews. Washington Avenue Temple," Evansville-Vanderburgh County Library, Evansville, Indiana; "Present Age To Produce Great U.S. Writers, Louis Untermeyer Says," *Evansville Press*, 31 October 1933, Historic Clipping File, Evansville-Vanderburgh County Library; untitled resolution objecting to planned talk by Darrow on evolution on 4 March 1926 by Quadruple Club, Indiana Church File, Evansville-Vanderburgh County Library; James E. Morlock, *The Evansville Story; A Cultural Interpretation*, (Evansville, Indiana: Creative Press, 1956, revised 1981), 183; Darrel E. Bigham, *We Ask Only A Fair Trial; A History of the Black Community of Evansville, Indiana* (Bloomington: Indiana University, 1987), 45, 104–108, 124–25, 138, 149, 169–70, 181, 187, 219. [Pages of newspaper articles in Historic Clipping File are not indicated.]

54. Ervin Weil, "An Account of the Origin and Development of the Washington Avenue Temple Lecture Series from 1927 to 1938," Evansville, Indiana, 1974, Hebrew Union College Records, MS-5 Folder B-7/14, American Jewish Archives, Cincinnati, Ohio. [Subsequent newspaper articles are from the *Evansville Courier* in the Historic Clipping File for the dates noted.] "Author of 'Story of Philosophy,' Literary Sensation, To Appear Here," 13 March 1927; "Central Planning Body For Economic Problems Suggested by Nearing," 12 December 1930; "Capitalistic Age Passing, Thomas Says In Address," 17 January 1933; "World in Throes Of Despair, Noted Liberal Declares," 6 January 1938; "Noted Lecturers Of Three Races In City Tonight," 6 December 1931; "Mohammedan Journalist Leaves Deep Impression," 13 December 1922.

55. "World Unity Seen By Indian Scholar," 23 February 1928; "Villard Fearful Of Consequence Of Hitler's Rise," 2 February 1933.

56. Weil, "An Account"; Bigham, *We Ask Only A Fair Trial*, 170.

57. Donald K. Gorrell, *The Age of Social Responsibility; The Social Gospel in the Progressive Era, 1900–1920* (Macon, GA: Mercer University, 1988), 7.

Chapter Six

Du Bois

You Have Given Me New Strength and Vision

The shift in scholar-activist William E. B. Du Bois' thinking about race, from an abstract cultural concept and academic research to a realization that organizations were crucial in the struggle for dignity and equality, can be viewed in the larger societal context of the move towards social activism in the early twentieth century. After confronting racism in the North and South, he turned from research to participation. Initially, his path was with the "Talented Tenth" of the Niagara Movement, but later to the more broadly-based National Association for the Advancement of Colored People. His change in thinking paralleled the growth of the Open Forum lecture movement.

As with other low-paid academics and social service professionals at the time, public lectures were a vital element in his work life, providing needed additional income and an opportunity to carry his ideas directly to local communities. Many speeches, on a wide range of platforms, enabled him to put into practice a newly formed belief in the primacy of organizations over the heroic struggles of individuals. Among the locations where he spoke during the 1920s, the Beth-El Open Forum in Hammond served as a strong bridge for human relations. Although the major biographical studies of Du Bois have not examined such talks, we can uncover the impact of his visit on the Hammond planners and learn what the visit and the lecture movement meant personally to him.[1]

What brought the internationally known researcher and activist to the largely white community of 50,000 in Klan-ridden Indiana in 1926? The 1920 census counted 168 "Negro and other races" in the city. The larger population for commerce in the industrializing Calumet Region, the northwest corner of the state, was 110,000. Among the 200 Jewish families in the city, several men were leaders in civic activities. Using Du Bois' Hammond lecture as a focus, we can assess the effect of the Forum in strengthening human relations. By examining correspondence to and from him, other documents, contemporary publications, recent scholarship, and interviews, we can recapture the period, understand why and how he came to the city, and sense what the visit meant to him and the people he encountered.[2]

Du Bois' challenge to Booker T. Washington as "race leader" during the early twentieth century centered on the slower approach to equality of the Tuskegee Institute educator and his accommodation to white leadership. The young scholar's historical and sociological research at the time had begun to merge with his belief in an activist leadership, and he moved to a different level than Washington, one in which the organization rather than individual achievement became the focus. While the younger man understood the moral and political aspects of the race problem, he could not build a personal following or effective political machine as Washington had done. He concluded the answer was through group action.[3]

In developing the Niagara Movement in 1905, Du Bois and others sought to educate the African American community about protest, convey dissatisfaction with the prevailing race relations, and hew a path for young leaders. With an all-black membership, the Niagara Movement reflected his idea that the educated "Talented Tenth" should become the race leaders. Historian Elliott Rudwick writes that although the movement failed, mainly because of the social distance of the more educated leaders from the general community, the attempt to organize a national group of informed, independent and articulate citizens led five years later to the founding of the NAACP.[4]

The new organization offset the problem of class rather than mass leadership through extensive involvement of white liberals and a black secretariat to broaden its base. For Du Bois, Director of Publications and Research and editor of its widely read monthly, *The Crisis*, the secure financial backing initially provided an independent editorial and research forum. Others might fear white dominance in the new organization, but his position was clear in his mind and ideal in striving towards his goals. He became more cosmopolitan and self-confident, promoted an aggressive African American image, and helped lay the foundation for the Harlem Renaissance in the 1920s.[5]

Unfortunately, in a way similar to how Washington was bypassed a decade earlier, his strengths as a researcher and activist rather than an executive lessened his administrative effectiveness. Following the pattern of most organizations, the NAACP had passed through the initial excitement of the formation stage to the formal institutional level, requiring different leadership skills. He forged his way to leadership but was too independent to become an "organization man." Historian Charles F. Kellogg writes that the scholar-activist "not only wanted complete control of *The Crisis*, but he also wanted to be an executive officer on a level with other Board members in directing the work of the Association." Yet, his "personal antagonisms prevented his working with most Board members and staff" and he was "difficult to control."[6]

James Weldon Johnson, the organization's Secretary and his close associate during the 1920s, wrote in 1933 that Du Bois' "lack of the ability to unbend in his relations with people outside the small circle has gained him the reputation of being cold, stiff, supercilious [and] limited his scope of leadership." Du Bois recognized his own shortcomings, when he wrote in his 1940 autobiography, that his leadership was one solely of ideas. "I never was, nor ever will be, personally popular."[7]

The extensive correspondence that Du Bois carried out during this period frequently focused on the need for more income than the organization could provide. He required a decent level of financial support for his family, for the historical and sociological research that was so important to him (on both personal and societal levels), and for the global activism that he had embarked on, in the reconfiguration of national boundaries after the World War. The source of additional income for these three areas lay in a full schedule of paid public lectures, as is revealed in his *Papers*. While the NAACP had early found speeches the most effective means of reaching the masses, the method was controversial within the organization's leadership. From 1910 to 1919, Du Bois traveled in nearly every state and in several foreign countries, delivering 424 speeches to nearly 200,000 people. "When the Board chided him in 1919 for spending too much time on lectures that had no direct relation to the work of the Association," Kellogg writes, "he replied that after expenses his income from lectures totaled $2,050, an average of $228 a year." Du Bois said that the speeches furthered the Association's goal of propaganda and were not for profit. During the 1920s, he charged $50 to $75 for each talk, with travel expenses paid by him. He usually scheduled his own appearances although the national Open Forum Speakers Bureau arranged some of them.[8]

An example of the extensiveness of his speaking is reflected in the listing of his "wayfaring" (his phrase) in the May 1923 *Crisis*. He had traveled 7,500 miles and had another 1,000 remaining before he returned to the office. He had delivered thirty lectures to 7,200 whites and 4,350 blacks at ten branches of the organization, four churches, three Christian associations, and two women's clubs, and he had ten more to deliver. His messages were on the economic basis of the nation's social divisions, the "Negro's" contributions in the Great War, the impact of European economic imperialism, and what the future might hold.[9]

Although a calendar of the February 1926 speaking tour that brought him to Hammond is not included in Du Bois' *Papers*, other lectures are listed on a day-by-day basis and are illustrative of his busy schedule. For example, in

May 1926, he spoke in Washington, D.C., Dover (Delaware), Washington again, South Boston (Virginia), Roanoke, Charleston, Savanna, Atlanta, Knoxville, Terre Haute, Mounds (Illinois), Cleveland, Dayton, Detroit, St. Louis, and Nashville, before returning in early June to New York City. In March 1928, he was at an afternoon program in the Chicago area and another location in the evening. The next day, he was at a morning lecture and an evening event, and on the following night, at still another site. Later in the month, he spoke in Ann Arbor, Detroit, Grand Rapids, Minneapolis, Chicago again, St. Louis, Jefferson City, and Kansas City. In the February 1926 circuit, the Open Forum Councils in Chicago and Cleveland arranged some of the lectures.[10]

Continuing his May 1923 report, Du Bois wrote that the audiences gave him careful attention, sometimes manifesting approval, and the newspapers were uniformly courteous. In this circuit, he remembered friends, "new and old who rose like developing souls out of mists of men and were kind, sympathetic, inspiring almost beyond conception—far beyond words." As much as his audiences appreciated him, directly connecting with people had a significant impact on his own sense of self. He never went on a trip "without a choking sensation—a realization near to tears of the immense, the unfathomable gratitude and appreciation of the Negro American for his leaders and workers." He made no appeal to emotion, talked without gesturing, and scarcely raised his voice. "I began my talks without excuse or flattery and ended without peroration. I have simply reasoned with fact and logic and illustration."[11]

For many years, he wrote, white listeners shrank from his frankness and his "bitterness," as they termed it. They preferred "Mr. Moton" (Robert R. Moton), who had succeeded Booker T. Washington as head of Tuskegee Institute in 1915. Today, Du Bois wrote, white audiences no longer want "mush and shallow optimism" but stark and awful facts told with calm, unemotional insistence. Most of his listeners heard him with sympathy and rapt attention and received him with deep thoughtfulness. He concluded that they wanted the "truth."[12]

Despite the lecture tours, the organizational difficulties at the NAACP continued. Its financial problems had actually begun before he did any work for the organization. In his 1940 autobiography, Du Bois wrote, "I arrived in New York [in 1910] to find a bare office; the treasurer, Mr. Villard, said frankly: 'I don't know who is going to pay your salary; I have no money.'" By 1916, *The Crisis* had become self-supporting, bringing in needed income and reaching people around the world. In 1920, revenue from the magazine rose to $77,000, with four and a half million copies sold in its first decade. The organization's financial difficulties continued, however, and *Crisis* revenue began to fall off in early 1924. For Du Bois, the postwar years were, in general, one of immense effort and discouraging turmoil. "I was nervous and restless [and] ranged the country from North to South and from the Atlantic to the Pacific in series of lectures, conferences and expositions."[13]

On May 13, 1925, Dr. Hedwig Stieglitz Kuhn of Hammond wrote Du Bois, inviting him to speak at the Beth-El Open Forum. Born into a cultured, highly educated Jewish-Christian German American family in Chicago in 1895, she was a physician and civic activist for many years in Hammond. Her initial contact with Du Bois may have been as a young woman through her uncle, Alfred Stieglitz, the renowned photographer. In 1914, Stieglitz presented in New York City the first exhibition of African sculpture as a medium of art expression rather than object of ethnographic interest. Although Kuhn worked closely with Temple Beth-El congregant Arthur Weiss, when he was the Open Forum moderator and later as business manager of the Kuhn Clinic, she most likely did not identify herself as Jewish. The invitation to speak should be seen as coming from the liberal intellectual leadership of Hammond rather than the congregation, even though the series was held at the temple.[14]

In her letter, Kuhn reminded Du Bois that when she visited him in the East during the previous year, they spoke about his coming to the Open Forum in Hammond. He told her during the 1924 visit that he would have other Chicago engagements in the February 1926 period, and she was now writing to set the date. All of the Tuesday night dates in February were open and so he was free to choose the most suitable one for her "small group." She said "those of us who know your work & are so warmly in back of it feel that it would mean a very great deal to have you come to this difficult industrial district." In Hammond, "there is a small nucleus of rare souls here on whom revolve the intellectual & spiritual future of large groups of people smothered in . . . prejudices and ignorances."[15]

Her group, she continued, was denting the surface and finding a most fertile soil. "The famous Indiana Klan will undoubtedly discover us to be even more 'dangerous' than they do now—but I have had several pitched battles with them & am only eager to reduce their ranks still more." She wrote there are many people in Hammond "who knowingly & unknowingly crave your message, many who are groping blindly for a path that doesn't lead to emptiness & uselessness." She hoped that in the "spirit of utmost cooperative fellowship" he would speak in Hammond. She concluded, "with happy remembrances of the few moments you gave us when I was in the East."[16]

The outcome of her letter and subsequent correspondence occurred on Tuesday evening, February 23, 1926. The *Lake County Times* reported that "Dr.

Du Bois" was entertained at dinner by Rabbi Max Bretton of Temple Beth-El and friends at the Elks Club. The dinner was being held prior to the NAACP leader's lecture at the Beth-El Open Forum that evening. The event took place fifteen months after the newspaper reported that "a cross blazed in every park of Hammond" when the Ku Klux Klan swept to victory in the November 1924 election.[17]

Kuhn's warm, hand-written letter was typical of the voluminous correspondence Du Bois received, reflecting the deep feeling that drew people of diverse cultures, countries and economic backgrounds to him. As was true with many of his correspondents, she was able to relate to him from a combination of idealism, intellectualism, and activism, in addition to their personal contact.

On September 25, 1925, Du Bois wrote Bretton that he would speak at the Open Forum in Hammond on the following February 23rd. If two other engagements could be arranged, the charge would be $75.00, from which he would pay his own expenses. If there weren't any additional lectures, the charge would be $100.00. He was available to speak during the week or possibly the week before.[18]

In the months preceding the Hammond lecture, Du Bois' correspondence in his *Papers* and his writings in *The Crisis* convey a wide array of work and personal activities. In addition to editorial and research responsibilities, the correspondence records his many concerns. He was involved with important administrative problems at Fisk University and Howard University. Always accessible, he was responding to requests for advice from aspiring writers, planning Pan-African activities and research projects, commenting on the Sweet case in Detroit (in which a physician defending his home against a mob was charged with murder), and arranging for "The Star of Ethiopia" pageant on African history for the following June in the Hollywood Bowl. He was also replying to numerous requests for his books, photos of himself, recommendations for reading, and financial assistance from strangers, friends and relatives. His letters were always prompt, brief, clear and right to the point. Reflecting his sense of history and knowing the importance of primary documents for research, he saved carbon copies of his letters, as well as the letters from his correspondents. In turn, Du Bois' executor, historian Herbert Aptheker, ensured that everything, including his personal and business matters, was given to the University of Massachusetts, Amherst, where the materials became 79 reels of microfilm and are now widely available in libraries and becoming digitalized.[19]

Besides his Hammond talk on February 23rd, Du Bois began filling up his calendar with other lectures for the month: 4th Youngstown, 5th Columbus, 6th Fort Wayne, 7th Detroit, 8th Toledo, 11th, 12th, or 13th Tulsa, 20th

Chicago, and 21st Indianapolis. On the 28th, he would be in Cleveland in the morning and Elyria in the afternoon. Other speeches were scheduled, and one instance of overbooking resulted in a "greatly disappointed" audience in Beloit, Wisconsin, when he failed to appear.[20]

On October 9th, Bretton responded to Du Bois, confirming the February 23rd lecture date, the $75.00 fee, and the topic, "The Future of the Darker Races." The talk was on a list of lectures from which local organizations could choose. The rabbi said he would endeavor to obtain several more lecture sites in the vicinity and was "looking forward with a great deal of joy to your coming."[21]

Du Bois spoke on the same topic at Temple Ohabei Shalom in Brookline, Massachusetts, on January 10th, and at the Detroit Open Forum on February 7th. The Brookline talk was followed in the evening by a speech in Boston at Ford Hall Forum. The Ford Hall talk was his first broadcast on radio, an important milestone in extending his message deeper into America. From 800 miles away, in Huntington, West Virginia, Walter A. Smith, a building contractor, told Du Bois in a moving hand-written letter that he had listened to the Ford Hall talk over the radio with his wife. "We are glad you had the opportunity of using the radio to bring facts to so many you could not reach otherwise. . . . We appreciate very much what you are doing for the race."[22]

An editorial praising the upcoming Beth-El Open Forum lecture series appeared in the *Lake County Times* on November 6th. While the editor commented on several of the lectures in the series, the only notation for the Du Bois talk was "Colored" in parentheses after his name. The paper congratulated the congregation on the excellence of the schedule.[23]

An article announcing the lecture appeared on the front page of the *Times* on February 23rd. It was headed "NOTED COLORED EDITOR NEXT ON PROGRAM"—a few inches below "INDIANA KLAN HOLDS SUNDAY MEETING AT KOKOMO." The promotional tone of the Forum article suggests that Arthur Weiss, the moderator, or Hedwig Kuhn wrote it. The public was urged to attend the program, "to hear this great man and outstanding personality whose life has been one immense dedication of energy, thought, love, and pain, in the hope of teaching lesser man true greatness of the inner soul." Du Bois was "brilliant, keen, balanced, fascinating." He makes "no sentimental appeal to the emotions of his audience," but outlines, very simply and clearly, "the far vision of great ideals he so modestly personifies."[24]

A front-page report on the talk the next day, which was also likely written by Weiss or Kuhn, was headed "COLORED EDITOR ASKS WELCOMING HAND FOR NEGRO." The article noted that Du Bois spoke on "The Future of the Colored Races," attempting to show inferentially that "the negro [*sic*] is the equal of the white man but oppressed." The attempt by science to prove inferiority of the race, such as through brain weights and shape of head, has not been successful. Du Bois declared there is "a growing determination in the darker world against the white man's methods of holding down the less fortunate races." He referred to the postwar conferences on India and South Africa. "The ordinary reaction of civilization toward people who want to advance should be the welcoming hand. Force isn't going to accomplish the permanent submission of the black race."[25]

In the word "Colored," the newspaper was using the vocabulary of the day. More important than the word was that the message and the messenger reached much further into the white community, thanks to the newspaper report. The wise advice of Mary Crawford fifteen years earlier, on the vital importance of publicity, was shaping societal awareness in the industrial heartland.

A copy of "The Future of the Colored Races" is not included in his *Papers*, or listed in the bibliographies of his published writings. Five years earlier, when he spoke on the same topic at Ford Hall in Boston, he was quoted in the newspaper that "white business men have organized the darker world so as to get all the profit possible out of labor and raw materials." The struggle for the monopoly of this labor and these raw materials, he said, "led to the world war." Even if he changed some of his words over the five years for his Hammond talk, he was likely just as straight-forward in his message, causing some discomfort to the largely white audience.[26]

In the same period that he spoke on "The Future of the Darker Races" in Brookline, Detroit and Hammond, Du Bois published an article on the theme in *Foreign Affairs*, the new prestigious national journal. In that article, "Worlds of Color," he described the "inevitable spread of the knowledge that the denial of democracy in Asia and Africa hinders its complete realization in Europe." He foresaw that "quickened India, the South and West African Congresses, the Pan-African movement, the National Association for the Advancement of Colored People in America, together with rising China and risen Japan—all these at no distant day may come to common consciousness of aim."[27]

Although no independent description of Du Bois' Hammond lecture was written at the time, a number of listeners commented through the years on his oratorical skills. In 1913, historian William H. Ferris wrote that he heard him lecture a few years earlier in a "masterly way" on John Brown. "Du Bois possesses a philosophic and comprehensive grasp of great movements in history and a light, graceful touch in making the past live again." He "is not a mob orator [but] can hold the attention of an audience and impress his thought upon it." Ferris describes "his self-possession and perfect command of himself upon the platform and . . . his quiet, easy manner of speaking, his well modulated voice and his delightful flow of words." However, while the mantle of Frederick Douglass had fallen on Du Bois, "he lacked the magnetism to gather . . . his race around him, lacked the fire and the force to electrify vast crowds, and lacked the generalship to bind the masses together."[28]

Historian and English professor J. Saunders Redding remembers hearing Du Bois speak in 1922 or 1923. Redding describes a careful, meticulous person, with a daintiness that did not fit the popular concept of a dynamic leader. He had a delicately structured, clear, clipped voice, a "probing, deliberate, impersonal light[,] like sparks struck off from tempered steel." However, there was "nothing of radiance; nothing mercurial, magnetic, gay," as by temperament he was "reserved, even aloof." While noting that his addresses were usually brilliant and as carefully developed as works of art, his delivery was "deadpan, in-taking (as if he must reappraise his utterances), not out-going." He has been called a dull platform speaker, "because he has no oratorical flair, because he never talks down to an audience, and because audiences are what they are."[29]

In the introduction to the scholar-activist's collected speeches in 1970, historian Philip S. Foner writes that Du Bois was a frequent fixture on the lecture platform, always linking the subject of the hour with the special problems facing black people around the world. Foner notes that while he was "no impassioned orator," he spoke in the "same clear, beautiful and dignified prose [as his] writings." His speeches "always had a remarkable effect on the listener." Foner also quotes the *Manchester Guardian* on a speech in London in 1911, where Du Bois spoke "with astonishing mastery, lucidity and perfection of phrase." The newspaper noted that "the manner was spontaneous yet every sentence was in place[,] an example of oratory exactly suited to its purpose."[30]

Novelist Henry Miller, who was grateful to Du Bois for publishing his first article, once heard him address a largely Jewish audience on the Lower East Side in New York. He remembers an impeccable diction, vast erudition, and "a challenging, straightforward way of speaking which won me over . . . immediately." When Du Bois came to the platform, he had "the air of a sovereign mounting his throne," and his very majesty silenced any demonstration. There was no "rabble-rouser in this leonine figure—such tactics were beneath him [but his words] were like cold dynamite." Miller writes that "he could have set off an explosion that would rock the world," but instead wanted to leave the audience "stunned rather than moved to action." Miller regrets that Du Bois lacked the passionate spirit, the touch of fanaticism of a John Brown.[31]

Following his talk in Hammond, Du Bois exchanged several letters with Kuhn. Referring to their visit with her father, Julius Stieglitz, who was Chairman of the Chemistry Department at the nearby University of Chicago, Du Bois wrote that he had "enjoyed tremendously the music at the University, the ride in the Ford and the experiences of Hammond." Continuing their warm communication, he said "it was a privilege to meet your father." She asked Du Bois for his photograph, knowing how busy he was, to "give us the added inspiration of a tangible bit of yourself in our lives."[32]

After Kuhn received his picture, with the lecture and visit still in mind, she wrote him about the "spiritual entity grown inside of me like a blossom in fertile soil." The impact "will ever reach deeper & further into the far corners of thot [*sic*] and feeling." She also thanked him for printing an article she had written. The anonymous essay, "The Truth Shall Make You Free," (the author "A White Woman,") appeared in the April 1926 issue of *The Crisis*. The deep feelings she described a year earlier about the article to A. G. Dill, the magazine's Business Manager, had now come forth. The printed story related in a very personal way the question of whether race prejudice is instinctive and incompatible, or acquired and artificial. In her letter, she said her friends were "surprised at my ability to boil such complex feelings down [to] the elemental crystals of fact."[33]

Kuhn later wrote an especially moving letter to Du Bois on the letterhead of the Chicago Lying-in Hospital, as she recuperated from a difficult Cesarean section. She expressed concern that she would not be able to attend the upcoming NAACP convention in Chicago. Even while convalescing, she sought to arrange a talk in Hammond or nearby Gary by Walter White, the organization's Assistant Secretary and an author she admired. She also conveyed her regards to "Johnson." Her reference was to James Weldon Johnson, NAACP Secretary during those years, who would speak at the Hammond Forum in 1927 and again in 1933.[34]

While the immediate reasons for Kuhn's correspondence were the Open Forum and Du Bois' work, she also expressed deep feelings to him about her children. It was her "proud hope to build the foundation of clear sweet thinking and feeling in these little souls so they can later enrich themselves at the hearths of many nations and many races." She was grateful, for "you have given me new strength and vision . . . the foundation is laid true and strong." She asked to contribute her energy and effort "to the great evolution."[35]

Writing in *The Crisis* after his visit to Hammond, Du Bois reflected about "my annual pilgrimage to see The Problem at first hand." He had traveled "nine hundred miles over land and river, by field and village, city and town, through poverty and wealth, smoke and sunshine, across the vale of the Mississippi, through Ohio, Indiana, Illinois and Missouri . . . to Oklahoma." On such trips, he always felt "the thrill" in entering the land of slavery.

It was like the nerves in a plunge in icy waters. But I knew the afterglow would come. For who am I that should write of Negro problems and never know in my own body the "Jim Crow" car and street car, the black ghetto, the world "for colored" and "for white", the separate schools and streets and theatres, and Twin Worlds?[36]

Throughout his life, Du Bois lectured in many communities, both through the Open Forum and on other platforms. The speeches brought needed income for his family, research, and global activism. They extended a broader perspective on race and religious relations in different regions, and spread his message, unfiltered, deeper into the country.

His personal correspondence and reports to NAACP members in *The Crisis* convey his appreciation of warm welcomes in homes and the impact he had on a wide range of people. Nor was the 1926 visit his last contact with Kuhn. In a 1940 letter on peonage in Georgia, an Ohio pastor wrote Du Bois, "you may recall that I visited you something like a year or two ago with Dr. Hedwig Kuhn."[37]

The scholar-activist profoundly moved Kuhn, Weiss and Bretton when he came to Hammond in February 1926. In turn, he was touched by their welcome and the knowledge of the impact of his visit, similar to "the deep thoughtfulness" with which he was received during his cross-country lecture tour in May 1923. The solid human relationships that developed during his appearance in Hammond can also be viewed in the context of the wider African American-Jewish American interactions in the Harlem Renaissance of the 1920s.[38]

In recapturing the 1926 visit to "this difficult industrial district," the Open Forum is now seen from the double perspectives of engendering social justice and human relations during a turbulent period in American history and in the personal life of the scholar-activist. In 1928, on the twentieth anniversary of the lecture movement, Du Bois wrote that he had "spoken many times before Forums in all parts of the East, Middle and Far West." He had found the movement "the straightest step toward practical, intelligent democracy that is being taken today." In 1937, Kuhn characterized the people who came to the lectures as a "sturdy core of thinking, fact seeking citizens." Without Du Bois referring specifically to the Hammond visit, the time he spent in the city was surely proof of his 1928 statement that "the Open Forum in America is one of the few bright and reassuring spots."

NOTES

1. Of the many studies on Du Bois, David L. Lewis's two-volume work, *W. E. B. Du Bois; Biography of a Race, 1868–1919*, (New York: Henry Holt, 1993), and *W.*

E. B. Du Bois; The Fight for Equality and the American Century, 1919–1963, (New York: Henry Holt, 2000), is the most thorough. However, while he conveys the large individual and organization aspects of Du Bois' life and career, he does not examine the public lectures at the local community level.

Radora Susan Drummer, in *Transformational Leadership in the Life of W. E. B. Du Bois, 1900–1930* (Ph.D. diss., Michigan State University, 1995), applies that theory of positive group change to the scholar-activist's visionary, intellectual, inspirational, and shared leadership. Although Drummer does not look at the local lecture circuit, she writes that "he was able to exercise transformational leadership characteristics more perfectly in his role as a public servant to the masses." (335) This insight suggests a focus for future research on his community presentations. As shown by his impact in Hammond, on both the human relations level and as an Open Forum lecturer, the educated, liberal white middle class in the country might be viewed in a similar focus to the "masses."

2. The city's population grew from 36,004 to 65,559 in the 1920s. U.S. Department of Commerce, Bureau of Foreign and Domestic Commerce *Statistical Abstract of the United States*, 1935, (Washington, D.C.: 1935), 22–23; *Fourteenth Census of the United States Taken in the Year 1920*, vol. 3, *Population 1920 Comparison and Characteristics*, (Washington, D.C., 1922), 304; *Smith's Directory of Hammond, Indiana and West Hammond, Illinois, 1923–1924*, (Dorchester, Massachusetts: Smith Publishing, 1923), 21; telephone interview by writer, Arthur Friedman, Munster, Indiana, 24 November 1996; Hammond Chamber of Commerce, *Pep-In-Calumet*, 27 October 1924.

3. In the extensive literature on Du Bois, the role of organizations in his activities has received special attention. See Francis L. Broderick, *William E. B. Du Bois; Negro Leader in a Time of Crisis*, (Stanford: Stanford University Press,1959), 55–118; Elliott M. Rudwick, *William E. B. Du Bois: Propagandist of the Negro Protest*, (Philadelphia: University of Pennsylvania Press, 1960, 2nd edition 1968), 148, 304; John A. Martin, Jr., *A Study of Two Contrasting Types of American Negro Leadership; Booker T. Washington and William E. B. Du Bois*, (Omaha: Municipal University of Omaha, M.A. thesis, 1962), 89–105; August Meier, *Negro Thought in America, 1880–1915; Racial Ideologies in the Age of Booker T. Washington*, (Ann Arbor: University of Michigan Press, 1963), 190–206; William Toll, *The Resurgence of Race; Black Social Theory from Reconstruction to the Pan-American Conference*, (Philadelphia: Temple University Press, 1979), 145–59; Joseph P. De Marco, *The Social Thought of William E. B. Du Bois*, (Lanham, Maryland: University Press of America, 1983), 63–103; Manning Marable, *William E. B. Du Bois; Black Radical Democrat*, (Boston: G. K. Hall, 1986; Boulder, Colorado: Paradigm Publishers, 2005), 52–98.

4. "Niagara Movement," *Dictionary of American History*, 5: 92–93. The social distance between the educated and less educated segments in the Niagara Movement, coupled with Du Bois' inexperience as a social action leader, is described most completely in Elliott Rudwick, "The Niagara Movement," *Journal of Negro History*, (July 1957) 17:177–200; repr., August Meier and Elliott Rudwick, eds., *The Making of Black America; Essays in Negro Life and History—The Black Community in Modern America*, (New York: Atheneum, 1969), 2:131–48.

5. Appointed Director of Publicity and Research of the NAACP in 1910, Du Bois had the title changed to Director of Publications and Research in a reorganization meeting in December 1914. Charles F. Kellogg, *NAACP; A History of the National Association for the Advancement of Colored People, 1909–1920*, (Baltimore: Johns Hopkins Press, 1967), 1: 91, 100; Lewis, *W. E. B. Du Bois; Biography of a Race*, 406, 497.

6. Charles F. Kellogg, "The NAACP and *The Crisis*," in Rayford W. Logan, ed., *W. E. B. Du Bois; A Profile*, (New York: Hill and Wang, 1971), 146, 153.

7. Ibid., 146, 153; James W. Johnson, *Along This Way; The Autobiography of James Weldon Johnson*, (New York: Viking Press, 1933; repr. 1968), 203–204; Du Bois, *Dusk of Dawn; An Essay Toward an Autobiography of a Race Concept*, (New York: Harcourt, Brace, 1940), 303.

8. Kellogg, "The NAACP and *The Crisis*," 139.

9. Du Bois, "Opinion," *The Crisis; A Record of the Darker Races*, May 1923, 7.

10. *The Papers of W. E. B. Du Bois*, (Sanford, NC: Microfilming Corp. of America, 1980–1981; repr. Ann Arbor, Michigan: University Microfilms, 1986), reels 15–19, 77–78, hereafter Du Bois *Papers*.

11. Du Bois, "Opinion," 8–9.

12. Ibid.

13. Du Bois, *Dusk of Dawn*, 225, 295.

14. Kuhn's father, Julius Stieglitz, was born Jewish in New Jersey and educated in Germany where he met his future wife, who was a liberal Christian. In 1892, he began a long tenure in teaching chemistry at the University of Chicago. He became a leading researcher and played an important role in the defense effort during World War I. His brother was Alfred Stieglitz, the renowned photographer. The 1914 exhibition was "the first anywhere to present African sculpture 'as a medium of art expression' rather than an object of ethnographic interest." Richard Whelan, *Alfred Stieglitz; A Biography* (Boston: Little, Brown, 1995), 336. Biographical information on the family is found in "Julius Oscar Stieglitz," Leo M. Glassmann, ed., *Biographical Encyclopedia of American Jews*, (New York: M. Jacobs & L.M. Glassmann, 1935), 534; "Julius (Oscar) Stieglitz," *Who Was Who in America*, 1187; "Julius Stieglitz," *Dictionary of American Biography*, Suppl. 2, 11:630–31; "Julius Stieglitz," *American National Biography*, 20:767–68; Sue D. Lowe, *Stieglitz; A Memoir/Biography*, (New York: Farrar Straus Giroux, 1983), 92.

15. Letter, Hedwig S. Kuhn, Hammond, Indiana, to Dr. W. E. B. Du Bois, New York, New York, 13 May 1925, Du Bois *Papers*, reel 16. (Because of variations in inside addresses and signatures, subsequent citations to correspondence will be "Kuhn," "Du Bois," and "Bretton.")

16. Ibid.

17. "Colored Editor Asks Welcoming Hand For Negro," *Lake County Times*, 24 February 1926, 1; "A Cross Blazed In Every Park Of Hammond," *Lake County Times*, 5 November 1924, 1.

18. Letter, Du Bois to Bretton, 25 September 1925, *Papers*, reel 16.

19. Du Bois *Papers*, reels 15–19; *The Crisis* (September 1925–February 1926), passim; letter to writer, 18 August 2011, Robert S. Cox, Head, Special Collections & University Archives, W. E. B. Du Bois Library.

20. Du Bois *Papers*, reel 77; telegram, Kathleen Foss, NY, to W. E. B. Du Bois, in care of Max Bretton, Hammond, Indiana, 23 February 1926, Du Bois *Papers*, reel 19.

21. Letter, Bretton to Du Bois, 9 October 1925, Du Bois *Papers*, reel 16; letter to writer, Linda Seidman, Special Collections & Archives, University Library, University of Massachusetts at Amherst, 2 February 1993.

22. Flier, Temple Center, Temple Ohabei Shalom, Brookline, Massachusetts, 10 January 1926; Open Forum Speakers Bureau, Chicago Office, Instructions for Engagement at Detroit Forum on 7 February 1926, Du Bois *Papers*, reel 19; letter, Walter A. Smith, Huntington, West Virginia, to Dr. W. E. B. Du Bois, New York, NY, 10 January 1926; letter, W. E. B. Du Bois, New York, NY, to Walter A. Smith, Huntington, West Virginia, 20 January 1926; letter to writer, 30 January 2007, James E. Casto Local History Room, Cabell County Public Library, Huntington, West Virginia.

23. "The Beth El Lecture Course," *Lake County Times*, 6 November 1925, 4.

24. "Noted Colored Editor Next On Program, *Lake County Times*, 23 February 1926, 1.

25. "Colored Editor Asks Welcoming Hand For Negro," *Lake County Times*, 24 February 1926, 1.

26. "Colored Races Of World In Ferment," *Boston Globe*, 13 December 1920, 14; "The Future of the Darker Races" as a speech is not included in Herbert Aptheker, ed., *Annotated Bibliography of the Published Writings of W. E. B. Du Bois* (Millwood, New York: Kraus-Thomson Organization, 1973), or in Paul Partington, ed., *W. E. B. Du Bois: A Bibliography of His Published Writings* (Whittier, California: Partington, 1977; rev. 1979). It is also not in the *Papers* that are being digitalized. Letter, Robert S. Cox.

27. W. E. B. Du Bois, "Worlds of Color," *Foreign Affairs*, (April 1925), 3:423–44. William P. Bundy, "The History of *Foreign Affairs;* Notes on the History of *Foreign Affairs* (1994), writes: "From the first, true to its credo, the magazine showed itself hospitable to authors who might not have been considered in the mainstream. One of these, a personal friend of Armstrong, was the distinguished African-American intellectual W. E. B. Du Bois, whose first of five *Foreign Affairs* articles, in 1925, defined the 'Color Line' as the key problem of the twentieth century. [Hamilton Fish Armstrong managed the New York City office and publishing operations of the journal.] Coolidge was delighted with this article, commenting (as Armstrong recalled in his memoir) that this was partly because it made him 'squirm under the conclusions.' [Archibald Cary Coolidge edited the publication from Harvard University, where he taught.] Other issues of race and colonialism were frequently covered." http://www.cfr.org/about/history/foreign_affairs.html (accessed August 6, 2011).

28. William H. Ferris, *The African Abroad, or His Evolution in Western Civilization, Tracing His Development Under Caucasian Milieu*, (New Haven, Connecticut: The Tuttle, Morehouse & Taylor Press, 1913; repr. New York: Johnson Reprint Corporation, 1968), 2:910–11.

29. J. Saunders Redding, "Portrait . . . W. E. Burghardt Du Bois," in William L. Andrews, ed., *Critical Essays on W. E. B. Du Bois*, (Boston; G. K. Hall, 1985; repr. *American Scholar* (Winter 1948–49), 18:93–96, 23–27.

30. Philip S. Foner, ed., *W. E. B. Du Bois Speaks; Speeches and Addresses, 1890–1919* (New York: Pathfinder Press, 1970), 1:8–10.

31. Henry Miller, *The Rosy Crucifixion, Book Two: Plexus* (New York: Grove Press, 1963, 1965), 559–66.

32. Letters, Du Bois to Kuhn, 11 March 1926; Kuhn to Du Bois, 13 March 1926, Du Bois *Papers*, reel 19; "Julius Stieglitz," *Who Was Who in America*, 1187.

33. Letter, Kuhn to Du Bois, undated, Du Bois *Papers*, reel 19; A White Woman [author is "Anonymous"], "The Truth Shall Make You Free," *Crisis*, April 1926, 296–97; letter, Kuhn to A. G. Dill, 23 June 1925, ibid., Du Bois *Papers*, reel 19. Even though the writer is anonymous, the feelings, writing style, and subject of the essay, a medical student discovering the roots of prejudice, point to Kuhn.

34. Letter, Kuhn to Du Bois, 3 June 1926, Du Bois *Papers*, reel 19; brochures, *Beth-El Open Forum, Fourth Season 1927–28*, and *Hammond Open Forum, Season 1933–34*.

35. Letter, Kuhn to Du Bois, undated, Du Bois *Papers*, reel 19. The letter was possibly written in March 1926 as Kuhn says that she is expecting a child in a few months.

36. Du Bois, "Opinion," *The Crisis*, April 1926, 267–68.

37. Letter, Rev. Donald L. West, Bethel, Ohio, to Du Bois, 23 March 1940, *The Correspondence of W. E. B. Du Bois, Selections, 1934–1944*, vol. 2, edited by Herbert Aptheker (Amherst, Massachusetts: University of Massachusetts Press, 1976), 228–29.

38. David L. Lewis, *When Harlem Was in Vogue* (New York: Oxford University Press, 1981), Chapter 4, "Enter the New Negro," passim.

Chapter Seven

Looking Ahead

An America To Be

The vision and commitment of the founder of the Open Forum, the administrative skills and idealism of the secretary who was *not* "all but absent from history," two courageous communities in Klan-ridden Indiana, and the strong interrelations impact of a visit by the leading African American scholar-activist of the period convey the essence of this public lecture movement. Understanding the initiative provides fresh insight into the nation's history and broadens our awareness of personal and community courage, democratic planning, and broad-based learning. The fact that the movement came to 200 to 300 cities for various periods of time, during the first decades of the twentieth century, ensures there is much to discover. Even when a series did not continue past the initial introduction of the concept, newspaper reports and other records await researchers in local libraries and archives.

The roots of most of the Ford Hall Forum leaders in Boston developed in middle-class, Protestant, Victorian America. They went beyond their personal pasts, sharing a faith in the centrality of every individual and self-improvement. They recognized a growing societal interdependence. Leaders in other cities might have different backgrounds, and participants would range from longtime residents to recent immigrants or the working class, but they all held to the same democratic faith.

The leaders, whether in Boston or Indiana, also recognized the cruel and unjust belief in society that individuals can rely solely on their talents to control their fate. Such a certainty was no longer possible in industrializing, class-defining America. For this reason, the forward-looking founders, as well as other clergy and lay leaders in the local communities, might very well be considered "progressives." George Babbitt could complain: "All talk and discussion—Lord! Sitting there—sitting there—night after night—not wanting to do anything." He missed the point that his daughter and the audience at the lectures had begun a different journey at the beginning of the new century.

With the nation's socio-economic engine changing, historian David B. Danbom notes, church attendance and a sense of community declined. An increasing number of Americans felt a loss of autonomy and community, and so formed new groups to gain a sense of kinship and a feeling of efficacy. Coleman developed the Open Forum and Crawford and others implemented it around the country at exactly the right time to meet this need.[1]

What was evolving in the larger national sphere during this period, historian John C. Burnham writes, was an idealism marked by "the juxtaposition of a practical piecemeal approach to reform with a religious or quasi-religious vision of democracy." This "progressive ethos"—*not* "Progressivism"—is perhaps the clearest way to set the movement in historiographical context. In addition to the leaders believing in the power of public learning and the ability of the participants to shape their own lives (to some extent), they held to a very broad and inclusive approach to social problems. It was all made possible through a very American agency, a voluntary organization. Small-town virtues such as decency and brotherhood were transformed into a weekly gathering of neighbors—really a sense of family—whether in the thousand-seat Ford Hall auditorium or the basement social hall of a Jewish congregation in northwest Indiana, with one hundred folding chairs.[2]

In addition to the publicity acumen of Coleman and Crawford, the growth of the movement coincided with the rise of factual, impersonal reporting in newspapers. Julius Chambers, managing editor of the *New York Herald* and *New York World*, recounted some years later, all that was wanted was "Facts; facts; nothing but facts." Nelson Crawford, in his 1924 text, *The Ethics of Journalism*, held that newspaper inaccuracies and reporters giving the most space to those who provided "typed copies of speeches [and] ready-prepared interviews," encouraged the use of public relations specialists by organizations. Coleman and Crawford, with their clear understanding of the role of public relations in the new era, skillfully led the way. In 1912, Coleman wrote "there is no force in the world today more potent and far reaching than the force generated by rightly directed publicity." He was far ahead of his time when he urged that in "these new and reorganizing times," the press and the church—"two great agencies of democracy"—should cooperate. A new spirit was at work, with religion seeing the importance of social service and the press seeking determinant factors.[3]

As the two leaders provided the national model, local programs copied their techniques. Newspaper reports from many cities, particularly when Coleman was speaking at the opening program, reflect the national movement in the rhythm of the language and often the exact words. The goal of the local planners was to repeat the success of Ford Hall and the national movement in their community. They followed the model that was successful in Boston—broad-based local leadership, involvement of socially progressive clergy, articulate and often controversial speakers, the right moderator, and well-crafted publicity, both before and after the talks.

In addition to the readiness of newspapers to use the press releases and follow-up reports, the Open Forum had one other fortunate circumstance. It became a connection between the middle class and information (although not social action) and between the middle and working class and the "story ideal." It was not entertainment but rather an intellectual expansion of open-mindedness that took the audience away from the repetitive grind of home and work responsibilities and past the racial and religious barriers that were dividing the country. Especially after World War I, as faith in democracy began to lose out to fears of unreason—"the urban masses, the immigrants, the Jews"—national and local Forum leaders hewed to a different path. They sought a more hopeful, neighborly community, locally and nationally, no matter what was happening around it. In the Open Forum, the fraternal spirit envisioned by Walter Rauschenbusch met the neighborly community of John Dewey.[4]

As the movement had the potential to cross into Christian socialism, it is fruitful to explore why it did not move in that direction. The primarily Protestant founders of the Open Forum drew their inspiration from social justice ideals that all faiths were wrestling with but their approach was from an ethical rather than a theological or secular ideological basis. The national and local planners, most of the lecturers, and likely the majority of people who attended, whether they were traditionally religious or not, supported some structural changes in society.

But they did not want to overthrow the system entirely. They believed that justice could be established on earth through reform of the system. Just as most Social Gospel leaders maintained that justice could be achieved short of social reconstruction, so did the leaders of the Open Forum, national and local, ally themselves with a progressive/liberal agenda rather than socialism. Historian Jacob H. Dorn writes that one criterion for being categorized a Christian Socialist during this time was to support a concrete program of structural changes in the public sector. In 1915, minister and social justice advocate Harry Ward spoke at Ford Hall on "The Challenge of Socialism to Christianity," but his message was to bring "this great vision of the City of God . . . to be with us on the earth." Some day, by our actions, "there shall be upon this earth the land of peace and brotherhood and righteousness."[5]

While the movement did not make the shift into Christian Socialism, it did have elements of another perspective, the concept of "direct democracy." As political scientist David Held describes this model, direct democracy must be local and limited in numbers, and the social positions of the participants must not differ greatly from each other. The administrative functions must be relatively simple and stable and there must be a certain minimum development of training in objectively determining ways and means.[6]

Applying Held's formulation, the "Ford Hall Folks" and participants in other cities exemplified some aspects of the idea of direct democracy. In Boston and in the two Indiana cities, the movement was local, with relatively simple and stable administrative functions. As attendance was very large in Boston, the "Ford Hall Folks" consciously developed smaller group social and intellectual activities, seeking a greater sense of fellowship. Thanks to Crawford's writings on how communities could conduct successful Forums, booklets from the national office, and regional meetings, local committees were able to use the Ford Hall model. Minimal training was needed to work out ways and means. A central booking bureau was available, but some local committees, such as in Hammond, used their awareness of community, national and international issues, as well as personal contacts, to seek thought-provoking speakers on their own.

However, the direct democracy formulation of Held fails in one crucial way, and that is the social positions of Forum participants differed greatly from each other. This was the result of intentionally aiming to attract immigrants and a wide range of working people. The planners would also not seek to resolve value conflicts in the public process. They knew that democracy does not presuppose agreement on diverse values. Indeed, unanimity of opinion would have been anathema to Coleman's vision and the goals of the local planners. Their concern was the process.

In writing about the "Open Forum" in 2002—*not* the historical Forum movement—psychologist Arnold Mindell observes that the range of people, roles and feelings creates a "guesthouse attitude toward whatever comes to the door of one's attention." Although not referring to the lecture movement of a century earlier, Mindell views an Open Forum as a kind of "flu shot," in which the microcosm of society at a lecture receives a little flu to protect against greater harm. Open Forums, he writes, "tend to prevent violence by giving folks a bit of the potential trouble in the form of energetic discussion." (It is intriguing to see the same insight a century later that Coleman articulated.)[7]

Philosopher Judith M. Green carries this insight further in examining the thought of Jane Addams and other radical women of her generation. Green emphasizes that Addams realized a "commitment to democracy requires including *different voices* within processes of social inquiry." The social reformer believed that the "*social inquiry process must include as equals those affected by its results* if it is to . . . advance the transformative deepening of democracy." Effective social inquiry must involve expert, democratically minded social scientists and "*the whole diverse democratic communities.*" [Emphasis in original.] While not mentioning the historical Open Forum movement, Green ties in a concept of John Dewey to make her point, that "the quality of citizen-to-citizen conversation is of crucial significance in the development of deep democracy."[8]

Why was the Forum movement so important to the national and local planners, the hundreds of lecturers who traveled to distant cities, and the thousands of people who attended?

In 1920, law professor Zechariah Chafee, Jr., used the challenge of John Milton's *Areopagitica* in 1644 to frame the importance of the discovery and spread of truth in society. Milton asked, "who ever knew Truth put to the worse, in a free and open encounter?" Chafee said truth is "possible only through absolutely unlimited discussion." If Americanism means anything concrete, he wrote, it is tolerance for opinions widely different from our own, however objectionable they are. We have got to take risks: "Democracy is not a water-tight compartment." Rather, it is a great adventure and in order to prepare people for that adventure, they have to think for themselves on the problems of society. We must not simply teach the ideals of today; we must train Americans to make the ideals of tomorrow.[9]

In 1926, Everett Dean Martin, who was at the time directing the People's Institute at Cooper Union, where Coleman first conceived the Open Forum, wrote that education is a "spiritual revaluation of human life." The true task is to reorient the individual, to take a richer, more significant view of experiences. The goal is to be placed above, not within one's system of beliefs and ideals. Education had to be liberalizing, freeing the mind from the servitude of the crowd and self-interest—a perfect description of the Forum ideal.[10]

The Open Forum lecture movement had been acting on the principles enunciated by Chafee and Martin since 1908. Crawford, in her tribute to the movement on its twentieth anniversary, recognized that it is not until free speech begins to be denied, and open discussion at meetings threatened, that Coleman's contributions are recognized. "There has got into the community consciousness a firmly rooted idea that the way to arrive at truth is to have all sides of a question sincerely represented . . . and then give to the people in the audience a chance to gain further information about any given subject through that delightful forum necessary, the question period." She concluded that the Forum is a great contribution to Boston, to the nation, and to her as an individual.[11]

Beyond the movement's founders, personal letters from those who attended or spoke at the lectures convey the impact. On the fifth anniversary of the Ford Hall Forum, fifteen-year-old Philip Sagerman of nearby Cambridge, in his neatly hand-written, four-page letter, said the speakers "infuse a new spirit . . . to do our share in bettering our social and economic conditions." He added that my "enthusiasm reaches its zenith when a forceful question is asked and the speaker is in doubt how to answer it."[12]

Coleman and Crawford often quoted Russian Jewish immigrant Freda Rogolsky, who, in her own words, was transformed by the Forum into an American. In her 1913 letter, she wrote that the lectures "could be compared to the 'melting pot,' where we all come together, forgetting all prejudices, and are brothers listening to how we may better the conditions and make this world a better place." In her heartfelt words, "to think that we can have from the same platform a woman interested in schools, a Jewish Rabbi, a Christian minister, a Socialist, a Chinese woman, and a Jewish Philanthropist next week is more than I can understand."[13]

Other contributors to the two testimonial albums had either spoken at Ford Hall or were in comparable work and knew the value of the Forum approach. In 1913, Robert A. Woods, who had established the South End settlement house in the city, noted the marked change that had come to the area, with more tolerance and open debate. He credited Ford Hall as one of the chief influences of this societal change. In 1928, Will Durant, who had begun bringing forward his ten-volume, 9,000–page magnum opus, *The Story of Civilization*, called Coleman "one of the great educators of America."[14]

And the founder of the movement never lost his ability to envision a better future. In 1936, when Coleman was 69 years old, and had retired from the Ford Hall Forum and Babson Institute, he saw that:

> In auto and airplane we demolish time and space. With motion pictures we can see everything the world around. By radio we can talk across oceans and continents. Television is on its way. . . . The world is growing smaller and smaller. The universe is ever expanding to our astonished gaze.[15]

One final understanding of the Open Forum movement, without referring specifically to it, is found in a 1985 study by political scientist Robert Bellah and colleagues. They write about the importance of civic virtue, and ask if we can become citizens again, and seek together "the common good in the postindustrial, postmodern age?"[16]

The challenge is before us. Can twenty-first century Americans slow down in the fast-changing electronic universe and seek this perspective? Can the informed, reflective, respectful framework of the Great Books discussion method, Great Decisions foreign affairs discussions, and National Issues Forums on domestic issues spread further? Might the approach developed by Coleman in 1908 cross today's socio-economic barriers to local community meetings, into radio and television, through computer connections? Can we achieve the ideal, envisioned by poet Archibald MacLeish in 1939, of an America to be?

The visionary founders, courageous local planners, and thousands of participants in the Open Forum lecture movement have provided a path. Coleman said in 1920, "In a democracy, we cannot and will not take our ideas handed down from 'those up there,' but express our own thoughts even if they prove to be wrong." Hedwig Kuhn described in 1937 the reward of "Opinions differing, challenges being met with facts, . . . all angles being brought in, no . . . restrictions . . . ."[17]

The history and method of the movement have been recovered. If concerned Americans will it, the spirit can be recaptured. The final image of the Open Forum evoked by Herring—*the striking of mind upon mind*—is a model for public learning and civil discourse today.

NOTES

1. David B. Danbom, *"The World of Hope," Progressives and the Struggle for an Ethical Public Life* (Philadelphia: Temple University, 1987), 5–26.

2. John C. Burnham in John D. Buenker, John C. Burnham and Robert M. Crunden, *Progressivism* (Cambridge, Massachusetts: Schenkman Publishing, 1977), 4–16.

3. Michael Schudson, *Discovering the News; A Social History of American Newspapers* (New York: Basic Books, 1978), 77–85, 137–38; Coleman, *The Church and the Press*, 4–9.

4. Schudson, *Discovering the News*, 90, 131.

5. Jacob H. Dorn, "The Oldest and Youngest of the Idealist Forces at Work in Our Civilization," in Jacob H. Dorn, *Socialism and Christianity in Early 20th Century America* (Westport, Connecticut: Greenwood, 1998), 25, and "Introduction," xii; Harry Ward, "The Challenge of Socialism to Christianity," *Ford Hall Folks* (22 March 1914, Vol. II, Number 22), Scrapbooks, 4.

6. David Held, *Models of Democracy*, 2nd edition (Stanford: Stanford University Press, 1987, 1996), 163.

7. Arnold Mindell, *The Deep Democracy of Open Forums* (Charlottesville, Virginia: Hampton Roads Publishing, 2002), vii, 147.

8. Judith M. Green, *Deep Democracy; Community, Diversity, and Transformation* (Lanham, Maryland: Rowman & Littlefield, 1999), 42, 44, 78, 83.

9. Zechariah Chafee, Jr., *Freedom of Speech* (New York: Harcourt, Brace and Howe, 1920), 1, 34, 227, 376.

10. Everett D. Martin, *The Meaning of a Liberal Education* (New York: W. W. Norton, 1926), viii.

11. Crawford, letter to David K. Niles, Associate Director, Ford Hall Forum, 9 April 1928, Coleman Memorabilia, Babson.

12. Philip Sagerman letter, n.d., *Ford Hall Folks to George W. Coleman*, Babson.

13. Freda Rogolsky, quoted in *Ford Hall Folks*, Vol. 1, No. 10, 2 March 1913, 7, Scrapbooks, 4.

14. Letters, Robert A. Woods, Boston, to Coleman, Boston, 15 February 1913, *Ford Hall Folks to George William Coleman*, and Will Durant, New York City, to Coleman, Boston, 29 March 1928, *Letters of Appreciation*, Babson.

15. Coleman, *This Business of Living*, 59.

16. Bellah, et al, *Habits of the Heart*, 270–71.

17. "Forum Movement Has Auspicious Opening," *Terre Haute Tribune*, 15 November 1920; Kuhn, "Time Again for Open Forum."

Selected Bibliography

PRIMARY SOURCES

Amherst, University of Massachusetts, Papers of W. E. B. Du Bois. (Searched on microfilm; in process of digitalization.)

Babson Park, Massachusetts, Babson College Archives.

———. Coleman Memorabilia.

———. Ford Hall Folks to George W. Coleman, February 23, 1908–1913 (Testimonial Album).

———. Letters of Appreciation to George W. Coleman, Ford Hall Forum, 1908–1928 (Testimonial Album).

Boston, Boston Public Library. Ford Hall Forum Collection.

Cambridge, Massachusetts, Schlesinger Library, Radcliffe Institute, Harvard University. Radcliffe College Archives.

Rochester, New York, American Baptist-Samuel Colgate Historical Library and Archives, American Baptist Historical Society. (The collection has been moved to Mercer University.)

———. Ford Hall Scrapbooks.

———. George W. Coleman Alpha File.

———. Rauschenbusch Family Papers.

———. Sagamore Sociological Conference Files.

SECONDARY SOURCES

Ahlstrom, Sidney E. *A Religious History of the American People*, New York: Doubleday, 1975.

Alpern, Sara, et al, *The Challenge of Feminist Biography; Writing the Lives of Modern American Women*. Urbana: University of Illinois Press, 1992.

American Association for Adult Education. *Handbook of Adult Education in the United States.* New York: American Association for Adult Education, 1934.

Andrews, William L. ed. *Critical Essays on W. E. B. Du Bois.* Boston: G. K. Hall, 1985.

Antler, Joyce. *The Educated Woman and Professionalization; The Struggle for a New Feminine Identity, 1890–1920.* New York: Garland Publishing, 1987.

———. *Lucy Sprague Mitchell; The Making of a Modern Woman.* New Haven: Yale University Press, 1987.

Aptheker, Herbert, ed. *Annotated Bibliography of the Published Writings of W. E. B. Du Bois.* Millwood, New York: Kraus-Thomson Organization, 1973.

Atherton, Lewis. *Main Street in the Middle Border.* Bloomington: Indiana University Press, 1954.

Bailey, Gary L. "Losing Ground; Workers and Community in Terre Haute, Indiana, 1875–1935." Ph.D. diss., Indiana University, 1989.

Baker, Ray Stannard. *The Spiritual Unrest.* New York: Frederick A. Stokes, 1910.

Beard, Mary "The Legislative Influence of Unenfranchised Women," in *Women in Public Life,* James P. Lichtenberger, ed., vol. 55. Philadelphia: American Academy of Political and Social Science, 1914.

Beckley, Harlan. *Passion for Justice; Retrieving the Legacies of Walter Rauschenbusch, John A. Ryan, and Reinhold Niebuhr.* Louisville, KY: Westminster John Knox Press, 1992.

Bellah, Robert N., et al. *Habits of the Heart; Individualism and Commitment in American Life.* Berkeley: University of California Press, 1985; New York: Harper & Row, 1986.

Bessette, Joseph M. *The Mild Voice of Reason; Deliberative Democracy and American National Government.* Chicago: University of Chicago Press, 1994.

"Beth-El Social Center Open Forum Course; First Season Program, 1924–25," through "Hammond Open Forum; Nineteenth Season, 1942–1943," brochures, writer's collection.

Betten, Neil. "Nativism and the Klan in Town and City: Valparaiso and Gary, Indiana," *Studies in History and Society,*" vol. 4. Bellingham: Western Washington Press, 1973): 3–16.

Bigham, Darrel E. *We Ask Only A Fair Trial; A History of the Black Community of Evansville, Indiana.* Bloomington: Indiana University Press, 1987.

Bogardus, Emory S. *Democracy by Discussion.* Washington, D.C.: American Council on Public Affairs, 1942.

Brown, Richard D. *The Strength of a People; The Idea of an Informed Citizenry in America, 1650–1870.* Chapel Hill: University of North Carolina Press, 1996.

Brown, William A. *The Church in America; A Study of the Present Condition and Future Prospects of American Protestantism.* New York: Macmillan, 1922.

Buenken, John D., John C. Burnham, and Robert M. Crunden. *Progressivism.* Cambridge, Massachusetts: Schenkman Publishing, 1977.

Carr, Edward H. *What Is History?* New York: Viking, 1964.

Carter, Paul A. *The Decline and Revival of the Social Gospel; Social and Political Liberalism in American Protestant Churches, 1920–1940.* Hamden, CT: Shoe String Press, 1956. Reprint, 1971.

Cartwright, Morse A. *Ten Years of Adult Education; A Report on a Decade of Progress in the American Movement.* New York: Macmillan, 1935.

Chambers-Schiller, Lee. "The Single Woman: Family and Vocation Among Nineteenth-Century Reformers," 335–50, in Mary Kelley, ed., *Woman's Being, Woman's Place; Female Identity and Vocation in American History.* Boston: G. K. Hall, 1979.

Coleman, George W. *The Business of Living.* Boston: Ford Hall Forum, 1936.

———. *The Church and the Press*, vol. 7, *Messages of the Men and Religion Forward Movement.* New York: Funk & Wagnalls, 1912.

———. "The Contribution of the Open Forum to Democracy in Religion," *The Journal of Religion*, 2 (January 1922): 4–5.

———. *Democracy in the Making; Ford Hall and the Open Forum Movement—A Symposium.* Boston: Little, Brown, 1915. Reprint, 1917.

———. *The People's Prayers; Voiced By a Layman.* Philadelphia: Griffith & Rowland, 1914.

Connolly, James J. *The Triumph of Ethnic Progressivism; Urban Political Culture in Boston, 1900–1925.* Cambridge: Harvard University Press, 1998.

Cook, Blanche Wiesen. "Female Support Networks and Political Activism: Lillian Wald, Crystal Eastman, Emma Goldman," originally published in *Chryalis* 3 (1977):43–61. Reprint, Linda K. Kerber and Jane S. DeHart, eds., *Women's America; Refocusing the Past,* 3rd edition. New York: Oxford University, 1991, 306–25.

Cott, Nancy F. *The Grounding of Modern Feminism.* New Haven: Yale University, 1987.

Cowan, Ruth Schwartz. *More Work For Mother; The Ironies of Household Technology From the Open Hearth to the Microwave.* New York: Basic Books, 1983.

Crawford, Mary C. "'The Church's Call'—The Campaign to Date." *The Church Militant* (Episcopal Diocese of Massachusetts) March 1920: 6–7, 15–16.

———. *The College Girl of America; And the Institutions Which Make Her What She Is.* Boston: L.C. Page & Company, 1905.

———. "Getting to the Unchurched in Boston," *The Interior*, January 21, 1909, 40: 71–72.

———. *Goethe And His Woman Friends.* Boston: Little, Brown, 1911.

———. "How Our Women Workers Are Providing For Old Age," *The Survey*, April 10, 1909, 22: 95–99.

———. "New Occupations for Educated Women," *The Outlook*, June 27, 1903, 74: 517–22.

———. "One Way We Might Help the School," *Graduate Bulletin*, Boston School for Social Workers (October 1915): 5–6.

———. *The Romance of Old New England Rooftrees.* Boston: L. C. Page, 1902.

———. "The Story of the Ford Hall Meetings," *Ford Hall Folks*, March 15, 1914.

Curti, Merle. *The Growth of American Thought*, 2nd edition. New York: Harper and Brothers, 1943. Reprint, 1951.

Danbom, David B. *"The World of Hope," Progressives and the Struggle for an Ethical Public Life.* Philadelphia: Temple University Press, 1987.

Davies, Margery W. *Woman's Place Is At the Typewriter; Office Work and Office Workers, 1870–1930.* Philadelphia: Temple University Press, 1982.

Davis, Lawrence B. *Immigrants, Baptists and the Protestant Mind in America.* Urbana: University of Illinois Press, 1973.

Deutsch, Sarah. "Reconceiving the City: Women, Space, and Power in Boston, 1870–1910," *Gender and History*, 6 (2), August 1994: 202–23.

———. *Women and the City; Gender, Space, and Power in Boston, 1870–1940.* New York: Oxford University Press, 2000.

Dewey, John. *The Public and Its Problems.* New York: Holt, 1927. Reprint, Denver: Alan Swallow, 1954.

Diner, Steven J. *A Very Different Age; Americans of the Progressive Era.* New York: Hill and Wang, 1998.

Dorn, Jacob H. *Socialism and Christianity in Early 20th Century America.* Westport, CT: Greenwood, 1998.

Du Bois, William E. B. *The Correspondence of W. E. B. Du Bois, Selections, 1934–1944,* vol. 2. ed. Herbert Aptheker. Amherst: University of Massachusetts Press, 1976.

———. *Dusk of Dawn; An Essay Toward an Autobiography of a Race Concept.* New York: Harcourt, Brace, 1940.

———. "Worlds of Color," *Foreign Affairs*, 3 (April 1925), 423–44.

Dye, Nancy Schrom. *As Equals and Sisters; Feminism, The Labor Movement, and The Women's Trade Union League of New York City.* Columbia: University of Missouri Press, 1980.

Eisenstein, Sarah. *Give Us Bread But Give Us Roses; Working Women's Consciousness in the United States, 1890 to the First World War.* Boston: Routledge and Kegan Paul, 1983.

Ely, Mary L., ed., *Adult Education in Action.* New York: American Association for Adult Education, 1936.

———. *Why Forums?* New York: American Association for Adult Education, 1937.

Emerson, Ralph Waldo. "Self-Reliance" in *Essays*, 37–70. New York: Franklin Watts, 1987.

Ewen, Stuart. *PR! A Social History of Spin.* New York: Basic Books, 1996.

Fagin, Sophia. "Public Forums in Chicago." M.A. diss., University of Chicago, 1939. ("Dissertation" is on title page.)

Ferris, William H. *The African Abroad, or His Evolution in Western Civilization, Tracing His Development Under Caucasian Milieu,* vol. 2. New Haven, Connecticut: The Tuttle, Morehouse & Taylor Press, 1913. Reprint, New York: Johnson Reprint Corporation, 1968.

Foner, Philip S. ed., *W. E. B. Du Bois Speaks; Speeches and Addresses.* Vol. 1, 1890–1919. New York: Pathfinder Press, 1970.

Fisher, Dorothy Canfield. *Why Stop Learning?* New York: Harcourt, Brace, 1927.

Follett, Mary Parker. *The New State; Group Organization the Solution of Popular Government.* Reprint, University Park: Pennsylvania State University Press, 1998. New York: Longmans, Green and Company, 1918.

The Ford Hall Forum; 75 Years of Public Discourse. Boston: Ford Hall Forum, 1982.

Gary, Brett. *The Nervous Liberals; Propaganda Anxieties From World War I To the Cold War*. New York: Columbia University Press, 1999.

Gastil, John and Peter Levine, eds. *The Deliberative Democracy Handbook*. San Francisco: Jossey-Bass, 2005.

Goldstein, Jerrold. "Reform Rabbis and the Progressive Movement." MA thesis, University of Minnesota, 1967.

Gorrell, Donald K. *The Age of Social Responsibility; The Social Gospel in the Progressive Era, 1900–1920*. Macon, GA: Mercer University Press, 1988.

Gordon, Lynn D. *Gender and Higher Education in the Progressive Era*. New Haven: Yale University Press, 1990.

Grattan, Hartley. *In Quest of Knowledge; A Historical Perspective on Adult Education*. New York: Association Press, 1955.

Green, Judith M. *Deep Democracy; Community, Diversity, and Transformation*. Lanham, MD: Rowman & Littlefield, 1999.

Gundersen, Adolf G. *The Socratic Citizen; A Theory of Deliberative Democracy*. Lanham, Maryland: Lexington Books, 2000.

Handy, Robert T. "The American Religious Depression, 1924–1935," *Church History*, 29 (March 1960): 3–4, 13.

Hawley, Ellis W. *The Great War and The Search For a Modern Order; A History of the American People and Their Institutions, 1917–1933*. New York: St. Martin's, 1979.

Held, David. *Models of Democracy*, 2nd ed. Stanford: Stanford University Press, 1987, 1996.

Herring, John W. "The Open Forum," *Adult Bible Class Monthly* (November 1922): 321–22, 325. (Methodist Book Concern).

———. *Social Planning and Adult Education*. New York: Macmillan, 1933.

Herringshaw, Thomas W. *Herringshaw's National Library of American Biography*. Chicago: American Publishers' Association, 1909–1914.

Hewitt, Dorothy and Kirtley F. Mather. *Adult Education; A Dynamic for Democracy*. New York: Appleton-Century, 1937.

Higham, John. *Strangers In the Land; Patterns of American Nativism, 1860–1925*. New York: Atheneum, 1967.

Hofstadter, Richard. *The Age of Reform; From Bryan to F.D.R.* New York: Alfred A. Knopf, 1955.

———. *Anti-Intellectualism in American Life*. New York: Knopf, 1963.

Howard, George E. "Changed Ideals and Status of the Family and the Public Activities of Women," 27–37, in *Women in Public Life*, James P. Lichtenberger, ed., vol. 55. Philadelphia: American Academy of Political and Social Science, 1914.

———. *A History of Matrimonial Institutions*, vol. 3. Chicago: University of Chicago, 1904. Reprint, Humanities Press, 1964.

Howells, Dorothy Ella. *A Century to Celebrate: Radcliffe College, 1879–1979*. Cambridge: Radcliffe College, 1978.

Jacoby, Robin Miller. *The British and American Women's Trade Union Leagues, 1890–1925; A Case Study of Feminism and Class*. Brooklyn, New York: Carlson Publishing, 1994.

Kane, Paula M. *Separatism and Subculture; Boston Catholicism, 1900–1920.* Chapel Hill: University of North Carolina Press, 1994.

Keith, William. *Democracy as Discussion; Civic Education and the American Forum Movement.* Lanham, MD: Rowman & Littlefield Publishers, 2007.

———. "Democratic Revival and the Promise of Cyberspace: Lessons From the Forum Movement," *Rhetoric and Public Affairs,* (2002) 5 (2): 311–26.

Kellogg, Charles F. *NAACP; A History of the National Association for the Advancement of Colored People, 1909–1920,* vol. l. Baltimore: Johns Hopkins Press, 1967.

Kessler-Harris, Alice. *Out to Work; A History of Wage-Earning Women in the United States.* New York: Oxford University Press, 1982.

Kett, Joseph F. *The Pursuit of Knowledge Under Difficulties; From Self-Improvement to Adult Education in America, 1750–1990.* Stanford: Stanford University Press, 1994.

Kloppenberg, James T. *Uncertain Victory; Social Democracy and Progressivism in European and American Thought.* New York: Oxford University Press, 1986.

Kuhn, Hedwig S. "Time Again for Open Forum." *Hammond Business* (Hammond Chamber of Commerce), September 1937, 1.

Lasch, Christopher. *The New Radicalism in America, 1889–1963.* New York: Knopf, 1965.

Lewis, David L. *W. E. B. Du Bois; Biography of a Race, 1868–1919.* New York: Henry Holt, 1993.

———. *W. E. B. Du Bois; The Fight for Equality and the American Century, 1919–1963.* New York: Henry Holt, 2000.

———. *When Harlem Was in Vogue.* New York: Oxford University Press, 1981.

Lewis, Sinclair. *Babbitt.* New York: Harcourt, Brace, 1922.

Levine, Peter. *The New Progressive Era; Toward a Fair and Deliberative Democracy.* Lanham, MD: Rowman & Littlefield, 2000.

Love, Donald M. *Henry Churchill King of Oberlin.* New Haven: Yale University Press, 1956.

Lurie, Reuben L. *The Challenge of the Forum; The Story of Ford Hall and the Open Forum Movement—A Demonstration in Adult Education.* Boston: Richard D. Badger, 1930.

McGiffert, Jr., Arthur C. *No Ivory Tower; The Story of the Chicago Theological Seminary.* Chicago: Chicago Theological Seminary, 1965.

Madison, James H. *Through Tradition and Change; A History of the Hoosier State and Its People, 1920–1945.* Indianapolis: Indiana Historical Society, 1982.

Martin, Theodora Penny. *The Sound of Our Own Voices; Women's Study Clubs, 1860–1910.* Boston: Beacon, 1987.

Mattson, Kevin. *Creating a Democratic Public; The Struggle for Participatory Democracy During the Progressive Era.* University Park: Pennsylvania State University Press, 1998.

Mervis, Leonard Judah. "The Social Justice Movement of the American Reform Rabbis, 1890–1940." Ph.D. diss., University of Pittsburgh, 1951.

Meyer, Donald B. *The Protestant Search for Political Realism, 1919–1941.* Berkeley: University of California Press, 1961.

Meyer, Michael A. *Response to Modernity; A History of the Reform Movement in Judaism.* New York: Oxford University Press, 1988.

Moore, Leonard J. *Citizen Klansmen; The Ku Klux Klan in Indiana, 1921–1928.* Chapel Hill: University of North Carolina Press, 1991.

Milkis, Sidney M. "Progressivism, Then and Now," 1–39, in Sidney M. Milkis and Jerome M. Mileur, eds. *Progressivism and the New Democracy.* Amherst: University of Massachusetts Press, 1999.

Mindell, Arnold. *The Deep Democracy of Open Forums.* Charlottesville, VA: Hampton Roads Publishing, 2002.

Minus, Paul M. *Walter Rauschenbusch; American Reformer.* New York: Macmillan, 1988.

Muncy, Robyn. *Creating a Female Dominion in American Reform, 1890–1935.* New York: Oxford University Press, 1991.

Norwood, Stephen H. *Labor's Flaming Youth; Telephone Operators and Worker Militancy, 1878–1923.* Urbana: University of Illinois Press, 1990.

Paton, Lucy Allen. *Elizabeth Cary Agassiz; A Biography.* Boston: Houghton Mifflin, 1919.

Peffer, Nathaniel. *New Schools For Older Students.* New York: Macmillan, 1926.

Perkins, Agnes F. ed., *Vocations for the Trained Woman; Opportunities Other Than Teaching.* Boston: Women's Educational and Industrial Union, 1910.

Phillips, Clifton J. *Indiana in Transition; The Emergence of an Industrial Commonwealth, 1880–1920.* Indianapolis: Indiana Historical Bureau, 1968.

Posner, Richard A. *Law, Pragmatism, and Democracy.* Cambridge: Harvard University Press, 2003.

Purcell, Richard J. "John A. Ryan, Prophet of Social Justice." *Studies; An Irish Quarterly Review,* 35 (June 1946), 153–75.

Rauschenbusch, Walter. *Christianity and the Social Crisis.* New York: Macmillan, 1907; repr. 1913.

———. *Christianity and the Social Crisis*, ed. Robert D. Cross. New York: Macmillan, 1907. Reprint, New York, Harper & Row, 1964.

———. *Christianizing the Social Order.* New York: Macmillan, 1912; repr. 1915.

Rawls, John. *The Law of Peoples; With "The Idea of Public Reason Revisited."* Cambridge: Harvard University Press, 1999.

Rieser, Andrew C. *The Chautauqua Moment; Protestants, Progressives, and the Culture of Modern Liberalism.* New York: Columbia University Press, 2003.

Rochester, Stuart I. *American Liberal Disillusionment in the Wake of World War I.* University Park: Pennsylvania State University Press, 1977.

Rodgers, Daniel T. *Atlantic Crossings; Social Politics In a Progressive Age.* Cambridge: Harvard University Press, 1998.

Roosevelt, Eleanor "My Day." October 20, 1938, United Feature Syndicate, Inc. Eleanor Roosevelt Papers, Mount Vernon College, Washington, DC.

Rowden, Dorothy, ed. *Handbook of Adult Education in the United States.* New York: American Association for Adult Education, 1934.

Rudwick, Elliott. "The Niagara Movement," *Journal of Negro History,* 17 (July 1957): 177–200. Reprint, August Meier and Elliott Rudwick, eds., *The Making of Black America; Essays in Negro Life and History,* vol. 2, *The Black Community in Modern America.* New York: Atheneum, 1969, 131–48.

Schneider, Dorothy and Carl J. Schneider. *American Women in the Progressive Era, 1900–1920.* New York: Facts On File, 1993.

Schudson, Michael. *Discovering the News; A Social History of American Newspapers*. New York: Basic Books, 1978.

Scott, Anne F. *Natural Allies; Women's Associations in American History*. Urbana: University of Illinois Press, 1993.

Scott, Donald M. "The Popular Lecture and the Creation of a Public in Mid-Nineteenth-Century America," *Journal of American History* 66 (March 1980), 806–808.

Sharpe, Dores R. *Walter Rauschenbusch*. New York: Macmillan, 1942.

"A Short History of the Women's Educational and Industrial Union." Boston: Women's Educational and Industrial Union, brochure, [1995?]

Sinclair, Upton. *The Jungle*. New York: Doubleday, Page, 1906; Reprint, Viking Penguin, 1986.

Solomon, Barbara M. *In the Company of Educated Women; A History of Women and Higher Education in America*. New Haven: Yale University Press, 1985.

Solomon, Barbara Miller with Patricia M. Nolan, "Education, Work, Family, and Public Commitment in the Lives of Radcliffe Alumna, 1883–1928," 139–55, in Joyce Antler and Sari Knopp Birklen, eds., *Changing Education; Women as Radicals and Conservatives*. Albany: State University of New York Press, 1990.

Stanton, Elizabeth Cady. "The Solitude of Self," quoted in Linda K. Kerber, "Can a Woman be an Individual? The Discourse of Self-Reliance," 200–22, in *Toward an Intellectual History of Women; Essays*, Linda K. Kerber, ed., (Chapel Hill: University of North Carolina Press, 1997.

Stephen, Caroline Emilia. *Light Arising: Thoughts on the Central Radiance*. Cambridge, England: Heffer, 1908. Quoted in Martha Vicinus, *Independent Women; Work and Community for Single Women, 1900–1920*. Chicago: University of Chicago Press, 1985.

Steuer, Rabbi Ulrick B. "History of Congregation Beth-El," Dedication of Temple Beth-El, Hammond, Indiana, 1955.

Stubblefield, Harold W. and Patrick Keane. *Adult Education in the American Experience; From the Colonial Period to the Present*. San Francisco: Jossey-Bass, 1994.

Trusty, Lance. *Hammond; A Centennial Portrait*, 2nd ed. Norfolk, VA: Donning Company, 1990.

Ware, Caroline F., ed. *The Cultural Approach to History*. New York: Columbia University Press, 1940. Reprint, Port Washington, NY: Kennikat Press, 1964.

Weil, Ervin. "An Account of the Origin and Development of the Washington Avenue Temple Lecture Series from 1927 to 1938," Evansville, Indiana, 1974. Hebrew Union College Records, MS-5 Folder B-7/14, American Jewish Archives, Cincinnati, Ohio.

Westbrook, Robert B. *John Dewey and American Democracy*. Ithaca, NY: Cornell University Press, 1991.

White, Ronald C. Jr. and C. Howard Hopkins. *The Social Gospel, Religion and Reform in Changing America*. Philadelphia: Temple University Press, 1976.

Willkens, William H. R. "A History of the Adult Education Programs and Agencies of the American Baptist Convention," (abstract) *Dissertation Abstracts*, 19, 4–6, 1958.

Wilson, Margaret G. *The American Woman in Transition; The Urban Influence, 1879–1920.* Westport, CT: Greenwood Press, 1979.

Woods, Robert A. and Albert J. Kennedy. *The Zone of Emergence; Observations of the Lower Middle and Upper Working Class Community of Boston, 1905–1914*, abr. and ed. by Sam Bass Warner, Jr., 2nd ed. Cambridge: Massachusetts Institute of Technology Press, 1962, 1969.

Woolf, Virginia. "A Room of One's Own," *Identity and Respect.* Chicago: Great Books Foundation, 1997.

Worrell, Dorothy. *The Women's Municipal League of Boston; A History of Thirty-five Years of Civic Endeavor.* Boston: Women's Municipal League Committees, Inc., 1943.

Index